A Very Great Profession

The Woman's Novel 1914–39

NICOLA BEAUMAN

Virago

Published by VIRAGO PRESS Limited 1983
41 William IV Street, London WC2

Copyright © Nicola Beauman 1983

British Library Cataloguing in Publication Data
Beauman, Nicola
  A very great profession.
  1. English fiction—20th century—History and
  criticism   2. English fiction—Women authors—
  History and criticism
  I. Title
  823'.912'300355   PR830.S/

ISBN 0-86068-304-4
ISBN 0-86068-309-5

Printed in Great Britain by litho at
The Anchor Press, Tiptree, Essex

The cover illustration shows an illustration from
the film, *Brief Encounter* reproduced by courtesy
of The Rank Organisation

Contents

Introduction
*'Three new library books lay virginally on the fender-
stool'*   1

1 **War**
  'But for me – a war is poor fun'   14

2 **Surplus Women**
  *'Lord Lord! how many daughters have been
  murdered by women like this!'*   37

3 **Feminism**
  *'If I'd had still-rooms and linen rooms and dairies . . .
  I might never have wanted to get out'*   63

4 **Domesticity**
  'An ordinary domesticated female'   94

5 **Sex**
  'A pagan body and a Chislehurst mind'   121

6 **Psychoanalysis**
  'All that repressed libido'   147

7 **Romance**
  'Came the Dawn'   173

8   **Love**
   ' *"Oh, dulling," said my mother sadly. "One always*
   thinks that. Every, every time." '   198

Epilogue
'Things she would never know again'   225

Notes   236

Glossary   253

Index   263

A Very Great Profession was conceived ten years ago when I first saw the film of *Brief Encounter* on television. In it the heroine, Laura Jesson, goes into the local town every week to do a bit of shopping, have a café lunch, go to the cinema and change her library book. This is the highlight of her week. It was the glimpse of her newly borrowed Kate O'Brien in her shopping basket that made me want to find out about the other novels the doctor's wife had been reading during her life as 'a respectable married woman with a husband and a home and three children'.[1] (This is how she describes herself in *Still Life* (1935), the Noel Coward play upon which *Brief Encounter* (1945) was based.)

I wanted, also, to learn something about Laura's life, which, because it *was* so respectable, ordinary and everyday, has been little documented. She lived uneventful days and was, like Katharine in Virginia Woolf's *Night and Day* (1919), 'a member of a very great profession which has, as yet, no title and very little recognition, although the labour of mill and factory is, perhaps, no more severe and the results of less benefit to the world. She lived at home.'[2] History in the past has been about kings and queens and revolutions, and social history explains bastardy or spinning methods; but history is also about life as it is perceived in the minds of people living in a particular period.

1

When I 'did' history and English literature at school this was not something that exercised my mind. It seemed to me utterly unsurprising to be taught these 'subjects' by elderly, rather dry women with whom I was unlikely ever to have very much in common; and that the topics of the 'lessons' should be treaties, dictators, or (in 'social history', period three on Wednesdays) sanitation, factory acts and costume. And we were never bemused by the paradox that our parents rarely envisaged more for us than a home-based existence (even if we were thought liable to 'get in' to university, that was three years of respectable pleasure rather than a stepping-stone to a career); yet at school the values thrust at us were entirely male-biased.

Naturally Virginia Woolf's *A Room of One's Own* (1929) was not on our reading-list and it was not until some years later that I came across the passage in which she discusses another paradox – that the few female names most people remember shine like beacons on the pages of literature. And, 'if woman had no existence save in the fiction written by men, one would imagine her a person of the utmost importance; very various; heroic and mean; splendid and sordid; infinitely beautiful and hideous in the extreme; as great as a man, some think even greater'.[3]

In imaginative literature woman is of the highest importance; in everyday life she is insignificant.

> What one must do to bring her to life was to think poetically and prosaically at one and the same moment, thus keeping in touch with fact – that she is Mrs Martin, aged thirty-six, dressed in blue, wearing a black hat and brown shoes; but not losing sight of fiction either – that she is a vessel in which all sorts of spirits and forces are coursing and flashing perpetually.[4]

Mrs Martin, Laura and Katharine, Mrs 'Everywoman' are, in the pages of history, found to have vanished without trace, since 'by no possible means could middle-class women with nothing but brains and character at their command have taken part in any one of the great movements which, brought together, constitute the historian's view of the past.' Indeed, except in a few pioneering works like Iris Origo's *The Merchant of Prato*, Peter Laslett's *The World We Have Lost*, Molly Hughes's *A London Child of the 1870s* or Maud Pember Reeves's *Round about a Pound a Week*, little has been documented about the kind of ordinary, unremarkable dailiness that is the norm for the great majority.

A Very Great Profession tries to correct some of this imbalance and to present a portrait through their fiction of English middle-class women during the period between two world wars. To the women writers who made their voices heard in those years 'this curious silent unrepresented life,' as Virginia Woolf called it, did begin to have its own significance; many of the novels are remarkable works of fiction – and they are all memorable because of what they tell the reader about what women did, thought and felt at the time.

The 'woman's novel' between the wars was usually written by middle-class women for middle-class women. Novelists wrote for women leading much the same kind of lives as themselves, the leisured who could perhaps still afford one or even two servants, who were beginning to enjoy the new labour-saving devices such as vacuum-cleaners and refrigerators, and who would still have been considered unusual if they tried to do anything 'for themselves'. Middle-class families were at this period generally small and boys were often sent early to boarding school, so it is hardly surprising that time hung heavy on many women's hands and that novel reading was one of life's chief pleasures.

Since writers and readers formed a homogenous group it is clear that the woman's novel at this period was permeated through and through with the certainty of like speaking to like. Elizabeth Bowen described her own and her contemporaries' work in the following terms (with presumably unconscious criticism of her own novels):

Pre-assumptions are bad. They limit the novel to a given circle of readers. They cause the novel to act immorally *on* that given circle. (The lady asking the librarian for a 'nice' novel to take home is, virtually, asking for a novel whose

3

pre-assumptions will be identical with her own.) Outside
the given circle, a novel's pre-assumptions must invalidate
it for all other readers.[5]

But *within* that given circle writer and reader were linked by
their mutual 'pre-assumptions'; they spoke the same language,
were interested in the same kind of things, led the same kind of
lives. As a modern critic observed in 1973, with reference to
Elizabeth Taylor:

> Her detractors too often seem to me to be criticising her
> subject matter, as if to write about a part of the world
> where people take elevenses in the Tudor Tea Rooms, play
> bridge, and attend point-to-points were to be immediately
> discounted from making any claims to creating serious
> literature. But since there are human beings who *do* take
> elevenses, etc., it should follow that they are as worthy of
> being written about as anyone else.[6]

It was in the same year that I called on my former supervisor at
Cambridge and told her that I was proposing to write a book
about women novelists during the 1920s and 1930s. This dear,
white-haired, unashamedly intellectual don, the author of a
classic work on Virginia Woolf, was almost too appalled to
speak; her only comfort was that I might continue some of the
work pioneered by Queenie Leavis forty years earlier. From her
point of view, there were no twentieth-century women writers
worthy of critical attention, with the obvious exception of
Virginia Woolf and the possible exceptions of Rosamond
Lehmann and Elizabeth Bowen.

This was not an encouraging start. But all through the subsequent years of breeding, nurturing and nursery tea, I kept the
picture in my mind of Laura Jesson taking elevenses in the
refreshment room of Milford Junction and returning home with
her Boots library book. It seemed so strange that an enormous
body of fiction should influence and delight a whole generation
and then be ignored or dismissed. Much of my reading was
directed, too, towards finding out about Laura's life and preoccupations – which is why, when I came to write *A Very Great*

Profession, it seemed more revealing to construct the chapters by themes rather than by chronology, author or type of novel. And it soon became clear that those novels which school, university and critical dogma had chosen to ignore were, to me, infinitely greater and more memorable than those which had for so long and so regularly appeared on reading lists. A novel is 'good', I believe, because it moves the reader and feeds her imagination. And there are very few novels in this book to which this canon does not apply.

For me, as well, a good novel must usually be one with a distinctively 'feminine note', a novel which in some way or another illuminates female attitudes to experience, throws light on the texture of women's lives. Another modern critic once announced that he could 'gain no pleasure from serious reading . . . that lacks a strong male thrust, an almost pedantic allusiveness, and a brutal intellectual content'.[7] Sadly, or happily, I only read novels with these characteristics under duress – and have found among the novels discussed in the following pages greater enjoyment and excitement than I found in most of my reading of the previous twenty years, though they are clearly deficient in strong male thrust.

Writers and critics have frequently expressed their disgust at women novelists being restricted to a ghetto defined by sex and their reasons are perfectly understandable. But to anyone interested in the fiction written during the period between the wars it soon becomes clear that there *is* a category of fiction written for women – 'the woman's novel'. Not all of the novels under discussion in the following pages were written by women, but the majority were, and they all have an unmistakably female tone of voice. They generally have little action and less histrionics – they are about the 'drama of the undramatic', the steadfast dailiness of a life that brings its own rewards, the intensity of the emotions and, above all, the importance of human relationships.

Rebecca West once observed that 'nearly every good novel which has ever been written by a woman bears a stamp which proclaims beyond all doubt that it is the work of a woman'.[8] The hyperbole is deliberately provocative and ignores those male writers with the 'feminine note'. In this book, male novelists such

5

as E. M. Forster, Martin Armstrong and Denis Mackail who also write mostly about the personal, the small-scale and the every-day are obviously not excluded on the grounds of sex; nor are H. G. Wells or A. S. M. Hutchinson, who write about women's themes from a masculine stance.

The years between the wars were the heyday of fiction written by women. Novel writing was, finally, a respectable occupation and no longer could people like Mrs Honeychurch in *A Room with a View* 'abandon every topic to inveigh against those women who (instead of minding their houses and their children) seek notoriety through print'.[9] Middle-class women had time, warmth, freedom from drudgery and an intelligence unsullied by the relentless and wearying monotony of housework. And, as in Jane Austen's day, when her manuscript was hidden as visitors arrived, fiction was easy to pick up and put down, as well as quietly boosting the often bruised spirit.

Many potential male writers had died in the First World War. As Ivy Compton-Burnett observed:

> They say that before the first war there were four or five men novelists to one woman, but that in the time between the two wars there were more women. Well, I expect that's because the men were dead, you see, and the women didn't marry so much because there was no one for them to marry, and so they had leisure, and, I think in a good many cases they had money, because their brothers were dead, and all that would tend to writing, wouldn't it, being single, and having some money, and having the time – having no men, you see.[10]

And as Rebecca West pointed out, conceding that male novelists still held the major positions in the literary batting order, the preponderance 'of the female on the lesser fields of glory is as likely as not one of the consequences of the war. No doubt there lie many dead in France and in the East and under the seas who desired nothing better than to live and keep certain appoint-ments between their imaginations and pen and ink'.[11] While Madeleine Henrey speculated that 'brilliant moments mixed with bitter sorrow'[12] had produced the experience women needed for writing great works.

Yet this 'bitter sorrow' theory does not allow for the great mass of English fiction which has stemmed from personal, everyday concerns and has centred round heroines who would all have echoed Katharine in *Night and Day* when she reflected that 'the only truth which she could discover was the truth of what she herself felt'. And such heroines would, of course, have had to have the leisure for such preoccupations – which is another aspect of the extreme class bias of fiction, for, of all art forms, the novel is the one which belongs particularly to the middle classes; and it is still true today that

> there is an aspect of fiction of so delicate a nature that less has been said about it than its importance deserves. One is supposed to pass over class distinctions in silence; one person is supposed to be as well born as another; and yet English fiction is so steeped in the ups and downs of social rank that without them it would be unrecognisable.[13]

It is the 'ups and downs' within one class that have provided the English novel's most fruitful source. Women writers were ladies and they dealt with ladies, with what E. M. Forster called 'gentlefolk', part of the class to which

> most of us belong, the class which strangled the aristocracy in the nineteenth century, and has been haunted ever since by the ghost of its victim. It is a class of tradesmen and professional men and little Government officials, and it has come into power consequent on the Industrial Revolution and Reform Bills and Death Duties.[14]

It is neither the castle nor the hovel, the top drawer nor the bottom, but that large class of people in between who would prefer life to go on rather as it always has done, people of a comfortable frame of mind who cling, conservatively, on to the established moral framework.

Lucy Honeychurch in E. M. Forster's *A Room with a View* (1908) is typical of the kind of heroine who tries, usually in vain, to escape the polite, decent, discreet outlook on life with which she had grown up.

Hitherto she had accepted their ideals without
questioning – their kindly affluence, their inexplosive
religion, their dislike of paper bags, orange-peel and
broken bottles. A ̄Radical out and out, she learned to speak
with horror of Suburbia. Life, so far as she troubled to
conceive it, was a circle of rich, pleasant people, with
identical interests and identical foes. In this circle one
thought, married and died. Outside it were poverty and
vulgarity, for ever trying to enter.[15]

But travel abroad has entirely changed her vision of her suburban neighbours and among the Tuscan olive groves she learns
to feel 'that there was no one whom she might not get to like'.
When she returns to England she is deemed to have been purged
of the suburban Honeychurch taint – the ultimate accolade is
that now 'she is not always quoting servants, or asking how the
pudding is made'.

The heroine of the woman's novel does frequently ask how the
pudding is made. This kind of light, concerned, inoffensive yet
silence-filling question was one familiar to all middle-class
women at a period when the problem was which pudding rather
than no pudding at all. It would have been a question familiar to
Rachel in *The Voyage Out* who, after luncheon, used to go

shopping with one of my aunts. Or we went to see someone, or we took a message; or we did something that had to
be done – the taps might be leaking. They visit the poor a
good deal – old charwomen with bad legs, women who
want tickets for hospitals. Or I used to walk in the park by
myself. And after tea people sometimes called; in winter I
read aloud, while they worked; after dinner I played the
piano and they wrote letters. If father was at home we had
friends of his to dinner, and about once a month we went
up to the play. Every now and then we dined out; sometimes I went to a dance in London, but that was difficult
because of getting back. The people we saw were old
family friends, and relations, but we didn't see many
people . . . A house takes up a lot of time if you do it properly. Our servants were always bad, and so Aunt Lucy

8

used to do a good deal in the kitchen, and Aunt Clara, I think, spent most of the morning dusting the drawing-room and going through the linen and silver. Then there were the dogs. They had to be exercised, besides being washed and brushed.[16]

Familiar, too, to the heroine of *Diary of a Provincial Lady* (1930) by E. M. Delafield or to that of *Mrs Miniver* (1939) by Jan Struther, and familiar to countless others who, like Mrs Miniver, often passed their days something like this:

Every morning you awake to the kind of list which begins: – Sink-plug. Ruffle-tape. X-hooks. Glue . . . and ends: – Ring plumber. Get sweep. Curse laundry. Your horizon contracts, your mind's eye is focused upon a small circle of exasperating detail. Sterility sets in; the hatches of your mind are battened down. Your thoughts, once darling companions, turn into club bores, from which only sleep can bring release. When you are in this state, to be kept waiting for half an hour in somebody else's house is nothing but the purest joy. At home the footstool limps, legless, thirsting for its glue; the curtain material lies virginally unruffled; the laundry, unconscious of your displeasure, dozes peacefully at Acton: while you yourself are free.[17]

For women at home rarely had much real freedom. But undoubtedly library books brought their own kind of release, which is why Laura Jesson tried not to miss her weekly visit to Boots. At the beginning of *Still Life* she is described in the following terms:

Laura Jesson is sitting at the downstage table having tea. She is an attractive woman in the thirties. Her clothes are not particularly smart but obviously chosen with taste. She looks exactly what she is, a pleasant ordinary woman, rather pale, for she is not very strong, and with the definite charm of personality which comes from natural kindliness, humour and reasonable conscience. She is reading a Boots library book at which she occasionally smiles. On the chair beside her there are several parcels as she has been shopping.[18]

John Betjeman, too, was astute enough to realise that books from Boots were once as crucial a part of middle-class existence as country life, Harrods and proper meals.

Think of what our Nation stands for,
 Books from Boots, and country lanes,
Free speech, free passes, class distinction,
 Democracy and proper drains.
Lord, put beneath Thy special care
 One-eighty-nine Cadogan Square.[19]

Boots had provided women with reading material ever since it was first founded at the turn of the century. By the mid-1930s it was the largest circulating library of its kind, with over four hundred branches and half a million subscribers. The annual subscription seemed reasonable enough if one compares it with the £60 a year it cost Vera Brittain and Winifred Holtby to rent a flat in Bloomsbury with four rooms, kitchen and bathroom in 1923. (The housekeeping bill for them and a maid was less than £3 a week.)[20] In 1926 it cost 42s a year to get books out from Boots 'on demand', 17s 6d to be able to choose from all works in circulation and 10s 6d for the 'ordinary' service. This was cheaper than the small but exclusive London lending libraries such as Day's, Mudie's or the Times Book Club, but not as cheap as W. H. Smith's library.

Class distinction dictated even the type of circulating library to which a woman belonged. Virginia Woolf did not go to Boots but to Day's or Mudie's.

Day's at 4 in the afternoon is the haunt of fashionable ladies, who want to be told what to read. A more despicable set of creatures I never saw. They come in furred like seals and scented like civets, condescend to pull a few novels about on the counter, and then demand languidly whether there is *anything* amusing?[21]

Boots, on the other hand, was a far more broadly-based library, catering more for suburban shoppers than for fashionable ladies.

Until the Second World War the circulating library was an intrinsic part of social life. In 1933 a town like Poole, whose population was then 43,000, had a library which issued 6,000 books a week. Daphne, in *The Death of the Heart* (1938) by Elizabeth Bowen, is a library assistant. She is not actually fond of reading, but it matters to the management to have

> a girl who *is* someone, if you know what I mean. A girl who – well, I don't quite know how to express it – a girl who did not come from a nice home would not do at all, *here*. You know, choosing books is such a personal thing; Seale is a small place and the people are so nice. Personality counts for so much here. The Corona Café is run by ladies, you know.[22]

Electricity, the wireless set and the motor car were part of the considerable material advancement which the average middle-class household enjoyed in the 1920s and 1930s. But the growth of the lending library must also have had an enormous impact, given that twenty-five million volumes were exchanged among the Boots branches in 1925 and thirty-five million by the time of the outbreak of the Second World War. Generally the subscribers came in to the library with their book list, sometimes the girl behind the desk made suggestions. The Boots Staff Training Pamphlet stressed the importance of not suggesting a book unless the customer's taste was well understood. 'You have only to imagine a person sitting down at the weekend to enjoy a time of good reading to which they have looked forward, only to discover they have been given something which, to them, is utterly unreadable.' This happens all too often to Felicity in Denis Mackail's novel *Greenery Street* (1925) when she goes to her local circulating library.

> Twice, sometimes three times a week, she sets out with a bundle of books under her arm, goes up in one of Andrew Brown's lifts, presents herself at the desk which is labelled 'FAB to KYT' and smiles at the young lady who sits behind it. In Felicity's case the young lady always returns this smile and the following dialogue then takes place:

11

Felicity: 'I've brought two books back, and here's my new list. Have you got the first volume of *Indiscreet Reminiscences* yet?'

Attendant: 'I'm afraid they're all out still. But can I give you the second?'

Felicity: 'No, thank you. We've had that. Oh – I say – have you got *Spate*? No? Well, have you got *That The Swine Did Eat*? Oh, aren't you taking it? I see. Well, have you got *The Gutter*? Oh, but I'm *sure* it's published. I saw a long review of it in – Oh, yes; perhaps it was an advertisement. Well, have you got *The Braxingfield Mystery*? My husband is *always* asking for it. Oh; I see. Well, have you got anything on my list? And nothing on the old list, either? Well, what *have* you got, then?'

(The Attendant, who has been waiting for this moment, dives under the desk and fetches up about half a dozen novels, which she offers for Felicity's inspection.)

Attendant: 'Here are some of the latest, Mrs Foster.'

(Felicity looks at the backs of these works, and fails to recognise either their titles or their authors.)

Felicity (politely, but disparagingly): 'I don't think I – '

Attendant (briskly): '*Prendergast's Property* – that's a very pretty story.'

Felicity (doubtfully): 'Oh . . . I never seem to like books where the people are called Prendergast.'

Attendant: 'Well, what about *The Transept*? It's going very well, you know.'

Felicity (suspiciously): 'Is it religious?'

Attendant (surprisingly): 'Oh, no. It's about Rhodesia.'

Felicity (with conviction): 'I always hate that.'

(By this time, however, a small queue has formed behind her, which has the effect of weakening her critical judgement. The attendant realises this, and goes quickly ahead.)

Attendant: 'I think you'd like this, Mrs Foster. *Illumination*.'

(Felicity picks up *Illumination* and opens it. Nice

short paragraphs, anyhow; and quite large print.)

Felicity: 'All right. That'll do for one.' (The queue shows
fresh signs of impatience.) 'And – oh, very well. I'll
take *The Transept* for the other. Perhaps my husband
will like it.'

Attendant (more briskly than ever): 'Oh, he's sure to,
Mrs Foster.'

Felicity: 'Well, thank you very much. Good morning.'

Exit[23]

The Boots First Literary Course for librarians divided literature into categories, presumably so that the harassed attendant
could at least decide which type of book her customer would find
acceptable. One of the most popular (along with the detective
and the love story) was 'Light Romance'. The course lecturer
said: 'We often hear [women] say they like a "pretty book". I am
sure that your own taste in reading has developed far above this
level, but to a librarian books are but tools and it our duty to
supply them to our subscribers without questioning their taste.'
He lent rather more of his approval to Family Stories, defined as
being 'for those tired of romance' who are often seeking
something with some reality in it; the subscriber may define
these as a 'well-written book'.[24]

It would be safe to conclude that it was either a Light
Romance or a Family Story that Laura had in her basket, and
that Mrs Miniver was looking forward to reading when, one day
in 1938, she arrived home for tea.

Tea was already laid: there were honey sandwiches,
Brandy-snaps, and small ratafia biscuits; and there
would, she knew, be crumpets. Three new library books
lay virginally on the fender-stool, their bright paper
wrappers unsullied by subscriber's hand. The clock on
the mantelpiece chimed, very softly and precisely, five
times . . .[25]

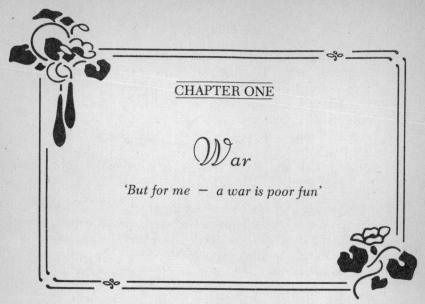

CHAPTER ONE

War

'But for me — a war is poor fun'

War is an essentially masculine occupation, part of E. M. Forster's 'great outer life . . . in which telegrams and anger count'.[1]

Along with the City, clubs, smoking rooms, shooting, sport and other middle-class male concerns it is by tradition alien to women's preoccupations. Yet war influences both the most important and the most minute details of women's lives, shaping them significantly enough to justify the sub-title of this book, 1914–39.

Women's writing is conventionally assigned to the department marked personal relations and emotional response – opposite the department marked masculine, anger and telegrams. R. Brimley Johnson, in his 1920 volume called *Some Contemporary Novelists (Women)*, suggested that women novelists did not mention the war very much because 'the truth about human nature is to be found in individual experience'[2] rather than in the broader sweep of the battlefield. This too is the common explanation for Jane Austen's disregard for the war across the channel, and is echoed by the editor of Virginia Woolf's letters who observes that there were signs of war everywhere: 'Yet so little did all this mean to her that her letters contain almost no reflection on it . . . She thought the war an inevitable outcome of male chauvinism.'[3]

Certainly the prevalent assumption during the Great War was that it was nothing to do with women. Not for them the sense of a new life starting, a great adventure towards which their whole previous existence had unconsciously turned. They could not cry out with an almost religious ecstacy:

> Now, God be thanked Who has matched us with His hour,
> And caught our youth, and wakened us from sleeping . . .[4]

Indeed, women had not been bred for the ritual of war. It is this point that echoes, clarion-like, from the biographies of the young men who went to war in 1914, for example from Nicholas Mosley's *Julian Grenfell* (1976):

> The pattern for men was not to ask questions, not to think, but to make jokes and to do one's duty: if this was not too difficult, it was perhaps because it was part of men's duty to fight and kill. It was like this in law, in politics, in business; with thought disencouraged, furious instincts were satisfied by ritual.[5]

And Julian Grenfell himself found no purpose in life until 1914 and then wrote to his mother: 'Isn't it luck for me to have been born so as to be just the right age and just in the right place – not too high up to be worried – to enjoy it the most?'[6]

Women could knit socks, nurse the wounded, even work in factories or on the land; but questioning the wisdom of their male superiors was quite out of order. There was little room for a woman to assume any sort of control, as Mr Britling's son points out in H. G. Wells's *Mr Britling Sees It Through* (1916):

> all this business could be done far better and far cheaper if it wasn't left to these absolutely inexperienced and extremely exclusive military gentlemen. They think they are leading England and showing us all how; instead of which they are just keeping us back. Why in thunder are they doing everything? Not one of them, when he is at home, is allowed to order the dinner or poke his nose into his own kitchen or check the household books . . . The

ordinary British colonel is a helpless old gentleman; he ought to have a nurse . . . This is not merely the trivial grievance of my insulted stomach, it is a serious matter for the country.[7]

Eventually women were allowed to make positive contributions to the war effort. Many were already used to working outside the home – in 1914 nearly six million out of the 19 million women over ten in Great Britain and Ireland were employed, mainly in industry, domestic service and commerce; and over the next four years this figure rose to 7.3 million, an increase in industry from 2.4 to 3.9 million.[8]

But now many middle- and upper-class women were anxious to be useful. At first there was little for them to do – as Vera Brittain wrote: 'Women get all the dreariness of war, and none of its exhilaration.'[9] *The Lady* (a journal for gentlewomen) offered its readers some consolation when it suggested:

The fact that one cannot bear arms does not excuse any one from helping their country's cause by fighting such foes as misery, pain and poverty . . . If we cannot in our innermost hearts feel really hopeful, we can at least pretend we do, and talk hopefully to those about us, write hopeful letters to distant, anxious friends, and do our very best to inspire a calm, courageous view of the situation among all with whom we come in contact . . . We can visit the smaller houses about us, and talk hopefully to those poor wives and mothers whose anxiety equals our own.[10]

Any efforts more positive than this were firmly squashed. When Elsie Inglis, a well-known woman doctor, offered a ready-made Medical Unit staffed by qualified women to the Royal Army Medical Corps she found her efforts unappreciated ('My good lady, go home and sit still,' the War Office told her) and was instead paid by the French government to take her unit to Serbia.[11] And when May Wedderburn Cannan carried out the orders of the War Office and upon mobilisation set up a hospital of sixty beds, she was told by the Red Cross Headquarters that they did not want it. (She offered it to a family connection at the

Military Base at Oxford and it was gratefully received.)[12] As
Cicely Hamilton commented in 1935: 'It was because British
authorities showed little enthusiasm for the idea of war hospitals
run by women that all our units were placed at the service of our
Allies – two or three in France, two or three in the Balkans, one
in pre-Bolshevik Russia.'[13]

Knitting was not always occupation enough, as Rose
Macaulay found:

> Was there a scrap or ploy in which you, the boy,
> Could better me? You could not climb higher,
> Ride straighter, run as quick (and to smoke made you sick)
> . . . But I sit here, and you're under fire.
> Oh, it's you that have the luck, out there in blood and muck:
> You were born beneath a kindly star;
> All we dreamt, I and you, you can really go and do,
> And I can't, the way things are.
> In a trench you are sitting, while I am knitting
> A hopeless sock that never gets done.
> Well, here's luck, my dear; – and you got it, no fear;
> But for me . . . a war is poor fun.[14]

(Later she was to write more heartfelt poems about the horrors of
the Great War.)

Even the Suffragettes, who had abandoned the Cause upon
the declaration of war, at first found little for their energies; and
despite the stories in the newspapers, initially women were not
employed in large numbers – for example, by March 1916
there were still only a hundred women bus conductresses in
London. The setting up of the Ministry of Munitions in 1915
gave some boost to the employment of women; things began to
change properly with the introduction of universal military con-
scription in May 1916, upon which the Government launched its
first concerted national drive to fill the places about to be
vacated by men.[15] Increasing numbers of women were soon to be
found working in industry (including munitions factories),
transport and commerce, while middle-class women turned to
organising, to driving motor vehicles and to nursing. By 1918
there were over one and a quarter million more women working

than there had been in 1914, and for many middle-class women the First World War brought with it their first opportunity for employment outside the confines of their home. As Cicely Hamilton observed just at the beginning of the Second World War:

> Long before the conflict had dragged to its end, the munition factories of the country were staffed to a great extent by women's labour; while with the need to increase the supply of home-grown food – a pressing need by 1917 – there came into being a body of volunteers for agricultural work; a body many thousand strong and known as the Women's Land Army. And in addition to the girls who laboured on the land and who worked in factories; in addition to the various corps attached to the Army, the Navy, and the Air Force, and the host of women employed in hospitals and convalescent homes, there was another host that worked in canteens and drove ambulances, cars and lorries. The old line of division between men's work and women's was broken down during the war.[16]

In E. M. Delafield's *The War-Workers* (1918) a group of women help run the Midland Supply Depot. They are all mesmerised by Miss Vivian, the Director, a woman who in normal life would have nothing to occupy her energies except petty social machinations but in wartime is in her element being queen bee. It is clear that the war is bringing her enormous personal satisfaction, allowing her scope to dominate, coerce, win adulation and yet assume an air of cheerful martyrdom. Her devotion to duty is absurd and the reader is left with the impression that the soldiers could have been billeted and the canteens supplied without so many pieces of paper being pushed about and so many women working to the limit of their endurance. The same point was made by Amber Reeves in her documentary novel *Give and Take* written in 1918 and published in 1923. Her setting is the fictional Ministry of Reconciliation and her purpose is to describe the petty and obsessive preoccupations of many of the characters.

Neither novel focuses at all clearly on the war, and because their main concern is character dissection they might just as well have been set in a girl's school. (Indeed both have some affinities with Clemence Dane's *Regiment of Women* (1917) which *is* set in a girl's school.) For, surprisingly, war work may have expanded middle-class women's horizons, but it provided relatively few themes for novelists. Although wartime experiences were described in those novels women wrote about nursing or ambulance driving, nevertheless, except in the autobiographies (such as *Testament of Youth*), the job remains incidental to the main theme, usually the heroine's intense and personal emotions about what is happening to her. Charlotte Redhead in May Sinclair's *The Romantic* (1920) goes out to Belgium as a volunteer field ambulance driver. She goes as part of a small group with the man she loves, John Conway. Under the stress of the work they do – braving shell bombardment to go out and bring in the wounded – it transpires that John 'funks'. As soon as she has fully realised his cowardice, this destroys her love. When he dies a coward's death no one has much sympathy and later, going back to England, Charlotte declares that she is not even sorry that he is dead. (Naturally, she is herself fearless and carelessly risks shells and bullets in order to get the men through.)

The war, although described as a backcloth to Charlotte's dawning realisation about John (a view of cowardice much ingrained in men and women at that time), is not at all important. Its causes or its wider implications are not even hinted at, the fact that she is a competent ambulance driver matters only in so far as it gives her a chance to compete on the same level with her lover. Similarly, in Enid Bagnold's *The Happy Foreigner* (1920) an English girl goes to France after the Armistice and drives a car for the French Army. Fanny is fearless, practical and optimistic. While driving through rain and snow, living with mud and rats and few creature comforts, she retains to the last a detached good cheer. As Katharine Mansfield observed: 'nothing can overwhelm her or cast her down, because it is her nature, and unchangeable, to find in all things a grain of living beauty. We have the feeling that she is, above all, unbroken.'[17]

There is very little detachment in Dorothy Canfield's *Home Fires in France* (1919). The eleven short stories that make up the volume give the reader a picture of civilian life in France during the war which is deadly and unforgettable, including a very moving short story called 'La Pharmacienne'. The first few pages describe the idyllic life of Madeleine who, awaiting the birth of her third child, is cosseted and cherished and idle. In the first days of August, Jules, 'in his wrinkled uniform, smelling of moth-balls', marches away and of course '*no* one had the faintest idea that his peaceful home town would see anything of the war'.[18] But after a brief period of terror and rumours, the village is horribly looted and its inhabitants are left with all their certainties destroyed virtually overnight; and Dorothy Canfield makes it clear that the plight of the civilians in France was often as ghastly as that of their menfolk in the trenches.

Though some grasped the full horror of the war, for many across the Channel it was viewed as nothing more profound than casualty lists, relevant to everyday life only if their tragedies became personal ones. What mattered to most middle-class people in England were 'the universal topics of maids and ration-cards', as Vera Brittain found in 1918:

> From a world in which life or death, victory or defeat, national survival or national extinction, had been the sole issues, I returned to a society where no one discussed anything but the price of butter and the incompetence of the latest 'temporary' – matters which, in the eyes of Kensington and of various acquaintances who dropped in to tea, seemingly far out-weighted in importance the operations at Zeebrugge, or even such topical controversies as those which raged round Major-General Maurice's letter to *The Times*, and the Pemberton-Billing case.
>
> Keyed up as I had been by the month-long strain of daily rushing to and fro in attendance on the dying, and nightly waiting for the death which hovered darkly in the sky overhead, I found it excruciating to maintain even an appearance of interest and sympathy. Probably I did not succeed, for the triviality of everything drove me to despair.[19]

The contrast between the life-and-death problems of wartime and the trivia of civilian life was a recurring theme. Soldiers on leave found that their friends and relations viewed the Front as something ghastly 'over there' that was nothing to do with them. People didn't really want to know, and this was so even in the parts of France that happened to have escaped the first-hand effects of war. A foretaste of the insularity that was to be a part of the 1914–18 war is given in May Sinclair's *The Tree of Heaven* (1917). To Frances and Anthony Harrison, the Boer War 'wasn't real'. When Frances's brother Maurice comes back from South Africa he tries to make them realise what he has been through; he evokes some lurid detail:

> Frances looked at him. He thought: 'At last she's turned; at last I've touched her; she can realise that.'
> 'Morrie dear, it must have been awful,' she said. 'It's *too* awful. I don't mind your telling me and Anthony about it; but I'd rather you did it when the children aren't in the room.'[20]

But this novel has a firm moral, and Frances and Anthony do finally learn to be touched by the reality of war and so do all their children. Dorothea, their daughter, is told by her lover as he departs for Mons in 1914 that 'it's *your* War, too – it's the biggest fight for freedom' and when he is killed, one of her chief regrets is all the time they wasted – 'All those years – like a fool – over that silly suffrage.' Her brother Nicky finds that it is 'absolute happiness' to go over the top. 'And the charge is – well, it's simply heaven. It's as if you'd never really lived till then; I certainly hadn't, not up to the top-notch'. Even Michael, who had originally funked the idea of enlisting, finally understands that this is the greatest War of Independence that has ever been.

> Now that he could look at it by himself he saw how the War might take hold of you like a religion. It was the Great War of Redemption. And redemption meant simply thousands and millions of men in troop-ships and troop-trains coming from the ends of the world to buy the freedom of the world with their bodies . . . He wondered how at this moment any sane man could be a pacifist.[21]

And the couple in May Sinclair's *Tasker Jevons* (1916) find that the war brings them happiness, for before the war Jimmy had been used to nothing more than exercising his genius. When he finds hidden reserves of courage in himself, he and his wife are brought close together. But this theme is very unusual, for most novelists depict their characters as being embroiled finally in terrible unhappiness because of the effects of the war. The fiancé killed at the Front was often and poignantly described, and then there was the frequent concomitant moral dilemma: 'I could bear it if I'd given myself to him that night – even for one night' (Dorothea in *The Tree of Heaven*).

May Sinclair's novels about war are among the very few propaganda books to have been written by a woman. (And *The Romantic* is quite unambivalent in its attitudes to cowardice in a soldier.) But their message is in fact two-pronged. For the author is at pains to point out that the miseries of peace can be as profound as those of war, and that peace definitely lacks the glory of war. The peaceful house in Hampstead, with its garden dominated by a tree of Heaven, has its tranquillity destroyed by the war but there is to be no ecstasy as a substitute. And this is the other moral, namely that without sacrifice there is no heroism, that only by loving and giving can we crush our self-absorption and selfishness, can we attain glory.

Clearly war is a natural theme for women because of the chance it provides for self-sacrifice; and, since women have been glorying in this for centuries, it is perhaps odd that more novelists did not avail themselves of the theme of war as an opportunity for women's sacrifice.

In the novels about nursing, the opportunities for self-abnegation are mingled with an awareness of the horror of war. Nursing was such hard work that no girl would volunteer to do it if she was uninterested in the joy of sacrifice; the emotional pleasure in serving heroes was restrained by the almost saintly devotion needed for the daily handling of men's wounds. And a degree of religious detachment was probably vital if a girl was to retain the necessary calm to make her a good nurse, as Enid Bagnold wrote in *A Diary without Dates* (1918): 'In all honesty the hospital is a convent, and the men in it my brothers.' But there were no war memorials for women who nursed their wounded brothers.

In *A Diary without Dates*, a series of autobiographical sketches, the reader is briefly immersed in the world of the Royal Hospital at Woolwich. Enid Bagnold was a Voluntary Aid Detachment nurse (VAD for short) and her book poignantly describes the back-breaking work, the tyranny of routine and the remorseless drudgery. The tone is resigned rather than grumbling, for the mood is one of self-sacrifice and more than once the author compares herself to a nun. The Sister in charge might be a Mother Superior and the hard work an act of piety to God. In the following passage, the young Enid Bagnold might as well be feeling her rosary beads and standing in the dim timelessness of a church:

> I lay my spoons and forks. Sixty five trays. It takes an hour to do. Thirteen pieces on each tray. Thirteen times sixty-five . . . eight hundred and forty-five things to collect, lay, square up symmetrically. I make little absurd reflections and arrangements – taking a dislike to the knives because they will not lie still on the polished metal of the tray, but pivot on their shafts, and swing out at angles after my fingers have left them.
>
> I love the long, the dim and lonely, corridors; the light centred in the gleam of the trays, salt-cellars, yellow butters, cylinders of glass.[22]

Yet the war itself does not really intrude, it is something remote. Certainly the men are in pain and their agony is greatly to be deplored. But what matters is the delight of nursing them back to health – when the ward is emptied and the ambulances hurry out of the yard there is no sigh of relief – on the contrary, 'the attack has begun . . . we shall get that convoy for which I longed'. Without the fighting there could be no nursing and

> when the ward is empty and there is, as now, so little work to do, how we, the women, watch each other over the heads of the men! And because we do not care to watch, nor are much satisfied with what we see, we want more work. At what a price we shall get it.[23]

There is a clear-sighted awareness of the opportunities for martyrdom and perhaps too little thought about the wider effects of the battle – yet within its limits *A Diary without Dates* is a great literary achievement.

The same disclaimer applies to another diary, that written by Lady Cynthia Asquith between 1915 and 1918. Although written entirely from the vantage point of the upper classes, the *Diaries* give an evocative portrait of this society as it limped into the post-war world. Life 'for the duration' was a question of keeping going in the face of grim odds; grief had to be dealt with as speedily and sensibly as possible and, because the pleasures of civilian life continued virtually unabated, Cynthia Asquith fell ill only *after* the Armistice – when she had to accept that the dead would not clamber to their feet off the schoolroom carpet and continue with their games. She wrote in October 1918:

> I am beginning to rub my eyes at the prospect of peace. I think it will require more courage than anything that has gone before. It isn't until one leaves off spinning round that one realises how giddy one is. One will have to look at long vistas again, instead of short ones, and one will at last fully recognise that the dead are not only dead for the duration of the war.[24]

While normal life went on, it was punctuated rather than dominated by grief. When her brother was reported killed in 1916 and the news had to be broken to her sister-in-law she wrote that 'the poignancy of what followed was so inconceivably beyond anything in my experience that I don't feel as if I could ever be unhaunted by it for a minute'.[25] But most days passed relatively phantom-free, not because she was callous but because far-off fighting seems so unreal to those at home. When, for an ecstatic moment, she thinks her brother might after all be alive she writes:

> *Oh*, that was *my cruellest moment*! I really believed and my heart had bounded with joy for a second. That one can so hope shows how little one has really taken it in. His being so far away, unseen for so long, and the way the news has trickled in makes it quite impossible to realise.[26]

24

So life goes on:

Saturday, 6th January 1917
Swam before breakfast. Went a-shopping – bought a blouse. Beb [her husband] returned and we went to the Metropole to lunch. The course restrictions involve a great deal of mental arithmetic at meals. One is only allowed two courses, but some things count as half a course . . .

Beb was on duty, so I had one of my little Creamery dinners and went straight to bed. I am in best looks. Marie Bashkirtseff is always apologetic when she makes a similar entry in her diary, but why should one be? Today I could really pass a great deal of time very happily just looking at myself in the glass. It's extraordinary how one's whole outline seems to alter, as well as complexion and eyes.[27]

And even when she takes a hand at nursing, the serious side of the war is deftly brushed aside.

Thursday, 29th March 1917
I was caught in a heavy hail storm on my way to Fortnum and Mason to order some fun-foods for Beb, and only got back just in time to change into my uniform and go out to lunch at Bruton Street. I have blossomed out into the outdoor uniform – dark blue *crêpe-de-Chine* veil and the orthodox cloak. It is very becoming, but I feel self-conscious in it and walk in terror of being called on for a street accident. What could I say, but 'Give him air'?[28]

The joy of Cynthia Asquith's *Diaries* consists in entering into a real world and into the mind of someone humane, unabashed, tender but realistic. The reader is aware that during the war years she never really 'faces up' to the cataclysm around her, but admires her for having the energy and the spirit to keep going. And the ending is almost more moving than what has gone before because, with the breaking off of the diaries, comes the acceptance of truth and of this we are given only a small glimpse. Clearly, however, the innocent child of the Edwardian era has been forced to face up to the scale of the tragedy around her.

Full acceptance came eighteen years later when she published her novel *The Spring House* (1936). Presumably Cynthia Asquith, reading her diaries some years after the war, had seen herself in a not altogether favourable light and wrote a novel in order to exorcise her inevitable feelings of self-loathing. As her diaries were not published until after her death she did not have a reading public to correct her negative impressions, to tell her that although the diaries reveal some extremely feminine, self-centred and perhaps 'silly' aspects of her character, she is revealed as someone quite exceptional. Yet her attempts at atonement in *The Spring House* do not succeed. The plot is blatantly autobiographical but the heroine, Miranda, is denied a happy ending. She discovers that she is in fact illegitimate and that her moral principles are the product of a vague sense of loyalty to her mother's deeply felt sense of virtue and propriety – now seen as merely an 'outward seemliness' that have cheated her of the chance of a few days of happiness with her now dead lover. She sails for Canada, determined to make a fresh start with her husband, only to find a letter announcing that he is no longer heart-whole. So Miranda is left with nothing except a last beautiful letter from her lover and a vague determination to face the future bravely.

Very little of the writing rings true and the war is a mere backcloth to the trivial machinations of the heroine. This was now less forgivable, since the late 1920s and early 1930s had seen a revival in novels about the First World War, in most of which war is the fundamental, inescapable fact and the characters its victims. But at the time of the war most writers lacked the necessary detachment to see it as anything other than a background to individual behaviour. Some of them were unable to settle to anything concentrated once hostilities broke out, or were firmly discouraged by publishers from mentioning anything political or military. The shining exception to this generalisation was H. G. Wells. He believed with great sincerity that it was no use blaming others for the folly of war, for we all were to blame for the antics of our fellow men: and forgiveness is all.

Mr Britling sees the truth of this in the climax of *Mr Britling Sees It Through*, one of the greatest of all the books to emerge from the First World War. When fighting began in

1914 he took much the same line as his fellow Englishmen which was

> to treat it as a monstrous joke. It is a disposition traceable in a vast proportion of the British literature of the time. In spite of violence, cruelty, injustice, and the vast destruction and still vaster dangers of the struggles, that disposition held. The English mind refused flatly to see anything magnificent or terrible in the German attack, or to regard the German Emperor or the Crown Prince as anything more than figures of fun.[29]

But by the time the war was six months old, Mr Britling has run the entire gamut of emotion from rage to despair to, finally, compassion.

> This thing was done neither by devils nor fools, but by a conspiracy of foolish motives, by the weak acquiescences of the clever, by a crime that was no man's crime but the natural necessary outcome of the ineffectiveness, the blind motives and muddleheadedness of all mankind . . . These Germans were an unsubtle people, a people in the worst and best sense of the words, plain and honest; they were prone to moral indignation; and moral indignation is the mother of most of the cruelty in the world . . . Is there not, he now asked himself plainly, a creative and corrective impulse behind all hate? . . . He was no longer thinking of the Germans as diabolical. They were human; they had a case. It was a stupid case. How stupid were all our cases! . . . He whispered the words. No unfamiliar words could have had the same effect of comfort and conviction . . . 'Father, forgive them, for they know not what they do.'[30]

Mr Britling learns forgiveness, Cynthia Asquith has to accept reality, the boys in *The Tree of Heaven* come to reject pacifism. But these are all 'quick reactions' and it was to be a decade before writers began to formulate their considered reactions. The public were alleged to be sick to death of war as a topic and hardly anything was allowed through the publishers' net. The exceptions were usually jingoistic, for example F. Tennyson

Jesse's *The Sword of Deborah* (1919) which was written at the request of the Ministry of Information and is about VAD and WAAC (Women's Army Auxiliary Corps) life in France. It ends thus:

> Not a woman I met, English or American, working in France, but said something like this, and meant it: 'What, after all, is anything we can do except inasmuch as it may help the men a little? How could we bear to do nothing when the men are doing the most wonderful thing that has ever been done in the world?'

Many fiercely resented the ostrich-like attitude demanded by publishers and provided by writers. Katharine Mansfield, for example, was shocked by Virginia Woolf's *Night and Day* (1919). She wrote a fairly kind review of it ('we had never thought to look upon its like again!')[32] but wrote to John Middleton Murry:

> My private opinion is that it is a lie in the soul. The war never has been: that is what its message is. I don't want (G. forbid!) mobilization and the violation of Belgium, but the novel can't just leave the war out. There *must* have been a change of heart. It is really fearful to see the 'settling down' of human beings. I feel in the *profoundest* sense that nothing can ever be the same – that, as artists, we are traitors if we feel otherwise: we have to take it into account and find new expressions, new moulds for our new thoughts and feelings . . . We have to face our war.[33]

But such feelings were exceptional immediately after the war. Only one novel – the wonderful, incomparable *William–An Englishman* which Cicely Hamilton published in 1919 and which won the Femina Prize in that year – expresses some of this immediacy. This masterpiece is understated and low key but is nevertheless a deeply profound comment on the impact of war on two 'ordinary' people.

William is a clerk in the City who inherits a small private income upon the death of his mother. 'His mind was blank and virgin for the sowing of any seed' and by chance it is Socialism

that is sown there. He 'devoted himself to what he termed public
life – a ferment of protestation and grievance' and becomes by
turns a steward, a heckler and a full-blown speaker. 'As a matter
of course he was a supporter of votes for women' and so he meets
Griselda, 'his exact counterpart in petticoats; a piece of blank-
minded, suburban young womanhood caught into the militant
suffrage movement and enjoying herself therein'. 'Like William,
she had found peace of mind and perennial interest in the hearty
denunciation of those who did not agree with her.'

They marry, these two like-minded souls, 'cocksure, contemp-
tuous, intolerant, self-sacrificing after the manner of their kind'.
As pacifists, they are little interested in the assassination of Franz
Ferdinand and set off serenely for four weeks' honeymoon in a
remote woodman's cottage in the Belgian Ardennes. The days
pass idyllically until eventually their distance from the 'daily
whirl' begins to pall. They start to regret the lack of letters and
newspapers in their remote hideaway.

> William pined unconsciously for the din and dust of the
> platform and Griselda missed the weekly temper into
> which she worked herself in sympathy with her weekly
> *Suffragette*. She missed it so much that at last she was
> moved to utterance – late on a still, heavy evening in
> August when once or twice there had come up the valley a
> distant mutter as of thunder.[34]

There are only the vaguest forebodings of the future: the
farmer's family seems to have gone in a hurry and a newly made
mound by the gooseberry bushes looks very much like a grave.
They set off, baggage in hand, eagerly anticipating their return
to civilised life. At first they think the three German soldiers they
meet are merely impertinent. 'Neither William nor Griselda had
ever entertained the idea of a European War; it was not
entertained by any of their friends or their pamphlets.' But soon,
in a scene that is written with unusual verbal power, the reality
of the war is brought home to them. They are forced to watch the
local mayor and the village schoolmaster being shot. We see the
scene through William's eyes:

Never before, in all his twenty-eight years, had he seen a

man come to his end; so far death had touched him only once, and but slightly, by the unseen passing of a mother he had not loved; thus the spectacle of violent and bloody dying would of itself have sufficed to unnerve and unman him. To the natural shrinking from that spectacle, to his natural horror at the slaying of helpless men, to his pity and physical nausea was added the impotent, gasping confusion of the man whose faith has been uprooted, who is face to face with the incredible. Before his eyes had been enacted the impossible – the ugly and brutal impossible – and beneath his feet the foundations of the earth were reeling.[35]

Now the tone of the novel changes to one of dark, nightmarish sombreness. Cicely Hamilton was too subtle a writer to spell out her moral – that, for all their participation in big issues and real life, William and Griselda are in fact completely naive and horribly unprepared for what confronts them. After the shooting, William endures the horrors of forced labour, eventually escaping to go and search for Griselda. He finds her finally; and she who had been so open, so laughing, so supremely confident, cannot tell him what has happened – 'but his own eyes had seen that she turned from him as if there was a barrier between them, as if there was something to hide that yet she wished him to know'. It is the shock of the rape which kills her: all through their flight into the countryside it is apparent that her body and soul have been irreparably wounded. She never speaks to William again (at one point, very humanly, he feels 'a sort of irritation at her long and persistent silence'); but she is past words and 'died very quietly in the straw at the bottom of the cart'.

The feelings of the new husband are poignantly described and what is particularly well evoked is the deep love this insignificant London clerk has for his rather unmemorable wife. And at the same time there is the larger awareness, that even though Griselda had been proud to wear 'a badge denoting that she had suffered for the Cause in Holloway' she had no conception of real suffering, which killed her when she met it. William, who is left desolate and alive, is changed in a way that Griselda would probably have been had she lived. His hatred for the German soldiers turns him into staunch patriot and he intends henceforward to devote his life to his country. Glory is not to be his: first he is rejected by the army and then he is only allowed to push pieces of paper about. He dies, albeit in a bombing raid, not in a trench, and his death is not heroic. But in his small way, the reader feels, he has made his contribution.

William—An Englishman was certainly not written as a patriotic novel. But it has a moral which almost transcends patriotism which is that everyone matters in his own way, that integrity is the important quality and that the little, secondhand clerk has his grandeur as much as the swash-buckling soldier. Cicely Hamilton shows the effect of the enormous, uncontrollable might of war upon the lives of the petty, the unimportant and the ordinary. She also makes the point that was made by Sheila Kaye-Smith a year earlier – that soldiers die not for an abstract concept of patriotism but for their own corner of their country: 'They had not died for England – what did they know of England and the British Empire? They had died for a little corner of ground which was England to them, and the sprinkling of poor common folk who lived in it.'[36]

The grandeur of the ordinary is a concept that is central to most women's lives, a concept that the later, more detached writing about the war was to display to the full. A 'second wave' of war fiction started in 1928–9 with Siegfried Sassoon's *Memoirs of a Fox-Hunting Man* and Robert Graves's *Goodbye to All That*. By this time the reading public was able to accept fiction about the ten-years distant war and writers wanted to publish it; in 1928 the reader could start to view those years with some historical perspective. In *The Hounds of Spring*, a bestselling novel by Sylvia Thompson published in 1926, the real story concerns a heroine who thinks her lover is dead and marries someone else and her subsequent moral dilemma when he reappears. But the author (who was one of that bright Oxford generation that included Vera Brittain, Winifred Holtby and Margaret Kennedy) manages to give her novel some more resonance than that of plot. She suggests that women are entirely altered by grief while men fit it in to their lives.

There was no anger, not even amazement, any more in her grief – that had come at first, like a storm – [but] horror and misery and resentment, shaking the foundations of her happiness and beliefs, destroying all the rare complex beauty of her outlook and changing, by what seemed sheer devastation, the very confirmation of her character. Edgar himself had taken John's death as one more and most intimate tragedy in the prolonged horrors of the war, but it hadn't, he knew, 'changed' him, altered his whole *tempo*, as it had Cynthia's; hadn't taken so much from him. Yet . . . whatever had gone, in youth and gaiety and pride, she had gained 'something' – the knowledge didn't explain itself verbally in [her] mind – which made her, not only to him but absolutely, greater, finer and more sensitive than she had been . . . He kissed her hand – thought with an ache of love and pity which held him speechless, 'It *is* worst of all for *her* . . . for women; they are most at the mercy of the fate of those they love.[37]

Sylvia Thompson also expressed the view that women in particular need safety and order unless they are to disintegrate, that lacking their own resources they will instinctively clutch at any passing straw to avoid drowning:

[Zina had] been brought up, we all had (madly, considering the condition of the world) to an accepted security, social, financial, moral: to postulate safety. And when the whole fabric thundered to atoms like that, she instinctively played for safety, to get back even a kind of skeleton of her native security. It was only too grimly natural.[38]

But neither of these two theories about women are anything to do with war except in its most personal aspects – the war caused the crisis in Zina's life, but of its wider effect we learn very little. On the other hand, we *do* gain a good deal of insight into the way women behave faced with tragedy and it was this personal aspect which lent the novel its wide appeal.

A more depersonalised approach to tragedy was that of the American Mary Borden, who did not try to publish her work about nursing until 1929 – or perhaps she wished to but had to keep it in a bottom drawer for ten years. Her book *The Forbidden Zone* consists of some poems and sketches which she produced between 1914 and 1918 during four years of hospital work with the French Army, and five stories that she wrote after the war. Of the title the author writes in the short preface:

> I have called the collection of fragments 'The Forbidden Zone' because the strip of land immediately behind the zone of fire where I was stationed went by that name in the French Army. We were moved up and down inside it; our hospital unit was shifted from Flanders to the Somme, then to Champagne, and then back again to Belgium, but we never left 'La Zone Interdite'.[39]

The title refers to the forbidden zone on the battlefield, to the boundaries of common sense and understanding which in wartime are pushed impossibly back and thus mark off forbidden territory, and to the areas in life which are to a woman forbidden, which are a masculine preserve. It is of the women watching the men slaughtering each other that one might say 'theirs not to reason why' and certainly Mary Borden does not ask questions, she merely describes exactly as it was to her stoical but appalled gaze.

Her experiences as a nurse were quite different from Enid Bagnold's because at a hospital just behind the front line the nurses have to endure infinitely more, and Mary Borden describes what she saw in a succinct prose style which has affinities with Ernest Hemingway's in *A Farewell to Arms* (1929).

> I had received by post that same morning a dozen beautiful new platinum needles. I was very pleased with them. I said to one of the dressers as I fixed a needle on my syringe and held it up, squirting the liquid through it: 'Look. I've some lovely new needles.' He said: 'Come and help me a moment. Just cut this bandage, please.' I went over to his dressing-table. He darted off to a voice that was shrieking somewhere. There was a man stretched on the table. His brain came off in my hands when I lifted the bandage from his head.

When the dresser came back I said: 'His brain came off on the bandage.'

'Where have you put it?'

'I put it in the pail under the table.'

'It's only one half of his brain,' he said, looking into the man's skull. 'The rest is here.'

I left him to finish the dressing and went about my own business. I had much to do.

It was my business to sort out the wounded as they were brought in from the ambulances and to keep them from dying before they got to the operating rooms: it was my business to sort out the nearly dying from the dying. I was there to sort them out and tell how fast life was ebbing in them. Life was leaking away from all of them; but with some there was no hurry, with others it was a case of minutes. It was my business to create a counter-wave of life, to create the flow against the ebb. It was like a tug of war with the tide.[40]

One of the purposes of this grim detail is to make it plain that in wartime women can be as staunch and as heroic as any man. And then war work could also mean 'freedom, exhilarating activity and romance', as it did for the heroine of Mary Borden's 1931 novel *Sarah Gay*. Working in France

she had been happy, surrounded by sights, sounds and smells that made the colonels of infantry, who came back from the front line to the hospital to pin military medals on the breasts of their dying men, turn pale with horror.

She made a good nurse, strong, serious, quick and not squeamish. She didn't seem to mind what she had to do; would scrub big, yellow feet, empty bedpans or hold a dying man in her arms, unaffected, apparently, by the smells of dirt, sweat, blood or gangrene. Sometimes she would go out behind the wooden hut where the men lay in their iron beds and be sick. Sometimes, alone in the cubicle where she slept, she would sob, stifling her face in her rough pillow, but no one knew this; and the surgeons realized that they could count on her to fight stubbornly and efficiently for the flickering lives of the broken battered men they sent her from the operating room. They marvelled at her British phlegm and gave up, quite soon, any attempt at the badinage that relieved their grim intercourse with the other nurses. She remained aloof from them, but with her helpless men she was different. She had learned the Poilu's argot and talked to them as if she were one of them, exchanging childish jokes with them while she dressed their hideous wounds, a friendly smile on her lips, her eyes grave, intent and professional.[41]

Women did not give their lives in the 1914–18 war, but this was the last war in which this was to be so, for modern air warfare kills men and women indiscriminately. When Vera Brittain wrote *Testament of Youth* (1933) she was remembering a war whose impact was uneven both between class and sex. The major impact was of course against the 'tommy', although popular myth would have us believe that the 'officer' class was the one which suffered the huge losses. But, as Robert Wohl has pointed out, out of 700,000 British combatants killed in the war only 37,000 were officers; the literate have kept their memory fiercely alive while the tommies have not had the good fortune to be similarly enshrined in myth.[42]

The impact on women was more enduring: often their lives were irrevocably warped. No one can read *Testament of Youth* without tears and it is a great tribute to Vera Brittain's prose style that she holds the reader enthralled through nearly seven hundred pages. She describes her childhood in provincial Buxton, her brief spell at Oxford, her growing love for Roland Leighton and her four years of nursing. Yet the relentless dramas of the war years leave her emotionally numbed, and although she finally finds a new love she makes no pretence that it will be anything but a very good second-best to the dead Roland, who embodies so much tragedy and so much heroism. For this is one of the most haunting themes of the few novels written by women whose lovers were killed in the war: they may find someone else but they will never replace what they have lost.

May Wedderburn Cannan, for example, describes in her

autobiography how her fiancé Bevil Quiller-Couch dies of pneumonia just after the Armistice: in 1924 she meets a new love who 'wore loose brown tweeds and had a bull-nosed Morris two-seater and was nice to my dog'. These affectionate but unpassionate phrases are echoes of the words written by May Wedderburn Cannan in her one novel *The Lonely Generation* (1934). In it, Delphine loses her lover Bobby, and five years later is wooed by Hugh, 'the perfect friend'. When she seeks the advice of an old family friend she describes him in phrases which are friendly, resigned, tender, but not lover-like: 'So she told him, quietly, soberly, as befitted a tale not of bright morning, but of evening; a tale of a new riding on an adventure, lovely, but sad for an earlier hour.'[43]

The dead can easily retain their romance, that is their pre-rogative. And at least the heroines of these books, by making it plain that they would never forget, revealed a strength and a compassion that many others in fact curiously lacked. They revealed, also, an idealism to which subsequent generations had to adjust themselves. This consisted partly in a moral and religious repulsion to war and also, more importantly, in an almost mystical reverence for the dead heroes. For many women who came to maturity during and after the First World War no living man could ever have the golden qualities of the dead, an attitude which has had far-reaching effects on the cultural and social life of England in the present century. There were too the 'surplus' women who never married, those with dead fiancés and those who never found a husband after so many millions had been killed – and whose lives were spent working or caring for elderly relatives. The past, and the dead that were part of it, became for many of far greater interest and glory than the unspectacular tawdriness of the present.

> I like to think of you as brown and tall,
> As strong and living as you used to be,
> In khaki tunic, Sam Browne belt and all,
> And standing there and laughing down at me.[44]

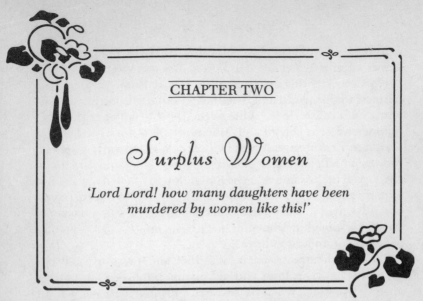

CHAPTER TWO

Surplus Women

*'Lord Lord! how many daughters have been
murdered by women like this!'*

'Members of the professional and business classes marrying within the nineteenth century had normally been brought up in large families, seven or eight being usual numbers, and only higher ones attracting attention.'[1] Thus Ensor in his classic account of late Victorian England published in 1936. The theme of Eleanor Mordaunt's novel *The Family* (1915) explored the effects of this *largesse*, being about the destructive effect of the large Victorian family when the parents proved ineffectual. They went on 'having child after child, content with trimming up the cradle afresh, in pink and blue ribbons and muslin. As though human beings were always babies, could live in the cradle!'[2]

And it was the girls who suffered most, for all they could do was stay at home waiting to marry; if hope finally died, they occupied themselves with domestic duties, social engagements, extended visits to relatives and other feminine pursuits. Without a husband to give them a home of their own, the unmarried daughter was forced to stay at home, dwindling into Aunt Laetitia or Great-Aunt Cecily, passing her days observing the joys of others. Very few complained, but filled their lives with notions of duty, respectability, kindliness and of course Godliness. By the time they were middle-aged they had become

a familiar and indeed indispensable part of the domestic landscape, a figure well known in fiction and memoirs.

Florence Nightingale's frustration was unusual. ' "What is my
business in this world and what have I done this fortnight?" she
wrote on July 7th, 1846. "I have read the 'Daughter at Home' to
Father and two chapters of Macintosh; a volume of *Sybil* to
Mamma. Learnt seven tunes by heart. Written various letters.
Ridden with Papa. Paid eight visits. Done Company. And that is
all." ' And in the same year she jotted down: ' "Oh if one has but
a toothache . . . what remedies are invented! What carriages,
horses, ponies, journeys, doctors, chaperones, are urged on one;
but if it is something the matter with the *mind* . . . it is neither
believed nor understood." '3

She wrote her tract *Cassandra* in 1852 and it was privately circulated seven years later and not openly published for another
seventy-five years, when Ray Strachey printed it as an appendix
to *The Cause* in 1928. It is a rousing castigation of the lot of
unmarried middle-class women who had neither the need, the
means or the chance to fend for themselves.

> The family uses people, *not* for what they are, nor for what
> they are intended to be, but for what it wants them
> for – its own uses. It thinks of them not as what God has
> made, but as the something which it has arranged that they
> shall be. If it wants someone to sit in the drawing-room,
> *that* someone is supplied by the family, though that
> member may be destined for science, or for education, or
> for active superintendence by God, i.e. by the gifts within.
>
> This system dooms some minds to incurable infancy,
> others to silent misery.4

Although most middle-class women were less rebellious than
this, the circumstances of the unmarried daughter of the house
were very similar. Her opportunities were drastically limited by
the demands of propriety and the restricted possibilities for
education and paid work. But few grumbled, taking it for
granted that they, the unlucky, should stay meekly at home and,
whether they were still waiting for a husband, or, once they
were over thirty, had gently given up hope, their occupations

were much the same, probably very like Jane Osborne's in *Vanity Fair* (1848):

> It was an awful existence. She had to get up of black winter's mornings to make breakfast for her scowling old father, who would have turned the whole house out of doors if his tea had not been ready at half-past eight. She remained silent opposite to him, listening to the urn hissing, and sitting in tremor while the parent read his paper, and consumed his accustomed portion of muffins and tea. At half-past nine he rose and went to the City, and she was almost free till dinner-time, to make visitations in the kitchen, and to scold the servants; to drive abroad and descend upon the tradesmen, who were prodigiously respectful; to leave her cards and her papa's at the great, glum, respectable houses of their City friends; or to sit alone in the large drawing-room, expecting visitors, and working at a huge piece of worsted by the fire, on the sofa hard by the great Iphigenia clock, which ticked and tolled with mournful loudness in the dreary room.[5]

Little had changed outwardly over seventy years later for Katharine Hilbery who, as *Night and Day* (1919) opens, is to be found 'in common with many other young ladies of her class . . . pouring out tea'.

> She had the reputation, which nothing in her manner contradicted, of being the most practical of people. Ordering meals, directing servants, paying bills, and so contriving that every clock ticked more or less accurately in time, and a number of vases were always full of fresh flowers was supposed to be a natural endowment of hers.[6]

She is beset by the same paraphernalia of clocks, servants and tea as was Jane Osborne and, like Florence Nightingale, is forced to read her mathematics books secretly in her bedroom since it was only at night 'that she felt secure enough from surprise to concentrate her mind to the utmost'. Yet, given that the domestic trappings had remained the same over the years, it is obvious that for Katharine everything else has changed a great deal.

She is free to make choices. Not as free as her daughters will be in the England of the 1920s (the novel is set pre-1914), but far freer than her immediate predecessors. For one of the most memorable qualities of *Night and Day* is its historical awareness; in contrast to the timelessness of, for example, *The Waves*, this earlier novel by Virginia Woolf is an elegy on time – or rather, tradition – past when the conventions of society held sway. The climax comes when Katharine rejects what tradition has handed down to her and realises that

> the only truth which she could discover was the truth of what she herself felt – a frail beam when compared with the broad illumination shed by the eyes of all the people who are in agreement to see together; but having rejected the visionary voices, she had no choice but to make this her guide through the dark masses which confronted her.[7]

Previously she had accepted that 'the rules which should govern the behaviour of unmarried women are written in red ink, graved upon marble, if, by some freak of nature, it should fall out that the unmarried woman has not the same writing scored upon her heart'. But now, for Katharine and other women like her, the red ink was fading and the tradition was relaxing its hold. To what had they owed this change in circumstances?

From about the mid-nineteenth century, middle-class women had been forced into the role of 'angel in the house', increasingly debarred from any form of occupation; 'they became custodians of the moral conscience, the repository of all virtue, and as such were obliged to live apart from the sordid everyday cares of material life'.[8] But as the century drew to a close, economic retrenchment had become an increasing necessity among the middle classes, and as a result family size decreased. There were now fewer unmarried daughters at home, but home itself was smaller and the way of life less lavish. And with fewer siblings and smaller households, the daughter of the house became less of an essential prop, and one which it was increasingly difficult to maintain.

At the same time the chances of finding a husband were diminishing since that constant proportion of surplus women ever present in the population had dramatically increased because of the demands of the Empire. The colonies offered steady employment and attracted three hundred thousand young males every year in the thirty years or so leading up to 1914. Not all of them could come home on leave in search of a bride, nor were they all lucky enough to find one among the young women who came out to the Colonies on a visit in order to husband-hunt. Yet many women were eager to abandon the comfort of the drawing room for the rigours of the tropics – they were grateful to find a husband and if a life in India was the price they had to pay, then they would pay it gladly.

The 1911 census demonstrates the difficulty of getting married: out of an average one thousand women 579 were married, 119 were widowed and 302 were unmarried.[9] Overall there was a female majority of 1.3 million, of whom some were too young for marriage and some were widowed; a 'surplus' that the First World War and the ravages of the 'Spanish' flu pushed up to 1.7 million by the 1921 census.

Thus growing numbers of unsupported middle-class women had begun to work as teachers and governesses and, by the beginning of the twentieth century, as 'typewriters', nurses and clerical workers; others began to enjoy the increasing opportunities for higher education. (Prior to inheriting her five hundred a year, the imaginary narrator of Virginia Woolf's *A Room of One's Own* 'had earned a few pounds by addressing envelopes, reading to old ladies, making artificial flowers, teaching the alphabet to small children in a kindergarten. Such were the chief occupations that were open to women before 1918.')

In a handful of late Victorian novels there appeared a type of woman who became known as the 'New Woman'. Olive Schreiner's *The Story of an African Farm* (1883), George Egerton's *Keynotes* (1893), Sarah Grand's *The Heavenly Twins* (1893), Grant Allen's *The Woman Who Did* (1895) and George Meredith's *Diana of the Crossways* (1895) have heroines who in various ways exemplify women who were struggling to throw off the stereotyped image of the middle-class woman and to grow into autonomous free spirits. By far the finest of this group of novels is George Gissing's *The Odd Women* (1893) which movingly constrasts the lives of four women who are 'odd' because, for various reasons, they are unmarried but not living at home.

Rhoda Nunn is a feminist who devotes her life to helping women to lead useful, independent lives; Alice and Virginia spend their days eking out their minuscule income rather than become companion helps to those better off than themselves, and their sister Monica rejects Rhoda's offer of help and quickly 'vanishes into matrimony' with a man who restricts her every impulse and tells her:

> Woman's sphere is the home, Monica. Unfortunately girls are often obliged to go out and earn their living, but this is unnatural, a necessity which advanced civilization will altogether abolish . . . If a woman can neither have a home of her own, nor find occupation in any one else's she is deeply to be pitied; her life is bound to be unhappy.[10]

But the Rhoda Nunns or Miss Minivers (*Ann Veronica*) or Mary Datchets (*Night and Day*) were in a minority; not many women could be described as is Mary in the following passage:

> She was some twenty-five years of age, but looked older because she earned, or intended to earn, her own living and had already lost the look of the irresponsible spectator, and taken on that of the private in the army of workers. Her gestures seemed to have a certain purpose; the muscles round eyes and lips were set rather firmly, as though the senses had undergone some discipline and were held ready for a call on them.[11]

For most middle-class women continued to be reared in the expectation that they stayed at home until marriage claimed them. And even though the high employment rate among the working class meant that by 1914 women made up one-third of the total labour force, novelists continued to ignore this vast proportion (some five million women) as a subject for fiction. The 146,000 female clerks who declared themselves in the 1911 census remained unlikely material for novels, which were still dominated by the love interest, by the subject of women's lives as, how and when they were rearranged by men.

Novels, being largely a middle-class art form, tend to reflect middle-class expectations, and at this time the chief of these was that a woman should conform to the way of life so deplored by Ann Veronica when she realised that the world 'had no particular place for her at all, nothing for her to do, except a functionless existence varied by calls, tennis, selected novels, walks, and dusting in her father's house'.[12] Interestingly, by the time H. G. Wells wrote *Ann Veronica* in 1909 the heroine's rebellion was no longer as striking as it would have been two or three decades previously. But because he was the most popular middlebrow novelist of his time and was alert to a groundswell that already existed, his novel outshone in popularity all the other 'New Woman' novels from which it derived so much. For it is indeed a truism of literary history that the 'modern' is in fact only an echo of what is already there; novels that are too far before their time do not sell.

Thus it was only when the tide was beginning to turn, when women were beginning to nurture expectations wider than the confines of their parents' home, that novelists began to write about their plight. Before the second decade of the new century no one had chosen as heroine the type of woman living at home in the mid-nineteenth century, described by Edward Carpenter as having

> absolutely nothing to do except dabble in paints and music . . . and wander aimlessly from room to room to see if by chance 'anything was going on'. Dusting, cooking, sewing, darning – all light household duties were already forestalled; there was no private garden, and if there had been it would have been 'unladylike' to do anything in it . . . every aspiration and outlet, except in the direction of dress and dancing, was blocked; and marriage, with the growing scarcity of men, was becoming every day less likely, or easy to compass.[13]

Multiply this picture by thousands and here, among Carpenter's six sisters, one might assume there was material for a novel. But it would be a novel without a climax, with a beginning, certainly, and a middle, but no end. For what end can there be for the woman at home with no marriage prospects, no possibility of occupation more taxing than endlessly spinning out her days and with no chance in a servanted, affluent home to use up the little energy remaining to her after boredom, depression and psychosomatic illness have claimed their share?

The inactive woman can only be the heroine of a novel when the options are there; because then, even if she chooses to ignore these options, there is the dramatic tension which inevitably accompanies her longings, indecision or even decisiveness. So it was only when the possibility of of choice became a real one that fiction began to exploit this particular theme, to describe a fate familiar to so many but hitherto ignored in literature. Ignored, that is, as a figure of crucial interest, for obviously from Jane Austen onward the unmarried daughter at home was a familiar walk-on part.

The New Woman of the 1890s was a forerunner of the heroines of the 1920s. But both were unrepresentative. Thousands and thousands of women accepted the convention that they did not feel sexual desire, must not assert themselves, must not think of any occupation except living at home or vanishing into matrimony; in short they were unrebellious. Looking back, it seems remarkable that the agitation for the vote was not carried much further inside the middle classes. But before the 1914–18 war offered middle-class women the chance to work outside the home, most would have accepted their imprisonment and would have agreed with Frederick Harrison's article on 'The Emancipation of Women' in which he said that:

> The true function of women is to educate not children only, but men, to train to a higher civilization not the rising generation but the actual society. And to do this by diffusing the spirit of affection, of self-restraint, self-sacrifice, fidelity and purity . . . as mother, as wife, as sister, as daugher, as friend, as nurse, as teacher, as servant, as counsellor, as purifier, as example, in a word – as woman.[14]

And he declared that 'to keep the family true, refined, affectionate, faithful, is a grander task than to govern the state'.

But for the woman without children, and with servants to run the home, it was a life wherein nothing much happened, not much was expected and time was endlessly and depressingly spun out. *The Rector's Daughter* (1924) is a novel by F. M. Mayor about a heroine in exactly this mould. We are told early on about Mary that

> as time passed on her contemporaries married, or settled into spinsters with objects in life. The neighbourhood arranged its friendships. At the tea-parties she had neither the charm of novelty nor familiarity. She was rather a fish out of water with the married. She played games with their children better than they did, for she kept something of a child in her; but the Rectory never had to search for servants, so that the topic of registries was closed. She could not hunt; she cared for no sport; she was useless at committees; she did not like gardening. This cut her off. She longed for friends, but friend-making needs practice and beginning early in life, and her best friend-making years slipped by unused.[15]

Nothing ever changes for her, yet Mary keeps our involvement, despite the centre of interest shifting at times to her might-have-been lover's wife. At the end of the book all three meet for a matinée.

> 'Well, old thing, it *is* jolly seeing you again, and not changed one bit, except that you're so awfully fit. You haven't told me a thing about yourself. What do you do with yourself all day, without me to see that you don't get into mischief?'
>
> Mary thought of her busy, happy life. She compared it to Kathy's fullness; it seemed starvation.
>
> 'I don't think there's much to tell,' she said. 'I only –' She stopped; she felt herself near tears.
>
> 'I *say*!' cried Kathy. 'It's nearly the half-hour. We must fly. I loathe being late.'[16]

Mary's devotion to her father is a mixture of habit, inertia, gratitude and deference to the accepted, conventional way of life which for years had been good enough for thousands of women like her. It was not going to be an overnight event, women's growing dislike of their domestic chains and their new yearning for self-fulfilment. Mary is described as being unexceptional and perfectly conformist. Not for her any ideas of supporting herself and putting her mind to some use. Her one attempt at writing is smartly crushed by her father and her one hope of marriage is snatched from her through her own lack of assertiveness and her 'niceness'.

Yet her life is not entirely empty, and some see *The Rector's Daughter* as an optimistic novel, describing an empty, useless life which, nevertheless, *matters*. For Mary loves and is loved by all around her in her enclosed world, and even though fulfilment eludes her she has known compassion, tenderness and deep feeling.

And, of course, she has never done anything of which people might disapprove – for it was so important to be nice. 'No nice girl . . .' was a phrase often on parents' lips and to behave badly was a far, far greater crime than to leave one's brain quietly to wither or to spin out an existence in which nothing marked the passing of the years except the passing seasons. The amount of sacrifice that took place upon the altar of convention was greater than we can ever imagine, since of course it is impossible to assess how much might have happened if the gods of manners, status and what-people-might-think had not exerted their influence. And we, the generations that have grown up since those days, should never forget that one of our most hard-won freedoms is our ability to do things, to exist, without so continually and obsessively caring about how others see us.

The novelist who would most have delighted in this freedom and who wrote so often on the theme of the devouring of the individual's needs and emotions by society was E. M. Delafield. Specifically, in two of her novels she wrote about the daughter at home whose only chance of self-fulfilment was ruthlessly sacrificed to the demands of convention and its mouthpiece, the mother. Alex, the heroine of *Consequences* (1919), has an unhappy childhood, annoying Nurse because she is unable to charm and dissemble. The Convent at Liège to which she is sent continues the process of subduing all that within her is spontaneous and heartfelt. She longs to be good and clever but is too transparent to manage pretence and too ashamed to be herself. She emerges ill-equipped to cope with the contrast between the moral and physical rigours of Liège and the ruthless hedonism involved in 'coming out'.

> She had hated the physical discomfort of the conventual system, the insufficient hours of sleep, the bitter cold of the Belgian winters and the streaming rain that defiled the summers . . .
>
> It seemed to Alex that when she joined the mysterious ranks of grown-up people everything would be different. She never doubted that with long dresses and piled-up hair, her whole personality would change, and the meaningless chaos of life reduce itself to some comprehensible solution. Everything all her life had been tending towards the business of 'growing up'. Everything that she was taught at home impressed the theory that her 'coming out' would usher in the realities of life . . . but she was also rather bewildered. The contrast between all this preoccupation with her clothes and her appearance, and the austere mental striving after spiritual or moral results which had permeated the convent atmosphere, was too violent.[17]

Alex is swiftly thrust into what Virginia Woolf called 'the crowded dance of modern life' and for her it literally is a dance. She is completely and touchingly naïve which is hardly surprising given that the previous boundaries of her world had been defined by the nursery and the convent. Exhortations like ' "Never more than three dances with the same man, Alex, at the very *outside*. It's such bad form to make yourself conspicuous with any one – your father would dislike it very much" ' leave her bewildered and are impossible to reconcile with the success of her convent friend Queenie. When *she* appears 'every man in the little waiting group was pressing round her, claiming first possession of her attention . . . she dispensed her favours right and left, always with the same chilly, composed sweetness.'

But, although observed with interest by Alex's father, Queenie is pronounced 'not – altogether'. And Alex flounders in a world organised on lines understood by most people but which prove a confusion to her; she is never taught how to negotiate the tightrope between friendly flirtation and being '– altogether', that line at which social relationships with men come to grief unless clearly defined. She wants to be friendly but feels awkward, she wants to be part of a group but feels different. Unless chance in the form of a knight on a white charger is to play its part, the novel can only end tragically. For of course there is no possibility of Alex finding a job as an outlet for her energies and emotions, even if 'so many girls take up slummin' and good works now-a-days'.

She dutifully agrees to marry a man who abhors sentimentality and has to remove his pince-nez before gingerly touching the middle of her cheek with his lips. Then he polishes the glass before replacing it – 'It was the apotheosis of their anti-climax.' And, although E. M. Delafield's perceptions are sometimes not very subtle, she is always acute when she points out that depth of feeling is usually irreconcilable with convention.

> On making up her mind that she must break off her engagement, Alex, unaware, took the bravest decision of her life.
>
> She was being true to an instinctive standard, in which she herself only believed with part of her mind, and which was absolutely unknown to any of those who made up her surroundings.[18]

So now there is no future for the 'weakly impulsive' Alex. Her reputation is sullied, her chances ruined and, in any other household, she would adopt the role of stay-at-home daughter. But Lady Isabel has never been one for affection and views the idea of an unmarried daughter as not only a social stigma but a slur upon her own charms. She makes it plain that Alex cannot expect to stay at home indefinitely and that, unmarried, there is no future for her. There is nothing for Alex to do except return to the convent life which has so far, apart from life in the nursery, been her only reality. But her passionate if repressed feelings render her unsuitable for the rigorous, self-disciplined life of a nun. Released from her vows, she returns to her widowed sister in Hampstead; but her sister does not want her, no one wants her and she has no money. After a misunderstanding with her brother Cedric over money, she drowns herself in one of the ponds on Hampstead Heath. And the reader is left shaken and depressed. Why for so long and until so recently were female offspring reared to have no purpose in life other than to be kept by someone else? Why, with her tremendous and stifled potential for love, was Alex deprived of the chance to tend others, teach others or be of service to others?

E. M. Delafield does not have an answer but she places a large part of the blame upon mothers. *Thank Heaven Fasting*, written in 1932, is again about a girl whose mother has only reared her in order to marry her off, preferably as rapidly and suitably as possible. From her earliest days Monica is groomed for the future and she is far luckier than Alex in that she does have some idea of how her particular world works; for example, she understands what Mrs Ingram means when she, at frequent intervals, exhorts her never to 'fall in love with a man who isn't quite, *quite* –'.

She could never, looking backwards, remember a time when she had not known that a woman's failure or success in life depended entirely upon whether or not she succeeded in getting a husband. It was not, even, a question of marrying well, although mothers with pretty and attractive daughters naturally hoped for that. But any husband at all was better than none. If a girl was neither married nor engaged by the end of her third season it was usually said, discreetly, amongst her mother's acquaintances, that no one had asked her.[19]

Monica flirts with a cad, makes friends with a man in love with a married woman, and generally, despite her anxiety to please, fails to pull it off. Then her father dies and she becomes her mother's only solace.

She said that Monica was her only child – all that she had

left in the world. Sometimes she thought that Monica might want to leave her, and she couldn't bear it.

'Not that I'd ever grudge you your happiness, my precious one, but just for a few years more – I don't suppose it'll be for very long.'

Monica, sick with pity, understood.

Her mother wanted to save her face.

She wanted both of them to be able to say that Monica had deliberately chosen not to marry, so that she might devote herself to her mother.[20]

But finally, happily, from an old family friend whose ramblings tend to send Monica into a brown study and whose eyes are earnest and prawn-like, finally she receives a proposal. In church Monica is 'conscious of nothing, save that the moment towards which the whole of life had been tending had come at last'.

She was to have a life of her own, after all.

A home, a husband, a recognised position as a married woman – an occupation. At last, she would have justified her existence.

Up to the very last moment she had been afraid, and had known that her mother was afraid, lest something should happen to prevent her marriage.

Nothing had happened: she was safe for ever.

There was no further need to be afraid, or ashamed, or anxious, any more.

She prayed that she might be a good wife to Herbert, and that if ever they had a child it might be a son.[21]

Monica's mother displays her generosity by longing for her only child to marry. Many mothers who had never been taught to have any inner resources, to manage for themselves rather than battening on others, clung to their daughters like limpets. The mother in *The Heel of Achilles*, E. M. Delafield's 1921 novel, deludes herself into thinking she is doing the best for her daughter, when really she is overpossessive and does not want her to be independent. Her sister-in-law is provoked into telling

her that she is a 'monstrous egotist' – 'Nothing matters to you so
much as having the *beau rôle* . . . you care for nothing and
nobody on earth, except as it affects your self.' And the vicar
says, more gently, that 'one knows very well . . . that it is less
painful to endure bodily anguish than to watch it endured by
one's beloved . . . Beyond that there is a greater immolation.
That of relinquishing the privilege of suffering to another, and
accepting the pain of watching that suffering.'

Some women, having themselves been deprived of independence by society, have chosen, consciously or unconsciously, to
pass this deprivation on to their daughters (see, for example,
Mary Olivier); some have battened on to their children for
pleasure and self-aggrandisement; while others have clung to
their daughters out of selfishness and fear, usually disguised as
invalidism, loneliness or general helplessness. The deformities
imposed by society on women's lives have too often been passed
from mother to daughter.

But once the Great War had widened women's horizons, the
restrictions of domestic ties became doubly irksome to the
daughter left at home. Joan in Radclyffe Hall's *The Unlit Lamp*
(1924) is in this position. She wishes to be a doctor and because of
this and her unacknowledged affection for her governess she
refuses a proposal. Her mother's response is unusual: ' "Oh,
Joan, I am so glad! . . . It's the thought of losing you . . . I can't
face the thought of that – and other things; you know what I
mean, the thought of your being maltreated by a man, the
thought that it might happen to you as it happened to me." '[23]

From early on Joan doubts whether her mother really loves
her but the thought of her 'so small and so inadequate' prevents
her from escaping to London, to a flat, independence and
medical school. When her father dies and it transpires that he
had 'borrowed' her small inheritance she realises that she will
never get away. She is not harsh enough to resist the explicit
blackmail in her mother's outburst:

'I see,' she said; 'you and Milly wish to leave home, to leave
me now that I have no one else to care for me. You want to
hide me away in a tenement house, while you two lead the

51

life that seems amusing to you. This home is to be broken up and I am to go to London – my health doesn't matter. Well, I suppose I'd be better dead and then you'd be rid of the trouble of me.'[24]

This scene comes about half-way through the novel and the momentum lapses after that. To the reader it is obvious that Joan will never get away, but Radclyffe Hall gives us many potential but rejected false-starts before she finally brings the novel to its sad conclusion. One reason for the meandering construction may be that she, the author, was evidently unclear in her mind whether her theme was devouring mothers or the girl afraid of men because of the petty tyrannies she has, throughout childhood, watched her father inflict on her mother. In the final scene, Richard asks Joan yet again to marry him:

'How long is it to go on,' he cried, 'this preying of the weak on the strong, the old on the young; this hideous, unnatural injustice that one sees all around one, this incredibly wicked thing that tradition sanctifies? . . . I tell you, Joan, the sin of it lies at the door of that old woman up there in Lynton; that mild, always ailing, cruelly gentle creature who's taken everything and given nothing and battened on you year by year. She's like an octopus who's drained you dry. You struggled to get free, you nearly succeeded, but as quickly as you cut through one tentacle, another shot out and fixed on you.'[25]

But Joan, replying, is thinking more of her own nature than of her mother: ' "I shall never marry anyone. I am not a woman who could ever have married. I've never been what you call in love with a man in my life".' It is clear that Radclyffe Hall is implying that some unmarried daughters used their mothers as shields, almost welcoming the insidious grasp of the maternal tentacles if it protected them from recognising sides of their natures they would rather ignore. Yet whether Joan is rejecting men or revelling in the pleasures of martyrdom is not quite clear. She is certainly more complex than Rachel in Lorna Rea's *Rachel Moon* (1931), whose spirit of self-sacrifice is so highly developed that she barely regrets her lover who has told her sharply but truthfully, 'you're deliberately immolating yourself on a cheap altar; an altar of martyrdom and victimisation and pathetic frustration and all that'. Even her sister declares, 'you love yourself – the noble daughter, the self-sacrificing one'. Yet in her own way Rachel is perfectly happy, even if it is probable that the main inspiration for *The Unlit Lamp* and *Rachel Moon* did come from the frequent occurrence of the unmarried daughter chained unwillingly to the parental home by the claims of the elderly. At times these 'claims' were scorned. Even before the Great War, *The Times* of 19 April 1914 came out with a vigorous statement on this theme:

Every day a host of human vampires drain the life-blood of those who are their nearest and should be their dearest . . . the most usual species is the widowed mother with a daughter of any age from 20 to 50. The other children have gone out into the world to marry and to work, and incidentally to live their own lives in homes of their own. Clearly it is the duty of the one who is left to look after the little mother. That is the universal verdict of the world and the family. If she submits, if she sacrifices her youth and individuality on the altar of the Fifth Commandment, her doom is sealed. The longer she stays on with her mother the more impossible it is for her to break away. Day and night she is at her beck and call. Her opinions, her gifts, her ambitions she must keep in the background till they atrophy from want of use. She must come when she is called, go where she is sent, walk or drive cheek by jowl with the vampire who saps her vitality, write her letters, pay calls, 'do' the flowers, exercise the dog, order the dinner, pay the wages, engage and dismiss her servants, count the linen, keep the books, and, to speak generally, run the house for the vampire's convenience from the vampire's point of view . . . The vampire ('Such a devoted mother, my dear!') has them by the throat, and slowly but surely squeezes the life out of them and drains them of youth and joy and hope. In all the long catalogue of woman's real and fancied woes there is hardly one more infuriating and none more depressing to contemplate than the commonplace tragedies of these spoilt and wasted lives.

Mothers in fiction do not often get sympathetic treatment, unless they are the reincarnation of the loving maternal instinct like Mrs Ramsay in Virginia Woolf's *To the Lighthouse* (1927) or of aloof graciousness like Lady Spencer in Rosamond Lehmann's *The Weather in the Streets* (1936); or unless they are shown wanting nothing better than to get away from their ever-pressing daughter like Lady Slane in *All Passion Spent* (1931) by Vita Sackville-West. But it is rare for a woman novelist to portray a mother of the kind imagined by Joan in *The Unlit Lamp*. Her ideal kind of motherly love

> ought to be a patient, waiting, unchanging love; the kind that went with making up the fire and sitting behind the tea-tray awaiting your return. The love that wrote and told you that you were expected home for Christmas, and that when you arrived your favourite pudding would be there to greet you. Yes, that was the ideal mother-love; it never wanted but it never exacted. It was a beautiful thing, all of one restful colour.[26]

In *The Crowded Street* (1924) (originally called *The Wallflower*) Winifred Holtby wrote about a theme which E. M. Delafield often explored: that of a mother meaning well but having no idea how to introduce her children to the complexities of life (boys of course were meant to have this done for them at their public school). Muriel, like Alex in *Consequences*, is sent away to school and then finds it hard to reconcile its values with those of home. She too finds the rules and regulations of dancing particularly confusing (although she is lucky enough to confront them early on, when she is only eleven).

> Muriel's orderly mind registered a new item of information. The unforgivable sin at a party was to have no partners. To sit quietly in the drawing-room at home was a virtue. The same conduct in the Kingsport Assembly Rooms was an undesirable combination of naughtiness and misfortune. In order to realize the Party in its full magnifi-

cence, one must have a full programme. All else was failure. Enjoyment of the music, the people, the prettiness – all this counted for nothing. It was not the Party.[27]

Like so many young girls before and since, Muriel reflects ruefully on grown-up conventions.

Being grown-up was puzzling. It seemed to make no difference at all in most things, and then to matter frightfully in quite unexpected ways. It meant, for instance, not so much the assumption of new duties as the acceptance of new values.

Was she more stupid than other people, or did everyone feel like this at first? She was travelling in a land of which she only imperfectly understood the language.[28]

She too has a friend from school days (Alex has Queenie) whose purpose in the novel is to import sexuality. Clare is bohemian rather than 'not altogether', but the contrast with her friend is equally telling. Muriel's mother realises that Clare's visit must come to an end when Clare has too many dances with the only available eligible man: in any way she can, she is determined to thrust her own daughters in front of him.

But her world crumbles when her other daughter, Connie, announces that she is expecting a baby and derides her mother's two-faced attitude to men. On the one hand, she has kept her daughters at home in order not to spoil their chances of a good marriage, on the other hand, she is deeply upset when one of them has used her sexuality to lure her lover to her. (There is the same irony in May Sinclair's wonderful novel *The Allinghams* (1927) where Margaret is pronounced mad for wanting to show her naked body to her lover but her sister Angie is forgiven because she has succeeded in seducing her lover, and her illegitimate son reconciles her parents to her – see page 130.)

Connie is forced by her family to get married and to live a farming life, the descriptions of which anticipate Stella Gibbons's satirical *Cold Comfort Farm* (1932). But she dies in childbirth, Muriel rejects a proposal and Mrs Hammond has failed to marry off either of her daughters suitably. But she does not have one to keep at home with her because Muriel has found work in London. It is unclear whether we are meant to see this as a triumph or ignominy for Mrs Hammond. Certainly most mothers in fiction between the wars would have preferred to keep their daughters at home because their upbringing had so ill-equipped them to face life without a prop.

Mrs Powell in Lettice Cooper's novel *The New House* (1936) is of this type, but her attitude is described as both intolerably selfish and completely out of date. She has two daughters, Delia who has 'escaped' to a laboratory in London and the prospect of a harmonious, carefully considered marriage to a fellow-scientist, and Rhoda, who has stayed at home. Rhoda is clearly following in the footsteps of her Aunt Ellen: they both had had one chance of marriage and escape from home, but both had been incapable of showing their love. And like Mary in *The Rector's Daughter* and Muriel in *The Crowded Street* Rhoda is ignorant of the very meaning of the word seduction, let alone of its practice. She remembers:

> How often had she heard her mother and other people say critically, 'Molly (or Betty, or Peggy) is running after that young man' with an implication of intolerable condemnation? How often had she been told not to show off, not to look at herself in the glass, not to attract people's attention? Spoken and unspoken, her upbringing had forbidden her to invite love; had been based, she now saw, on her mother's unexpressed conviction that love was wrong.[29]

Rhoda's aunt had rejected a proposal because, for her, love for a parent had to take precedence over love for anyone else.

> Aunt Ellen was practised in resignation. She had been brought up to think it a virtue not to expect much. The virtue had been instilled into her by parents who had not envisaged the inevitable result, that she wouldn't get much; or, if they had, they had perhaps concluded that for their daughter virtue should be its own reward. It never occurred to Ellen, recalling those god-like parents out of the past, that they themselves had pursued and enjoyed a

lot of other rewards besides virtue. She had accepted their serene conviction that they were always right, just as she had accepted their view that it was a pity when 'the lower classes' became discontented or tried to do or have things 'above their station'. Ellen's father and mother had laid great stress on the duty of being satisfied, one which they were well able to perform themselves, and which suited them in their children, dependants and employees. I'm sure, Ellen thought, I ought to be very thankful. Such a happy home with Mamma for so many years![30]

And at the beginning of the novel Rhoda's thoughts are much the same, that it would be cruel to leave her mother for 'it was better to forego your own wishes, and enjoy the more rarefied happiness that came from being on the side of the angels'. Throughout the day on which she helps her mother to move from the decaying family mansion into a 'new house' she continually comes back to this question. We watch her 'terrible notions of duty' gradually being swayed by other considerations, her mother's petty demands, the tedium of the life mapped out for her and, in particular, her aunt's entrenched and rather annoying 'ways'. For example, there is an unselfishness so extreme that it only makes the recipients of any generosity feel guilty, 'which made you impatient with Aunt Ellen, when she would sit in the draughty chair and eat the burnt piece of toast, thrusting selfishness upon you against your will'.

Rhoda reaches a crisis in her life when the bareness of the family home and her own prospects force her to reassess both the past and the future. Aunt Ellen is there helping them to move house, anxious to help, trying to cheer up her sister, implacably resentful at the thought of change. 'Her tone had the automatic brightness and encouragement of someone who had lived with an elderly invalid for very many years, of someone who for very many years had begun two-thirds of her remarks with, "Never mind!" ' Suddenly Rhoda hears herself saying, 'Never mind!' 'She heard in her own voice the shallow, bright tone that she had heard so often in her grandmother's drawing-room when Aunt Ellen poked the fire, or picked up a dropped stitch, or closed the window.'

writing in the 1950s, described the surplus woman's successor in the following terms:

> There were legions of her kind during the nineteen-thirties, women from the age of thirty and upward, who crowded their war-bereaved spinsterhood with voyages of discovery into new ideas and energetic practices in art or social welfare, education or religion . . . They went to lectures, tried living on honey and nuts, took lessons in German and then went walking in Germany; they bought caravans and went off with them into the hills among the lochs; they played the guitar, they supported all the new little theatre companies; they took lodgings in the slums and, distributing pots of paint, taught their neighbours the arts of simple interior decoration; they preached the inventions of Marie Stopes; they attended the meetings of the Oxford Group and put Spiritualism to their hawk-eyed test.[35]

The unmarried girl no longer had to stay shyly at home. The Victorian emphasis on obedience to the demands of the family was gradually replaced by a slightly more permissive individualism, and blame was now sometimes attached to the mother who tried to keep her daughter at her side. In Rachel Ferguson's *Alas, Poor Lady* (1937), the real culprit is Mrs Scrimgeour who is selfish, thoughtless, evasive and lacking in any real concern for her children beyond that of trying to make sure they fulfil society's expectations of them. Given that she has far too many unmarriageable daughters, it is rather hard for her to ensure that they do what is required – which is to marry suitably. Yet she trains them neither to be attractive to men nor to find a way of occupying themselves. One daughter becomes a nun. Another expects a proposal and receives instead the news that the young man in question loves someone else. And a family inheritance is so badly invested and badly managed that the youngest daughter, Grace, is forced to become a companion help. She eventually ends up friendless in one room, courtesy of the Distressed Gentlefolk Protective Association – a victim of a way of life which anticipated nothing more than a round of leaving cards, waiting for people to call, directing servants and keeping up appearances – and which, when it failed, envisaged no substitute.

But at least unmarried women had during the 1920s ceased to have the humiliating status so familiar to their unmarried aunts; nor had the demanding mothers remained immune to the kind of criticism voiced by *The Times* in 1914. Even Virginia Woolf grumbled in her diary about her mother-in-law 'who is so "painfully sensitive" – so fond of cakes, so incapable of amusing herself, so entirely without any interest in my feelings or friends; so vampire-like & vast in her demand for my entire attention & sympathy . . . Lord Lord! how many daughters have been murdered by women like this!'[36] And it is made quite plain by Margaret Kennedy in her novel *Together and Apart* (1936) that the absolutely futile divorce would never have happened if the mothers-in-law had left their children alone. Only their 'well-meaning' interference stopped the couple from patching over a trivial quarrel, and so a normally harmonious family was needlessly destroyed.

As the shadow of the nineteenth century receded, the concept of the 'matriarch' became ever more obsolete. And there is during the 1920s very little deference to duty and a large amount of sympathy for those who have been ensnared in its name. Olivia, in *Invitation to the Waltz* (1932) by Rosamond Lehmann, feels terribly sorry for Miss Robinson who makes her dresses:

> she wouldn't get a husband: she hadn't a chance now. She was thirty. Letting I dare not wait upon I would, youth had gone by; and now the candour of her desires was muddied, her spark of spirit spent. Never would she do now what once she had almost done: walked out of the house and left them all whining and gone to London to earn her living . . . That was after the death of Mr Robinson . . . and Mother said I need all my dear daughters round me now, God willing we shall never part in this life, I feel it won't be long before I too Go Home.[37]

By the 1930s, then, women's lives were less constricted. On the one hand, their chances of marrying had greatly increased, for the men who had been schoolboys at the end of the Great War were now of a marrying age, while in addition some half a million men who had emigrated overseas in the difficult days after the war had now begun to return.[38] On the other hand, if they chose not to marry, the attitude of society was kinder than it had been before the Great War. Countless middle-class women lived independent lives in comfortable circumstances, supporting themselves through their own efforts and being able to choose whether to marry or to have a career. Cicely Hamilton commented in 1940 with justifiable pride:

> If a woman is destined to go through life unwed, my country of England has many advantages as a domicile; there are, I imagine, few parts of the world where the once traditional contempt for the spinster is more thoroughly a thing of the past. Time was – and not so very long ago – when the middle-aged Englishwoman who had not found a husband was considered fair game for the jester; by the humorists of the Victorian age she was always depicted as a figure of fun – an unattractive creature who, in spite of all her efforts, had failed to induce a man to marry her. That was the old maid as a past generation saw her – and as we do not see her today; we have too many unmarried women successful in business or professional life, distinguished in literature, science, and art, to be able to keep up that joke.[39]

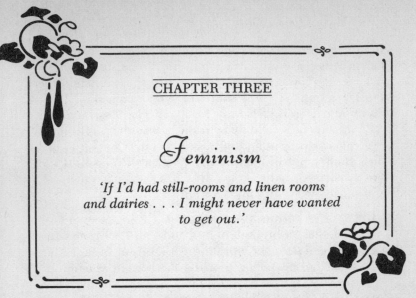

CHAPTER THREE

Feminism

*'If I'd had still-rooms and linen rooms
and dairies . . . I might never have wanted
to get out.'*

'My personal revolt was feminist rather than suffragist; what I rebelled at chiefly was the dependence implied in the idea of "destined" marriage, "destined" motherhood – the identification of success with marriage, of failure with spinsterhood, the artificial concentration of the hopes of girlhood on sexual attraction and maternity.'[1] Cicely Hamilton, who throughout her autobiography displays an unusually modest insight into the pleasures and difficulties of the unmarried woman, was always wary of 'the Cause', believing that its 'fanatical' aspects were inherently dangerous. Indeed, she went so far as to suggest that the militant suffrage movement was the beginning of the dictatorship movements 'which are by way of thrusting democracy out of the European continent' and that Mrs Pankhurst was the first of the European dictators because of her imperiousness and fanaticism. So, to her, the cause of Birth Control was of far greater interest because there could be no permanent advance in the position of women except 'under a system of voluntary motherhood'.

For most middle-class women, however, feminism, until the end of the First World War, was synonymous with the fight for the vote. The heroine of Elizabeth Robins's *The Convert* (1905) finds an object in life in the Cause and gives up 'managing things' (charity concerts) because she finds that 'there is work to do'. Ellen in Rebecca West's *The Judge* (1922) had, before she met her lover, displayed her independence of spirit because 'every Saturday afternoon [she] sold Votes for Women in Princes Street'. And Dorothy in May Sinclair's *The Tree of Heaven* (1917) displays hers not only by taking a first-class in Economics at Newnham but by attending meetings of the Committee of the North Hampstead Branch of the Women's Franchise Union. Here a vehement lady named Miss Blackadder harangues her minuscule crowd with some passion:

> 'Until you're enfranchised you are not going to own any *man* as father, or brother, or husband' (her voice rang with a deeper and stronger vibration) 'or lover, or friend. And the man who does not agree with you, the man who refuses you the vote, the man who opposes your efforts to get the vote, the man who, whether he agrees with you or not, *will not help you to get it*, you count as your enemy.'[2]

But Dorothy, too, opposes vehemence. She

> was afraid of the Feminist Vortex as her brother Michael had been afraid of the little vortex of school. She was afraid of the herded women. She disliked the excited faces, and the high voices skirling their battle-cries, and the silly business of committees, and the platform slang. She was sick and shy before the tremor and the surge of collective feeling; she loathed the gestures and the movements of the collective soul, the swaying and heaving and rushing forward of the many as one. She would not be carried away by it; she would keep the clearness of her soul . . . She would fight for freedom, but not in their way and not at their bidding.[3]

Dorothy retains the clearness of her soul, for, like Cicely Hamilton, her real revolt is feminist rather than suffragist. This is partly in her nature, and partly an inevitable consequence of the passing of time. By the second decade of the twentieth century, Dorothy has realised that the 'work to do' encompasses more than the question of votes, and leads her life accordingly;

yet when her lover, whom she had refused to marry because of her commitment to personal freedom, is killed in the retreat from Mons, her former cry of 'I think love isn't love and can't last unless it's free' has become meaningless to her.

This less than optimistic attitude to a woman's 'personal revolt' was often to be repeated in women's writing between the wars. The search for freedom and independence would either be brought to a halt by marriage; or the loss of the loved one would bring bitter regrets; or the determined would be shown to have given up, painfully, something to which their less singleminded sisters had capitulated. There are only a few equivalents in fiction to Cicely Hamilton's cheerful renunciation of marriage in favour of the rich and varied life that she created for herself.

Many of the 'New Woman' novels of the 1880s and 1890s already had plots where the search for freedom and sexual independence by the heroine is either cut short by marriage or later regretted. *Marcella* (1894) by Mrs Humphry Ward is only one of these. And novels written just before the First World War often portray heroines who struggle at first but soon defer gratefully to their lovers.

Lucy in E. M. Forster's *A Room with a View* (1908) tries to escape suburban ideals and towards the end of the novel she summons up the courage to tell her mother, amidst the hush of Mudie's circulating library, that she is thinking of sharing a flat for a little with some other girls.

'And mess with typewriters and latchkeys,' exploded Mrs Honeychurch. 'And agitate and scream, and be carried off kicking by the police. And call it a Mission – when no one wants you! And call it Duty – when it means that you can't stand your own home! And call it Work – when thousands of men are starving with the competition as it is!'

'I want more independence,' said Lucy lamely; she knew that she wanted something, and independence is a useful cry; we can always say that we have not got it. She tried to remember her emotions in Florence: those had been sincere and passionate, and had suggested beauty rather than short skirts and latchkeys. But independence was certainly her cue.

'Very well. Take your independence and be gone. Rush up and down and round the world, and come back as thin as a lath with the bad food. Despise the house that your father built and the garden that he planted, and our dear view – and then share a flat with another girl.'[4]

But no sooner have Lucy and her mother caught the train back to Dorking than she becomes engaged to be married and her brief clawing at freedom is rapidly ended.

In the same way Mrs Havelock Ellis shows her heroine deferring to received ideas of womanhood. In *Attainment* (1909) she describes Rachel deciding to use her private income to come to London, live with her maid in a flat and work for the poor. When she finally decides to give this up, a radical poet informs her that

you know in your heart that this game of puss-in-the-corner, called philanthropy, is no use to you. You are too sane and healthy for it. It's all right for love-sick girls and dyspeptic widows. It fills gaps. It will even do as a general introduction to realities for a girl of your make, but you'd rot if you stayed in it.'[5]

After some time attempting to form a commune called the Brotherhood of the Perfect Life, Rachel goes home and retreats into marriage. But at least her money has allowed her to have a taste of independence.

H.G. Wells was equally conventional, for he portrays the heroine of *Ann Veronica* (1909) as losing her assertiveness once she is in love. Some have criticised him for belittling Ann Veronica's aspirations. Most will conclude that he was a realistic middle-class novelist who was well aware of the boundaries of propriety and one who, while admiring the intelligent, free-spirited and free-loving woman, liked her, finally, to subdue her liveliness in deference to the male. The taming was for him as exciting as the wooing, which is why so many of his mistresses were writers whose minds he could respect. (They included

Violet Hunt, Dorothy Richardson, Rosalind Bland, Amber Reeves, Rebecca West and Elizabeth von Arnim.)

When Ann Veronica has finally realised that the world 'had no particular place for her at all', she runs away from home to study biology. Her father, in true Victorian fashion, divided women into either Angels in the House or prostitutes. 'His ideas about girls and women were of a sentimental and modest quality; they were creatures, he thought, either too bad for a modern vocabulary, and then frequently most undesirably desirable, or too pure and good for life.' But he could not visualise a woman living regardless of the approval of a man and it was vain for Ann Veronica to declare: ' "I want to be a human being; I want to learn about things and know about things, and not to be protected as something too precious for life, cooped up in one narrow little corner." '[6] In her father's eyes she is misguided and muddle-headed and he puts it down to the influence of fiction. ' "There was a time when girls didn't get these extravagant ideas . . . It's these damned novels. All this torrent of misleading spurious stuff that pours from the press. These sham ideals and advanced notions".'[7]

To Ann Veronica, Morningside Park, where she lives ('a suburb that had not altogether, as people say, come off') is impossibly stuffy, a place where her free spirit would of necessity wither. She anticipates the rebellion of Vera Brittain who, weary of passing her days 'in all those conventional pursuits with which the leisured young woman of every generation has endeavoured to fill the time that she is not qualified to use',[8] wrote in *Testament of Friendship*:

> I had read Olive Schreiner and followed the militant campaigns with the excitement of a sympathetic spectator, but my growing consciousness that women suffered from remediable injustices was due less to the movement for the vote than to my early environment with its complacent acceptance of female subordination.[9]

Being of an earlier generation, Ann Veronica's rebellion against female subordination *was* crystallised by the fight for the vote and she accepts that 'the Vote is the symbol of everything'.

The result of her joining the struggle for the Vote is imprisonment and a period of contemplation.

> As the long solitary days wore on Ann Veronica found a
> number of definite attitudes and conclusions in her mind.
> One of these was a classification of women into women
> who are and women who are not hostile to men. 'The real
> reason why I am out of place here,' she said, 'is because I
> like men. I can talk with them. I've never found them
> hostile. I've got no feminine class feeling. I don't want any
> laws or freedoms to protect me from a man like Mr Capes. I
> know that in my heart I would take whatever he gave . . .'
> 'A woman wants a proper alliance with a man, a man
> who is better stuff than herself. She wants that and needs it
> more than anything else in the world. It may not be just, it
> may not be fair, but things are so. It isn't law, nor custom,
> nor masculine violence settled that. It is just how things
> happen to be. She wants to be free – she wants to be legally
> and economically free, so as not to be subject to the wrong
> man; but only God, who made the world, can alter things
> to prevent her being slave to the right one.'[10]

She concludes that previously she had been driven by stark
egotism and that only now does she 'begin to understand Jane
Austen and chintz covers and decency and refinement and all the
rest of it'. And so the novel retires into romance, with Ann
Veronica open-eyed to the virtues of love and humility and her
gesture of defiance taking the form of living with a married man.
Wells was thereby fulfilling his own fantasies, which involved
subduing a spirited girl to the will of a good man while keeping
bourgeois morals at bay. The defiance of the first part of the
novel and the immorality of the second ensured that *Ann
Veronica* became a *cause célèbre*; for those middle-class parents,
and they were the majority, who assumed decency and
refinement to be unquestionably a part of life it was potentially
explosive and many forbade their daughters to read it.

Its danger was by far the greater because Wells was a respected middle-class writer. He could not be dismissed as a mere
oddity like the earlier feminist writers such as Olive Schreiner,

'George Egerton', Grant Allen or Sarah Grand. And he was additionally dangerous since he did not only show a young girl rebelling against the constrictions of suburbia: he also showed a girl who, once she has admitted to herself that she loves, declares her feelings and gets away with it. He wrote in 1934:

> The particular offence was that Ann Veronica was a virgin who fell in love and showed it, instead of waiting as all popular heroines had hitherto done, for someone to make love to her. It was held to be an unspeakable offence that an adolescent female should be sex-conscious before the thing was forced upon her attention. But Ann Veronica wanted a particular man who excited her and she pursued him and got him. With gusto . . . if I had been a D. H. Lawrence, with every fig leaf pinned aside, I could not have been considered more improper than I was.[11]

By the 1920s, feminism for some middle-class women became more a question of personal integrity, of women fulfilling themselves for themselves. To do this, they felt that they must fight for equality for women. As Winifred Holtby wrote:

> I am a feminist because I dislike everything that feminism implies. I desire an end of the whole business, the demands for equality, the suggestions of sex warfare, the very name of feminism. I want to be about the work in which my real interests lie, the study of inter-race relationships, the writing of novels and so forth. But while the inequality exists, while injustice is done and opportunity denied to the great majority of women, I shall have to be a feminist with the motto Equality First. And I shan't be happy till I get . . . a society in which sex-differentiation concerns those things alone which by the physical laws of nature it must govern, a society in which men and women work together for the good of all mankind, a society in which there is no respect of persons, either male or female, but a supreme regard for the importance of the human being.[13]

Winifred Holtby was following in the tradition of the 'Old Feminism' in her desire to see 'an end of the whole business'. She was unsympathetic to the 'New Feminism' which was far more politically orientated than the 'Old'. The doctrine of the 'New' feminists was defined by Eleanor Rathbone. In direct contradiction to the 'Old', they argued that the time had come to stop concentrating on equality, defined as demands for those things that men had and women were without, and to work for those things women needed 'not because it is what men have got but because it is what women need to fulfil the potentialities of their own natures and to adjust themselves to the circumstances of their own lives'.[14] The 'Old' feminists fought for equal pay, equal opportunities, equal rights, while the 'New' feminists were anxious to emphasise the differences between men and women and to use the basic fact of this difference as a starting-point for their efforts on women's behalf. Fifty years later these different approaches are still with us. The feminist movement in fact includes many 'feminisms' and indeed this has been a strength. Dora Russell is one example of a feminist who expresses both the 'Old' and the 'New' – declaring the need for equal rights, for laws which offer justice to women as well as men, but who believes in the necessity for women's own values and concerns to be developed and to be represented in our male-dominated society. If anyone asks me 'are you a feminist?' I say 'no, not if it means having aggressive, "anti-men" feelings.' But when pressed, I admit to being a passionate feminist in the sense that I want an end to the whole business as quickly as possible, even though I begin to think it will not be in my lifetime.

The feminist novels that were written between the wars tend to be in the tradition of the 'Old' feminism, being concerned less with the stark realities of either male or political oppression than with women's chances for self-fulfilment in a still unequal society. They were about the importance of the human being when that being happens to be female. Yet the solutions were far from clear-cut and many of the novels which try to show a female soul winging its way to the heights of self-development still end with the same old sop to convention, namely the heroine deferring gratefully to the protection of her male lover. In this respect the Ann Veronica theme set a pattern which was to be frequently imitated. There is for example *The Rebel Generation*

(1925) by Jo van Ammers-Küller, a Dutch novel which achieved some popular success in England when it was translated in 1928.

The novel is divided into three parts, set in 1840, 1872 and 1923. The first part describes a tyrannical father presiding undisputed over his cowering family. The women pass their lives in a round of ironing, sewing, cooking and petty economising, and the idea of a girl even thinking for herself is abhorrent. Thirty years later we see that even the ones who did marry suitably have led futile, unhappy lives, thinking only about their status in the eyes of others. They continue to bring up their daughters to believe that 'God's will is that a daughter should obey her parents and help her mother at home until she fulfils her proper destiny by marriage'. The one girl who escaped is now a writer, active on behalf of women's causes, unmarried and eager to bring freedom to the daughters of those with whom she shared her life thirty years previously. But the moral is that even emancipation does not bring happiness at least in the long run:

> They were so blissfully certain, all these ardent young things, that they possessed the one secret of true happiness and had found a complete solution for all the ills and grievances of womankind . . . although the lords of creation held 'blue stockings' in the most undisguised contempt, this did not in the least deter the women from their folly but seemed rather to egg them on to fiercer efforts.[15]

One of 'these ardent young things' escapes: she becomes a doctor and we see her in the 1920s when she goes back to Leyden to live with her nephew and his wife. Yet even she is surprised when the wife 'made out an irrefutable case against housekeeping, averring that it was a mere abstract idea. Only teachers of domestic economy and a handful of old frumps would dream of attaching any importance to it. Housekeeping to a modern woman is just ordering the meals, keeping the accounts and arranging the servants' work'. Freedom from drudgery there may be but clearly emancipation does not mean happiness for everyone. The daughter of this 'modern woman' declares angrily: ' "Hasn't Mother's precious *work* always been placed far before any 'old-fashioned domesticity' as you call it?" ' The author comments:

> The women of fifty years ago in despair at the barren aimlessness of their lives had sought happiness in intellectual development and the equality of the sexes. And now the younger generation were already proposing to reject the privileges their elders had so hardly won and to go back to the days of thraldom.[16]

So a young 'career woman' falls into her lover's arms.

> He was so different from the rest. *He* didn't care in the least whether she were clever. To him she was weak and dependent, just a little girl he longed to hold tight in his arms while she whispered that she loved him and would be his for ever and ever.
>
> And all at once she knew that it was just this kind of girl that she wanted to be; that all the things with which she had tried to fill her life were not such as brought lasting happiness to any woman.[17]

It is the same moral as Rose Macaulay was so fond of making. Each generation thinks it is unique but they are just treading a well-worn path. As Rome declares in *Told by an Idiot* (1923) ' "there's one thing about freedom . . . each generation of people begin by thinking they've got it for the first time in history, and end by being sure the generation younger than themselves have too much of it" '.[18] And her mother remembers

> in her own youth the older people talking about the New Girl, the New Woman. Were girls and women really always newer than boys and men, or was it only that people noticed it more, and said more about it? . . . The New Young Woman. Bold, fast, blue-stockinged, reading and talking about things of which their mothers had never, before marriage, heard — in brief, NEW.[19]

And G. B. Stern wrote on the same theme in *Tents of Israel* (1924) (published in America the following year under the title of *The Matriarch*). The novel is a family chronicle, complete with family tree, about the Rakonitz family. Traits of character are handed down from generation to generation and however hard members of the family try to escape it is impossible for them to do so. One of them tries. She

> would not be absurdly chaperoned, nor drilled into marriage; she was modern; she would not be ruled by the *jeune-fille* traditions of etiquette; she would make her own arrangements; she would make no arrangements at all; live as she liked; live free; snap her fingers at the out-of-date solemnities of dowry, and parents who 'approached' each other.[20]

But those around her react in the way that Ann Veronica's father had reacted – they assume she gets her foolish notions from books: ' "Modern girl, indeed! . . . all this idiocy of free love and light love and love for an hour – pagans up-to-date – isn't her own inspiration. She's been reading too much, silly goose." ' Both novelists were making the same point, one which Cicely Hamilton echoed:

> One of Nature's devices to save the world from stagnation is to implant in the breast of each generation a certain amount of contempt for the old-fashioned manners and outlook of its immediate predecessors; a contempt which youth, grown older in its turn, will receive from its own sons and daughters.[21]

The main theme of A. S. M. Hutchinson's *This Freedom* (1922) is whether the post-1918 world had changed for the better or worse. The novel's style is facile and its tone of voice sentimental, but it had a wide popular appeal. Yet, in the manner of bestselling fiction, the author flits from one moral stance to another, declaring roundly against one and then another, caring nothing for consistency but concerned only with airing all the arguments. For example, when Rosalie, the heroine, is a child the author sympathises with her for the servile position she holds in relation to the men in her family. But when she is adult and tries to fulfil her own aspirations, then she is condemned for not ministering to her husband and children. It may be a necessary ingredient of bestsellers that they do not offend anyone, paying lip service first to one, then to another; but the end result always appears unprovocative.

The opening of *This Freedom* is similar in some ways to that of *The Crowded Street*, which was to appear two years later, although Winifred Holtby can evoke the father's brutish selfishness while Hutchinson has to spell it out; he tells one what to think where a more subtle novelist works on the reader's perceptions indirectly. But the following passage from *This Freedom* must none the less be representative of something that happened daily throughout middle-class England:

> Her mother – her mother and her sisters and the servants and the entire female establishment of the universe – seemed to Rosalie always to be waiting for something from her father or for her father himself, or waiting for or upon some male other than her father. That was another of the leading principles that Rosalie first came to know in her world. Not only were the males, paramountly her father, able to do what they liked and always doing wonderful and mysterious things, but everything that the females did either had some relation to a male or was directly for, about or on behalf of a male.
>
> Getting Robert off to school in the morning for instance. That was another early picture.
>
> There would be Robert eating; and there was the entire female population of the rectory feverishly attending upon Robert while he ate. Six females, intensely and as if their lives depended upon it, occupied with one male. Three girls – Anna about sixteen, Flora fourteen, Hilda twelve – and three grown women, all exhaustingly occupied in pushing out of the house one heavy and obstinate male aged about ten! Rosalie used to stand and watch entranced. How wonderful he was! Where did he go to when at last he was pushed off? What happened to him? What did he do?[22]

When Rosalie grows up she works in a bank and lives in a lodging house. She is determined not to marry. But Cupid shoots his arrow and despite her good intentions she is smitten.

> And she told Harry: marriage should be a partnership – not an absorption by the greater of the less; not one part active and the other passive; one giving, the other receiving; one maintaining, the other maintained; none of these, but instead a perfect partnering, a perfect equality that should be equality of place, equality of privilege, equality of duty, equality of freedom. 'Harry, each with work and with a career. Harry, each living an own life as every man, away from home, shutting his front door upon that home and off to work, leads an own and separate life. Harry –.'[23]

Hutchinson comments, in his sickly, pompous way: 'Do try to imagine her, tremulous in this her vital enterprise, tremulous in this wonder that her armies found.'

At first 'it all worked splendidly':

> In those early years, when two were in the nursery and as yet no third, there wasn't a sign that Harry, who had married for a home, ever could say 'I have a right to a home.' He had, and he was often saying so, the most perfect home. He came not home of a night to a wife peevish with domestic frets and solitary confinement and avid he should hear the tale of them, nor yet to one that butterflied the day long between idleness and pleasures and gave him what was left. He came nightly to a home that his wife sought as eagerly as he sought, a place of rest well-earned and peace well-earned.[24]

But as time goes on, life is not so easy. Outwardly all is contentment, Harry a successful barrister and Rosalie a successful banker, their children nurtured by devoted nannies and governesses, summers by the sea at Cromer with their parents' undivided attention, good nature and cheerfulness perpetually since 'children, she held, ought not to see their parents bad-tempered or distressed or in any way out of sorts or out of control'.[25] So Rosalie is 'able to come to her children only when all her undivided attention and wholehearted love could be given to them'. Yet something jars. The children seem too self-contained, they are not spontaneous in their affection. Harry never admitted to his wife that he felt this until the day when she announces that she wishes to go to the East for a year on business and he is finally driven to saying that, yes, he *does* think that men are different from women and that she *should* shoulder the greater burden of domesticity.

Rosalie looks at her children properly for the first time and, noticing that her eldest child claims not to believe in Bible stories, decides to leave the office. But it is too late. She cannot reclaim her children's love and she cannot be happy at home. So, much against Harry's will, she returns to work. To have rejected your maternal duty *twice* is going too far, and retribution strikes hard. Of her children Hugo is imprisoned for felony and goes out to the colonies; Doda dies after a backstreet abortion; and Benjie kills himself. At the end Harry and Rosalie are left with their granddaughter and the moral is clear: 'She has all her meals with them. There's no nurse . . . She trumpets in her tiny voice, "Lessons, lessons. On mother's knee! On mother's knee!" '

This Freedom was written at a time when middle-class women were beginning to take for granted that they could accept paid employment should they so wish. Many working-class women had always worked. Yet after the First World War, women of all classes in paid employment were seen no longer as patriots serving their country but as selfish 'limpets' who would not give up their jobs to the men in need of work. Most middle-class women escaped being thus stigmatised by working only as a way of filling in time between school and marriage. And those who continued once they were married often found the same problems as Rosalie or as Laurence, the heroine of Storm Jameson's *Three Kingdoms* (1926).

The theme of this novel is stated in the first chapter when Laurence fights against her sister-in-law's calm belief that 'I have a life. You just try being the wife of a rising young publisher and the mother of a publisher's three daughters and see whether it's a whole time job or not . . . There can't be more than one centre to a marriage. And if the man isn't the centre, it's an unhappy marriage.' Laurence leaves her son to be cared for by

someone else, goes to work in an advertising agency and discovers, as did Rosalie,

> the difficulty of doing decently three jobs of work. She saw
> that neither her son nor her husband got the best out of her,
> and the Napier Advertising Service had just been taught
> that there were times when it ran neither first, second,
> nor third, but was left out of the running
> altogether – scratched at the post . . .
>
> If she could do eight or nine or ten hours' work in seven at
> the office, she could, beginning at nine, get away at five
> every day. That meant two hours for Sandy, not counting
> Saturday afternoon and Sunday, and every evening for
> Dysart, if he wanted her.
>
> 'It's all a question of getting down to it,' she said.
>
> She got down to it with methodical ardour and a fair
> measure of success.[26]

But after many vicissitudes she too accepts that she cannot
cope. ' "A woman like me . . . can't do three things . . . a
woman ought not to be a mother at all if she isn't prepared to do
it properly." '[27] And Laurence realises that her sense of
frustration is an outcome of modern life – in the past women
had played a crucial role in running their homes, but since the
Industrial Revolution the housewife's traditional skills had
become redundant, with a consequent lessening of her sense of
worth: ' "If I'd had still-rooms and linen rooms and dairies . . . I
might never have wanted to get out." ' So Laurence returns
north to the family home and concludes that the best life has to
offer is the ability to cherish another. Of course, as she recognises, 'the ideal itself is a little out of fashion' but that is to be her
main commitment: to cherish, to get away to the country as
often as possible, and to keep her brain ticking over with a part-
time job ('Come in one day a week. Take stuff home to read . . .
do some editing for me', a kindly publisher tells her).

Laurence's perceptive recognition of the waning role of
women and her desire to do useful work clearly owes something
to Olive Schreiner's *Woman and Labour* (1911), which is a plea
for women to emerge from the parasitic role that has been thrust

upon them by modern life. Schreiner points out that in our society women's work has contracted and, with the division of labour, many women have been forced into parasitic dependence on men:

> Exactly as in the earlier conditions of society an excessive and almost crushing amount of the most important physical labour generally devolved upon the female, so under modern civilised conditions among the wealthier and fully civilised classes, an unduly excessive share of labour tends to devolve upon the male.[28]

The male can certainly have no grounds for complaining that modern life has deprived him of an active role or 'reduced him to a condition of morbid inactivity'. But women have been robbed almost wholly 'of the more valuable of her ancient domain of productive and social labour'.

> Our spinning-wheels are all broken . . . Our hoes and our grindstones passed from us long ago . . . The history of our household drinks we know no longer . . . Day by day machine-prepared and factory-produced viands take a larger and larger place in the dietary of rich and poor, till the working man's wife places before her household little that is of her preparation . . . The army of rosy milkmaids has passed away for ever, to give place to the cream-separator and the, largely, male-and-machinery manipulated butter pat.
>
> Year by year, day by day, there is a silently working but determined tendency for the sphere of woman's domestic labours to contract itself; and the contraction is marked exactly in proportion as that complex condition which we term 'modern civilisation' is advanced.[29]

Olive Schreiner would not allow for compromise. Her book ends with this famous and rousing homage to idealism:

> Always in our dreams we hear the turn of the key that shall close the door of the last brothel; the clink of the last coin that pays for the body and soul of a woman; the falling of

78

the last wall that encloses artificially the activity of woman
and divides her from man; always we picture the love of
the sexes, as, once a dull, slow, creeping worm; then a
torpid, earthy chrysalis; at last the full-winged insect,
glorious in the sunshine of the future.[30]

Laurence had once had these kind of ideals but is forced into the
kind of compromise that has been the lot of all married women
since they emerged from the linen room. (The theme recurs in
several of Storm Jameson's novels, for instance in *Company
Parade* (1934): the conflict between domestic life and work
remains, but the heroine in the later novels often abandons husband and child for her work, however guiltily.) E. M. Delafield
wrote a novel which treats the dilemma in a humorous way, in
which she shows a woman who has, for purely selfish motives,
cherished her career too much and her family too little. *Faster,
Faster* (1936) could not have been written before the 1930s since
at the heart of the novel is the assumption that the career woman
is here to stay. But given that women want to work, to what
extent should their families be sacrificed? (It was the question
asked by the daughter in the Dutch novel *The Rebel Generation*,
although the children never ask *directly* why Mother's precious
work should always come first.)

Claudia, the heroine, has qualities similar to those of Alice in
Rebecca West's short story 'The Salt of the Earth' which had
been published the year before (see page 168.) She puts herself
second continually, stretching herself in all directions and never
complaining, taking all burdens on her shoulders both at home
and in the office of the agency she runs. She, like Alice, will not
accept that she adores martyrdom, abhors the role of second
fiddle and actually runs her life only to suit herself and not, as she
always pretends, because she is devotedly serving others. As in
the Rebecca West story, her relations try and disillusion her but
she will not listen. Her sister tells her that 'you like seeing yourself
as Atlas supporting the world' and tries to make her see that she's
'posing' – ' "Aren't you, all day and every day, acting as the
perfect, selfless mother, the sole support of them all, the woman
who's gallantly working herself to death?" '

Claudia, again like Alice, dies. And the last chapter shows her family completely happy, free of her stranglehold, able to live unencumbered by the guilt caused by another's martyrdom. And yet Claudia had played out her role on the assumption that she was indispensable and that without her the whole edifice would crumble. She is a classic example of the woman who insists on doing everything, refusing to delegate to anyone, being self-deprecating and 'honest' while forcing those around her into roles of dependence when they would be much happier thinking for themselves. She also epitomises the woman who prefers to have a paid job but continues her domestic role as an excuse for martyrdom.

Dorothy Canfield's brilliant novel *The Home-Maker* (1924) dissects another aspect of this theme. The novel, set in America, is about a deeply unhappy marriage in which the husband is inefficient at his job and has lost all respect for himself and the wife is so frustrated by having to stay ineffectually at home watching his incompetence that she has become a martinet. But the husband, Lester, has a crippling accident and his wife, Evangeline, gets a job as a sales assistant. And so life takes a wonderful turn for them both, with Lester able, from his sick-bed, to cherish and understand his children and his wife able to excel in the way she had always longed for and escape the family's dependence on her.

There are memorable descriptions of father and children together, for example an eight-page scene in which Lester allows his son to learn how to use an egg-beater. It is perfectly clear that Evangeline is happy and fulfilled earning more money than her husband had ever dreamed of and he is equally happy bringing up the children with tenderness and love. But then one night Evangeline sees her husband turning over in his sleep, for the first time since his accident.

> She was a wicked woman. God be merciful to me, a sinner. She had no heart. She did not want her husband to get well. She did not want to go home and live with her children.
>
> But she must. She must! There was no other way . . . If Lester got well, of course he could not stay at home and keep house and take care of the children . . . no able-

bodied man ever did that. What would people say? It was out of the question. People would laugh at Lester. They would laugh at her. They would not admire her any more. What would people say if she did not go back at once to the children? She who had always been so devoted to them, she whom people pitied now because she was forced to be separated from them.[31]

When Lester realises he can walk again, his reaction is the same. He is sick at heart at the thought of going back to his loathed job and seeing his children shrivelling into the timid souls they had been before his accident; for now he has learnt to understand his wife's faults and virtues as well as his own.

Eva had passionate love and devotion to give them, but neither patience nor understanding. There was no sacrifice in the world which she would not joyfully make for her children except to live with them. They had tried that for fourteen dreadful years and knew what it brought them. That complacent unquestioned generalization, 'The mother is the natural home-maker'; what a juggernaut it had been in their case! How poor Eva, drugged by the cries of its devotees, had cast herself down under its grinding wheels – and had dragged the children in under with her. It wasn't because Eva had not tried her best. She had nearly killed herself trying. But she had been like a gifted mathematician set to paint a picture.[32]

Lester wonders whether he and his wife could exchange roles but he knows this is impossible. Tradition decreed 'that men are of worth in so far as they achieve . . . material success, and worthless if they do not'.

Why, the fanatic feminists were right, after all. Under its greasy camouflage of chivalry, society is really based on a contempt for women's work in the home. The only women who were paid, either in human respect or in money, were women who gave up their traditional job of creating harmony out of human relationships and did something really useful, bought or sold or created material objects. As for any *man's* giving his personality for the woman's work of trying to draw out of children the best there might be in them . . . fiddling foolishness! Leave it to the squaws! He was sure that he was the only man who had ever conceived even the possibility of such a lapse from virile self-respect as to do what all women are supposed to do. He knew well enough that other men would feel for such a conception on his part a stupefaction only equalled by their red-blooded scorn.[33]

After a night of agonised mental torment Lester makes up his mind to sham and persuades the doctor into the conspiracy. He has accepted that society would not condone his role of home-maker if it was voluntary but if he continued to be forced by illness to be the wife then it would admire him for his pluck.

Ironically, had Lester wanted to stay at home in order to paint or write, society would accept this – as long as he did not also bring up his children himself. For Cyril Connolly's classic observation that 'there is no more sombre enemy of good art than the pram in the hall' is universally accepted as a truism – no self-respecting male could hope to do creative work within earshot of tiny feet. Whether women can is another question, which makes the theme of creativity and women crucially important in any discussion about feminism.

Very few novels by women in the period 1914–39 described a woman finally giving up love and marriage for her career. The moral was almost always that in order to be happy, to fulfil herself as a woman, it was important for her to sacrifice, to dote and – eventually – to self-abnegate. After all, the staple readership of the circulating libraries was largely women who had done just this, or, if they were unmarried, they were presumed to be longing not to be. But there were a few exceptions, apart from the novels of Storm Jameson already mentioned. One of these, *Mainspring* (1922) by V. H. Friedlaender, was described by Winifred Holtby in a 'Letter to a Friend':

> The theme is to some extent similar to that of *This Freedom*, but differently worked out. The heroine is an artist who eventually renounces the man she loves for the

sake of her art. It is a hard thing to do well, but the author somehow has made it convincing both that the girl would act so and that her pictures would be worth it.[34]

The heroine, Bridget, decides that to marry her lover would be to sacrifice her genius. Bolstered by the unstinting praise of a world-famous art-critic she gives her lover up.

> It was done; it could never be undone. And all for what – for what? *That she might paint!*
>
> In that moment it seemed to her that she had surely touched the limits of human folly, so insignificant did she feel, so void of all power or inspiration, so impiously pre-sumptuous . . . Now she understood what it would mean to fail. It would mean becoming one of that great, tragic army of women without a mainspring; mateless women drifting despairingly away from their youth, clutching at straws of memory and hope as they passed, finding them break, ending on the pitiless rocks. It would mean the sense of loss and frustration, the fading face, the body weakening beneath the starvation of the mind; insomnia, nerves, disease; death before life, death without life.[35]

So she goes off to her garret, knowing what she will miss but determined to be a painter. We have to assume that she has 'a room of her own and five hundred a year'[36] for any woman at this period who wanted to be creative and was not married had to have a private income; women could not at this time think in terms of the part-time teaching job. They had either to make money by their art, or give it up to support themselves, or live off someone else's money. It is this latter assumption that permeated Virginia Woolf's discussions of women and fiction in *A Room of One's Own* (1928) and her related essays: the male literary tradition would continue to retain its grip as long as women remained financially dependent on men and as long as male-dominated conventions continued to hold sway.

The case against male self-importance is memorably put by Terence Hewet in Virginia Woolf's first novel *The Voyage Out* (1915). He is prompted by Rachel's frank admission that she

found Gibbon boring to wonder aloud at the stranglehold
exerted by men over women.

'The respect that women, even well-educated, very able
women, have for men,' he went on. 'I believe we must have
the sort of power over you that we're said to have over
horses. They see us three times as big as we are or they'd
never obey us. For that very reason, I'm inclined to doubt
that you'll ever do anything even when you have the vote.'
He looked at her reflectively. She appeared very smooth
and sensitive and young. 'It'll take at least six generations
before you're sufficiently thick-skinned to go into law
courts and business offices. Consider what a bully the
ordinary man is,' he continued, 'the ordinary hard-work-
ing, rather ambitious solicitor or man of business with a
family to bring up and a certain position to maintain. And
then, of course, the daughters have to give way to the sons;
the sons have to be educated; they have to bully and shove
for their wives and families, and so it all comes over again.
And meanwhile there are the women in the background
. . . Do you really think that the vote will do you any
good?'[37]

In this key passage it is clear that Virginia Woolf is describing
an ideal man who has no respect for the world of 'telegrams and
anger', one who can see things from the point of view of a
woman, who actually likes women. When Rachel describes to
him her particular 'accumulation of unrecorded life'[38] she is confused when Hewet tells her that he is interested in her description
because she is a woman. All the men in Rachel's sphere up till
now have provided for women, tolerated women, but have not
been interested in them. And here is one who can actually laugh
at the way men have organised society.

'There's no doubt it helps to make up for the drudgery of a
profession if a man's taken very, very seriously by everyone – if he gets appointments, and has offices and a title,
and lots of letters after his name, and bits of ribbons and
degrees. I don't grudge it 'em, though sometimes it comes

over me – what an amazing concoction! What a miracle the masculine conception of life is – judges, civil servants, army, navy, Houses of Parliament, lord mayors – what a world we've made of it! Look at Hirst now. I assure you,' he said, 'not a day's passed since we came here without a discussion as to whether he's to stay on at Cambridge or to go to the Bar. It's his career – his sacred career. And if I've heard it twenty times, I'm sure his mother and sister have heard it five hundred times. Can't you imagine the family conclaves, and the sister told to run out and feed the rabbit because St John must have the schoolroom to himself – "St John's working", "St John wants his tea brought to him". Don't you know the kind of thing? No wonder that St John thinks it a matter of considerable importance. It is too. He has to earn his living. But St John's sister – ' Hewet puffed in silence. 'No one takes her seriously, poor dear. She feeds the rabbits.'[39]

These lines have been engraved on my heart ever since I first read them in my teens and I believe they constitute one of the most important statements in feminist writing this century. They are also a clue as to why Virginia Woolf has been criticised by some for her failure to carry her feminism through into her novels. Early on in her writing life she had created a man who liked women, who was in an intellectual sense androgynous because he empathised so deeply with women. After that she turned to her primary interest, which was women. She was bored by the idea of anti-male carping or by creating more 'sympathetic' men; so she confined her attention to portraying the woman's perspective. When she tried, as in *Jacob's Room* (1922), to create a male point of view she endowed her hero with so much feminine perception that as a man he is unconvincing. In her other novels she describes the world through female eyes and men are very much the minor focus of interest. Only occasionally in her fiction does she lampoon male egoism, as in the following passage from *The Years* (1937) where Peggy is talking to a spare-time poet:

My people, he was saying . . . hunted. Her attention

wandered. She had heard it all before. I,I,I — he went on.
It was like a vulture's beak pecking, or a vacuum-cleaner
sucking, or a telephone bell ringing. I,I,I. But he couldn't
help it, not with that nerve-drawn egotist's face, she
thought, glancing at him. He could not free himself, could
not detach himself. He was bound on the wheel with tight
iron hoops. He had to expose, had to exhibit. But why let
him? she thought, as he went on talking. For what do I care
about his 'I,I,I'? Or his poetry? Let me shake him off then,
she said to herself, feeling like a person whose blood has
been sucked, leaving all the nerve-centres pale. She
paused. He noted her lack of sympathy. He thought her
stupid, she supposed.

'I'm tired,' she apologized. 'I've been up all night,' she
explained. 'I'm a doctor —'

The fire went out of his face when she said 'I'. That's
done it — now he'll go, she thought. He can't be 'you' — he
must be 'I'. She smiled. For up he got and off he went.[40]

Peggy is here ridding herself of temporary male domination.
But, as Virginia Woolf made explicit, the creative woman will
only ever be able to find her own style when she is free, independent and untrammelled by the burdens of domesticity; and
when she is unhampered by male traditions and impositions.
Until this day comes she has to charm, conciliate and tell lies, she
has to defer to 'the extreme conventionality of the other sex'[41] and
she even has to use an unwieldy male sentence unsuited for a
woman's use. But 'give her another hundred years . . . let her
speak her mind and leave out half that she now puts in'[42] and she
will write a masterpiece.

May Sinclair had written a novel in 1910 about a group of
writers struggling to do this without changing the accustomed
social patterns and conventions. *The Creators* is about the problem of reconciling marriage and writing. Three varying marriages are described but the most interesting is Jinny's, since
she becomes a well-known middlebrow novelist who is shown as
a warm, very human personality; whereas her fellow-writer
Tanqueray writes more 'difficult' fiction and has a moody, ego-
tistical character. ('He doesn't see anything except his genius.')

Jinny's problems begin when she has children and domestic life inevitably encroaches; the crisis comes when her adorable baby is six months and she tells the nurse to 'take him down to the bottom of the garden, where I can't see him'. Her husband, who has always admired her 'genius', finds his ideas have changed. He now regards genius

> as a malady, a thing abnormal, disastrous, not of nature; or if normal and natural – for Jinny – a thing altogether subordinate to Jinny's functions as a wife and mother. There was no sane man who would not take that view, who would not feel that nature was supreme. And Jinny had proved that left to nature, her womanhood, she was sound and perfect. Jinny's genius had had, as he put it, pretty well its fling. It was nature's turn.[43]

A compromise is reached in the form of a housekeeper and Jinny 'gave her mornings to her work, a portion of the afternoon to her son, and the evenings to her husband'. At first 'she was a fine juggler on her tight-rope' but then tension develops. Breakfast in bed helps, even if the relations deem it rather sad; eventually, however, her health breaks down and it is decided that her genius is a crime, 'a power in the highest degree destructive and malign, a power utterly disintegrating to its possessor and yet a power entirely within her own control'. Jinny is submissive but cannot escape retribution and her third child, a girl, is born dead.

So she goes away to Devon, but even there cannot find peace since it is there that she recognises that she loves Tanqueray. When she returns home on learning of her child's illness, rumours are rife that she has left her husband. But May Sinclair allows us no pulp novel reconciliation. The ending is inconclusive; marriage and creativity are irreconcilable unless one partner abnegates her entire being to the other's genius. And it is not in the nature of genius nor of men to be self-abnegating; so that when the creative partner is a woman the problem will be insuperable. And the only one of Jinny's friends who goes on writing is Nina, who lives true to her belief that 'virginity was the law, the indispensable condition'.

Cicely Hamilton must have approved of Nina, for her revolt against 'destined' marriage echoes Nina's belief. In *Marriage as a Trade* (1909), written the year before *The Creators* was published, she wrote:

> It is not, of course, actual sexual intercourse, legalised or the reverse, which renders a woman incapable of great creative art; it is the servile attitude of mind and soul induced in her by the influences brought to bear on her in order to fit her for the compulsory trade of marriage . . . their aim [is] to induce the girl who would eventually become a woman to conform to one particular and uniform type . . . Hence the crushing out of individuality, the elimination of the characteristics that make for variety and the development of the imitative at the expense of the creative qualities . . . The deliberate stunting and repression of her intellectual faculties, the setting up for her admiration and imitation of the ideal of the 'silly angel', have all contributed to make of her not only a domestic animal, more or less sleek and ornamental, but Philistine as well.[44]

A woman can, in short, only be successful in literature by discarding the 'conventional ideals of dependence' and cultivating an individual cast of mind – and marriage cannot align with these ideals.

Again and again women writers ask themselves whether they can juggle their work, their husband, their children and their friends, still have some time left for themselves *and* retain their sanity. As Anne Morrow Lindbergh observed in 1937:

> Isn't it possible for a woman to be a woman and yet produce something tangible besides children, something that stands up in a man's world? In other words, is it possible to live up to women's standards and men's standards at the same time? Is it possible to make them the same? (As the feminists do.)
>
> I have finally, through many stages, come round to the conclusion that for me, it isn't . . . I am not prepared to

sacrifice . . . those advantages and qualities that are truly feminine.[45]

For her the important aspect of a woman is that she should be 'rounded and receptive and sensitive in all directions'. And she feels optimistic:

> Oddly enough, you know, I feel that out of this new rounded life one is going to get 'tangible' results from women, too, but only as by-products and in *quantity*. But I feel that out of a truly feminine life some very great art might spring: something far more startling than anything we have seen from women yet – not much, but pure gold. A little of it has come already: Virginia Woolf writing about Mrs Ramsay in *To the Lighthouse*; Vita Sackville-West in *All Passion Spent*; the thread about marriage that runs through Rebecca West's *Thinking Reed*; some of Rosamond Lehmann's writing. There must be more, but I haven't read much lately. And in the other worlds of art and accomplishments. But never 'professional' in the sense that men's accomplishments are professional.[46]

Apart from the novels Anne Morrow Lindbergh mentions, which are indeed about 'truly feminine' lives, other writers worried at the problem of reconciling domesticity and writing. In *Far End* (1926), May Sinclair describes a novelist who is driven, by the pram in the hall and his baby's crying, to rent a room away from home. He has two affairs, one sensual and one intellectual, but before he and his wife have come to a parting of the ways his baby luckily passes the four-year-old milestone and stops crying, life gets back to normal and his wife can do his typing once more because she is not constantly alert for the baby's wails. And the Provincial Lady in E. M. Delafield's *Diary of a Provincial Lady* (1930) tries to 'find time for herself' – to manage her household and write short stories. Neither occupation ever quite succeeds in shaking off the other:

> June 3rd – Astounding and enchanting change in the weather, which becomes warm. I carry chair, writing materials, rug, and cushion into the garden, but am called

in to have a look at the Pantry Sink, please, as it seems to have blocked itself up. Attempted return to garden frustrated by arrival of note from the village concerning Garden Fête arrangements, which requires immediate answer, necessity for speaking to the butcher on the telephone, and sudden realisation that Laundry List hasn't yet been made out, and the Van will be here at eleven.[47]

As Virginia Woolf wrote: 'How any woman with a family ever put pen to paper I cannot fathom. Always the bell rings and the baker calls.'[48] E. M. Delafield was unusual in continuing, through financial necessity, to keep up the struggle both to write and to run her household. Sadly, she never wrote a novel in which the heroine is forced to earn a living by her diminished circumstances. Selina in Edna Ferber's novel *So Big* (1924) turns herself, after a tremendous struggle, into a businesswoman, as does the heroine of *Joanna Godden* (1921) by Sheila Kaye-Smith. Others take an interest in the world of money merely because they can no longer be content with the shrinking-violet role. In Amber Reeves's *A Lady and Her Husband* (1914), Mary is introduced to radical ideas by her daughter. When she learns the truth about the way her husband has been running his chain of teashops she feels it is hypocritical to continue with her former easy-going life – she realises that its comfort and luxury were entirely dependent on the exploitation of hundreds of overworked and under-paid waitresses. She determines to live a new, better existence, one which is not supported by the degradation of others. How passionate is her concern is not quite clear, but it is deep enough to make her leave her comfortable home and take lodgings while she works out her feelings. She is wonderfully contrasted to her husband, who is ordinary, uncorrupt, but all too human and comfortable to want to change.

Some women writers produced fiction with semi-autobiographical portraits of women who try hard to be creative and maternal simultaneously. The heroine of *Hostages to Fortune* (1933) by Elizabeth Cambridge soon gives up the unequal struggle to write a novel. 'By the time she had provided for their bodily needs she had little energy left for their affections. She didn't want to love anybody or to be loved. She wanted to sit down, and not even think.'[49] The heroine of Enid Bagnold's *The Squire* (1938) finds that maternity *is* creativity in a deeply satisfying way. And the heroine of Dorothy Canfield's *The Brimming Cup* (1921) finally decides that it is possible to be receptive and sensitive while continuing to cherish her brood. All the women in these novels see life as it is, accept their femininity and their role ungrudgingly and reconcile themselves to their loss of freedom. Ultimately it is true that 'if there was chicken, she took the leg; if there was a draught she sat in it'.[50]

It is not only the spirit of renunciation and self-sacrifice that debars women from being creative, nor their gentleness which forbids them the necessary ruthlessness to be creative. They are hampered also by their vitality, a quality remarked on by Rebecca West: she would have expected that

> women, with their greater faculty of being pleased by little things and imponderables, would write more and better poetry. The explanation [why not] lies perhaps in the unfortunate identity of the source of genius and the source of sexual attractiveness; vitality is the secret of both. This means that the women who are most fitted for the arts are the first to be called away to follow an occupation than which is none more continuously prohibitive of the listening attitude of mind which is the necessary prelude to the creative process.[51]

'The listening attitude of mind' is the faculty most women with children long to have back again – mostly they are merely listening for a cry from the nursery rather than for the faint breath of the muse. Even women without children find that the womanly role is not exactly conducive to creativity. Katharine Mansfield wrote to John Middleton Murry that

> the house seems to take up so much time if it isn't looked after with some sort of method. I mean . . . when I have to clean up twice over or wash up extra unnecessary things I get frightfully impatient and want to be working. So often this week, I've heard you and Gordon talking while I washed dishes. Well, someone's got to wash dishes and get

food. Otherwise – 'There's nothing in the house but eggs to eat.' [After] you . . . have gone I walk about with a mind full of ghosts of saucepans and primus stoves and 'Will there be enough to go round?' . . . and you calling (whatever I am doing) '*Tig*, isn't there going to be tea? It's five o'clock' as though I were a dilatory housemaid.[52]

Katharine Mansfield had no children and was also forced by her illness to be a good deal apart from her demanding husband. Others, such as Vita Sackville-West and Virginia Woolf, were married to men who revered their wives and were perfectly prepared to defer to their needs for peace and quiet. Even the unmarried, such as May Sinclair, organised devoted housekeepers and remote writing 'huts'. Margaret Kennedy always had nannies for her children, while Stella Benson, who had no children and an amenable husband, wrote to him firmly:

The only thing I cling to in the last resort [is that] I *must* put my writing first . . . I insist on being a writer first and a wife second . . . I wasn't *born* to be a wife to anyone, but to be a writer – however I am your wife, and I'm very glad I am; and if only you would realize that I can only be the kind of wife I am – only secondarily domestic – it would be much better.[53]

On the other hand, 'George Egerton', who *did* have a child, wrote towards the end of her life that 'until woman makes as deliberate a choice as a nun who never bungles her job because she accepts the sacrifice her vocation demands, she will never meet man, at his best, on equal terms as a writer – and perhaps not then.'[54]

Perhaps the last word should be Lady Slane's in *All Passion Spent* (1931) by Vita Sackville-West. She is the newly widowed wife of an extraordinarily distinguished man whose life has been heaped with honours. Upon his death she, at the age of eighty-eight, is firm in her resolve to do what she wants, which is to live peacefully in Hampstead and do whatever she feels like for the first time in her life. She thinks back over her life and remembers Henry's reaction when she asked where in the scheme of things there was going to be a studio for her? He had smiled again, more fondly and indulgently than ever, and had said there would be plenty of time to see about that, but for his own part, he fancied that after marriage she would find plenty of other occupations to help her pass the days.

Then, indeed, she felt trapped and wild . . . [yet] he had only taken for granted the things he was entitled to take for granted, thereby ranging himself with the women and entering into the general conspiracy to defraud her of her chosen life . . . She had her answer. She never referred to it again.

Yet she was no feminist. She was too wise a woman to indulge in such luxuries as an imagined martyrdom. The rift between herself and life was not the rift between the worker and the dreamer.[55]

And accordingly she subdued all her ambition to her love for her husband.

She was, after all, a woman. Thwarted as an artist, was it perhaps possible to find fulfilment in other ways? Was there, after all, some foundation for the prevalent belief that woman should minister to man? Had the generations been right, the personal struggle wrong? Was there something beautiful, something active, something creative even, in her apparent submission to Henry? Could she not balance herself upon the tight-rope of her relationship with him, as dangerously and precariously as in the act of creating a picture? Was it not possible to see the tones and half-tones of her life with him as she might have seen the blue and violet shadows of a landscape; and so set them in relation and ordain their values, that she thereby forced them into beauty? Was not this also an achievement of the sort peculiarly suited to women? of the sort, indeed, which women alone could compass; a privilege, a prerogative, not to be despised? All the woman in her answered, yes! All the artist in her countered, no![56]

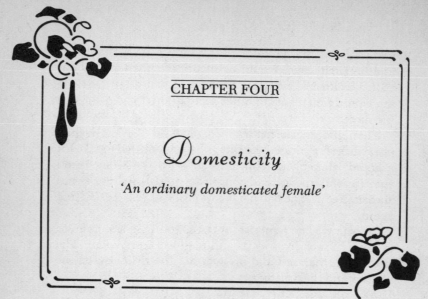

CHAPTER FOUR

Domesticity

'An ordinary domesticated female'

The marriage ceremony is the novel's conventional happy ending. But the ensuing domestic bliss is an unfruitful topic for fiction, presumably because it is even-tempered, everyday and therefore dull. In the first work of fiction she ever wrote, George Eliot apologised to her readers for writing about someone commonplace:

> 'An utterly uninteresting character!' I think I hear a lady reader exclaim – Mrs Farthingale, for example, who prefers the ideal in fiction; to whom tragedy means ermine tippets, adultery, and murder; and comedy, the adventures of some personage who is quite a 'character'.[1]

But she believes it would be to the reader's gain to be able to see into 'a human soul that looks out through dull grey eyes, and that speaks in a voice of quite ordinary tones'.

Yet, once Dorothea (in *Middlemarch*) is in turmoil no longer and has found her life's companion, the novel ends, with only a brief note to tell the reader what happened afterwards. And once Natasha has dwindled contentedly into a wife, Tolstoy tells us almost nothing about the texture of her life except that her upper lip is faintly and maternally shadowed with hair and that her main preoccupation is the colour of her babies' napkins.

Generations of female readers have regretted these omissions, believing that their 'quite ordinary tones' were as interesting a topic for fiction as the extremes preferred by Mrs Farthingale.

Male writers tended to ignore domesticity and female ones generally followed suit. As Cicely Hamilton pointed out:

> Women who have treated of maternity in books or pictures have usually handled it in exactly the same spirit in which it is commonly handled by men – from what may be termed the conventional or Raphaelesque point of view. That is to say, they treat it from the superficial point of view of the outsider, the person who has no actual experience of the subject.[2]

But, during the 1920s, women writers gradually began to write about basic, everyday middle-class female preoccupations such as married love, the bringing up of children, the finding and keeping of domestic help, the choosing and enduring of schools – describing the pleasures and pains of a generally rather steadfast daily life. A new kind of female writer was for the first time addressing herself to a new kind of female reader, asking questions such as Norah's in *A Note in Music* (1930) by Rosamond Lehmann.

> Why should this vampire family so prey on her and pin her down that even one afternoon's freedom became a matter of importance, to be regretted afterwards? Why should she let him for ever drain her to sustain himself? . . . Only, tonight she hated the active life, wanted to have a rest from this perpetual crumbling of the edges, this shredding out of one's personality upon minute obligations and responsibilities. She wanted, even for a few moments, to feel her own identity peacefully floating apart from them all, confined and dissolved within a shell upon which other people's sensibilities made no impression. But this was not possible, never for a second, in one's own home.
>
> What it is, she thought, ceasing with a jerk to indulge in self-pitying reflections, to be an ordinary domesticated female![3]

At first, few defied the convention that once a woman was married her life was of no interest unless she was, or was tempted to be, unfaithful to her husband. But E. M. Delafield broke new ground in this respect. She, of all her contemporaries, excelled at describing the everyday life of the upper middle-class women of England and in one of her best novels, *The Way Things Are* (1927), the 'love interest' is clearly a sop to convention rather than the main theme.

Laura, its heroine, married for the same reason as so many others (but is honest enough to admit this to herself).

> She had been rather anxious to be married, just when she first met Alfred.
>
> The war was over, and there had been a question of her returning home, which she did not want to do, and so many other people seemed to be getting married . . . She wanted the experience of marriage, and she was just beginning to be rather afraid of missing it altogether, because so many of the men belonging to her own generation had gone.[4]

Her life is perfectly happy in a rather uneventful way.

> Alfred had sometimes said, and frequently implied, that Laura was ruled by her servants.
>
> Laura, in return, said and implied that Alfred did not know anything at all about the domestic problem from the inside.
>
> She often felt that Alfred did not understand her, and that he still less understood what a difficult and fatiguing affair life was for her, and it also vexed her to know that their ideas differed widely on the important subject of Edward's and Johnnie's upbringing, but nevertheless, Laura knew that she and Alfred were what is called 'happily married' . . . they lived at Applecourt, which had belonged to the Temples for three generations, and the house had nine bedrooms, two bath-rooms and three sitting-rooms, and two kitchens and a pantry, and a good deal of passage-way, and a staircase with two landings, and no lighting whatever.

And there was – or, very frequently, there were not – a cook-general, a house-parlourmaid, and a children's nurse. A gardener received thirty-five shillings a week and a cottage and helped Alfred with the cleaning of the car, and worked in the garden and in the kitchen-garden.

Laura had been brought up in a house that entirely resembled Applecourt, except that it had been more comfortable, because everything had been much less expensive and difficult, in the time before the war.[5]

At the beginning of the novel, Laura is feeling, as usual, that life should have more to offer than daily confrontations with cook.

Gladys was twenty-six and Laura thirty-four. Gladys was the servant of Laura, paid to work for her. She had been at Applecourt only six months, and it was highly improbable that she would remain for another six. Nevertheless, it was Gladys who, in their daily interviews, was entirely at her ease, and Laura who was nervous.

'I'll just see what we've got in the larder.'

The attentuated remainder of the Sunday joint was in the larder, with half of a cold rhubarb tart and a fragment of jelly.

'Better make the beef into cottage pie,' said Laura. 'And what about a pudding for mid-day?'

As though these words possessed a magic, her mind, as she uttered them, became impervious to any idea whatever. Just as though the word 'pudding' had the power to stultify intelligence.

Laura looked at the cook, and the cook looked out of the little barred window of the larder, entirely detached.

'It's so difficult to think of a *new* pudding, isn't it?' said Laura pleadingly.

Gladys smiled, as though at a small jest.[6]

Laura's existence is beset with difficulties with her husband, children, neighbours, nanny or cook – but E. M. Delafield makes it quite plain by the satirical tones in which she describes these that as far as fiction is concerned their interest-value is second best. So her heroines face up to domestic trivia but they also devalue them: the reader may smile at and sympathise with their predicament, but it is ephemeral, what Virginia Woolf called 'the froth of the moment'.

> To know the outside of one's age, its dresses and its dances and its catchwords, has an interest and even a value which the spiritual adventures of a curate, or the aspiration of a high-minded schoolmistress, solemn as they are, for the most part lack. It might well be claimed, too, that to deal with the crowded dance of modern life so as to produce the illusion of reality needs far higher literary skill than to write a serious essay upon the poetry of John Donne or the novels of M. Proust. The novelist, then, who is a slave to life and concocts his books out of the froth of the moment is doing something difficult, something which pleases, something which, if you have a mind that way, may even instruct. But his work passes as the year 1921 passes, as fox-trots pass, and in three years' time looks as dowdy and dull as any other fashion which has served its turn and gone its way.[7]

But women readers, whose lives are of necessity filled with the minutiae of the material world, have always wanted to know about 'the outside of one's age' and there is no real reason, except that the conventions of criticism had so decreed, why fiction that describes it should lack staying power.

Why are Laura's troubles with cook more dowdy and dull than her troubles with her lover? The answer lies buried in the traditions of fiction in a culture which is class-bound and male-dominated. Yet the effect on the female reader, sixty years later, is to leave her with a desperate and almost perverted yearning for a mere crumb of everyday reality. We would be enchanted to find a novel written in the 1920s or 1930s which actually told us how a woman organised contraception. How did Mrs Dalloway hold up her stockings? What did the breast-feeding mother do about milk leaking on to her dress? Yet when an already well-established writer like Naomi Mitchison tried to be straightforward about matters such as contraception in *We*

Have Been Warned (1935), she encountered great difficulty in having the novel published.

There are many critics who would retort that this kind of domestic detail is of interest to no one, and there are some who would say that this is the trouble with women writers, anyway, that they avoid the large issues and concentrate on the trivial. It is only when women are certain of an overall female audience that they are free to explore one of the most basic of female preoccupations – the reconciliation and connections of the everyday with the issues which society defines as broader and more important. Virginia Woolf left the everyday out of her novels and confined it instead to her diaries and letters, to astonishing effect: there is no other diary of the twentieth century which conveys a woman's daily life in such absorbing detail. But it is literature's loss that this detail is excluded from the fiction, and there must be many readers who are now reading the novels with new delight because their imagination has been fed by the diaries with the everyday texture often so disastrously absent from the fiction.

So the true subject of *The Way Things Are* had to be Laura's love for Another Man and her resigned realisation that passion must not be allowed to destroy a home. To many female readers, however, the key issue is the heroine's role as the hub of a household, the focus without whom her dependents could not function, but who is forbidden a personality other than that of administrator and cherisher.

She would never give herself to Duke, but hers was not the Great Refusal that ennobles the refuser and remains a beautiful memory for ever.

The children, her marriage vows, the house, the ordering of the meals, the servants, the making of a laundry list every Monday – in a word, the things of respectability – kept one respectable. In a flash of unavoidable clear-sightedness, that Laura would never repeat if she could avoid it, she admitted to herself that the average attributes only, of the average woman, were hers.

Imagination, emotionalism, sentimentalism . . . what

woman is not the victim of these insidious and fatally unpractical qualities?

But how difficult, Laura reflected, to see oneself as an average woman and not, rather, as one entirely unique, in unique circumstances . . .

It dawned upon her dimly that only by envisaging and accepting her own limitations could she endure the limitations of her surroundings.[8]

Many novelists describe their heroines at home to show them in context, but they are scene-setting rather than touching the heart of things. Virginia Woolf avoided the 'accumulation of unrecorded life'[9] almost completely after her first two novels and there must be many readers who would feel more empathy with Clarissa Dalloway if her domestic trappings had been evoked with a little more enthusiasm and her sensitive psychological antennae with a little less. The following passage is an unforgettable description of Mrs Dalloway in her role as domestic centre − but it is sadly brief:

The hall of the house was cool as a vault. Mrs Dalloway raised her hand to her eyes, and, as the maid shut the door to, and she heard the swish of Lucy's skirts, she felt like a nun who has left the world and feels fold round her the familiar veils and the response to old devotions. The cook whistled in the kitchen. She heard the click of the typewriter. It was her life, and bending her head over the hall table, she bowed beneath the influence, felt blessed and purified, saying to herself, as she took the pad with the telephone message on it, how moments like this are buds on the tree of life.[10]

And why did no one portray, in fiction, the kind of lives described by Margery Spring Rice in *Working-Class Wives, Their Health and Conditions* (1939)? Might not *Round About a Pound A Week* (1913) by Maud Pember Reeves have had more impact if presented to the public as a novel? The answers are clear: for fiction to be believable it demands first-hand knowledge and involvement from the writer − write about what you know is a familiar exhortation to the aspiring novelist. It would have been quite impossible for any of the poor, struggling, coping women described in either of these two books to have won the time or quiet to put pen to paper; or for 'Mrs Britain' in Leonora Eyles's documentary book *The Woman in the Little House* (1922) to do the same:

> She makes an effort to do the bedrooms, and manages to make the children's bed; she cleans the front; she talks to the passing coalman about his child in hospital; she goes to the shop for onions and hears all about Mrs Wilson's lodger; she peels the potatoes and hushes the baby; she slaps Tommy again because he has fetched the breakfast tea-spoons off the sink and poked them down the drain; looking through the window to see if she can see a neighbour's child who would come and play with Tommy, she sees Mrs Allen, and has a quarrel with her because Johnny Allen hit her Peroy last evening – and then the children come home from school. She washes the breakfast plates and doles out the greyish-looking stew that smells violently of onions, carefully reserving the most meaty portions on a big plate for Mr Britain's tea.
>
> The children eat rapidly; they have noticed that, when the doling out was done there was about a teacupful left in the saucepan, and the first to finish will probably get it.
>
> Mrs Britain, with a sigh, sits down to her plateful, but just as she does so the baby cries again, and, pushing the comforter in his mouth, she takes him on her knee. Her body, which feels tired and needs to relax, gets no rest; it has to remain taut to hold the child and enable her to eat at the same time.[11]

Leonora Eyles was trying to make people sit up and take notice. She attempted the same thing in her fiction, but because *The Woman in the Little House* is so straightforward and commonsensical it undoubtedly had more effect. In her fiction she is overwhelmingly emotional; in her non-fiction she can come straight out with remarks like 'looking round Number 9 Taraline Street [Peckham], one is struck by its supreme inconvenience. *It was designed by men architects, and men don't live and move and have their being in their houses.*[12]

Twenty years later than Leonora Eyles, Edith Sitwell wrote, at the height of the 'people's war',

> I would like to have written of those unrecorded women . . . who have never found fame, but whose daily example has helped to civilise our race: the ordinary women in their hundreds of thousands, beings whose warmth of heart and love of country and family, whose unswerving loyalty and gallantry, and gay, not dour, sense of duty, are among the glories of Britain.[13]

One can only regret that she did not write about them. For the lives of the upper middle-class women who were described in fiction were not the same as those of these 'unrecorded women'; compared with working-class women their lives were cushioned and the reader needs to extend a different kind of sympathy to the woman who complained that 'life would be perfectly bearable if it were not for teeth and cooks' from that she bestows upon 'Mrs Britain'. It is an inescapable fact that while a small segment of British society was being articulately resentful about registry offices and the housemaids who 'used to give me notice as I tried to climb the stairs to my writing room',[14] the larger proportion of the population was living from day to day enduring appalling hardship.

In her autobiography, Naomi Mitchison describes being the hub of a large household, managing to entertain her friends and write novels only because of the attentions of servants and delivery-boys.

> So there we were and rooms were clean and tidy, the meals were cooked and served, orders to shops were delivered on time and there were at least three posts a day, all based on our being at the top end of the class structure. We could presumably have sat back and enjoyed it but we filled up all that lovely spare time which nobody seems to have today with our friends and children, ours and our friends' love affairs, our good causes and committees, Dick's bar work, my writing, interest in the other arts, letters, trips

abroad and as time went on the growth of social conscience.[15]

She expected her domestic life to run smoothly, was grateful when it did, but could not imagine life otherwise. It would not have been quite the thing for a woman of her social position to give up love affairs or a social conscience in order to do the housework herself, and in any case why should she have done so? The question might be asked with more relevance about the heroines of E. M. Delafield's novels, who often live in the country, do not entertain very much and have fewer children than the real-life Naomi Mitchison. I often think that Laura or the Provincial Lady would have been far happier giving up endless tussles with maids, cooks and nannies and doing the housework for themselves — but it occurred to very few to do this until they had to do so through necessity.

Sometimes the 'leisured' classes did not have it so easy. In an excellent explanation of 'the servant problem' Quentin Bell tries to make the modern reader have some imaginative understanding of what domestic life was like, even for the affluent.

Now, when Virginia Woolf went to Asham she found none of these [modern] commodities. To get there at all she had to walk or to bicycle for several miles or to go to the expense of a taxi or a fly. To make a light she had candles which dropped grease on the carpet, or lamps which smoked and had to be refilled with oil and trimmed every morning; heat was supplied by wood or coal — and coal was in short supply from 1916 to 1919; the coal had to be carried about in scuttles, grates had to be cleaned, fires laid, and if they were not competently managed they would fill the room with smoke or die miserably. In the country you got hot water by boiling it over a stove. Cold water had to be pumped up into a tank every day and Asham was furnished only with an earth closet. There were no refrigerators or frozen foods, a tin-opener was a kind of heavy dagger with which you attacked the tin hoping to win a jagged victory. All the processes of cooking and cleaning were incredibly laborious, messy and slow. There are still plenty of people who live in conditions of this kind or worse – far worse – but obviously in these circumstances someone must be perpetually at work if any kind of comfort or cleanliness is to be maintained.[16]

It was fortunate that, just as servants were becoming a rare luxury, houses were becoming somewhat easier to run. For example, by the end of the twenties there were 30,000 vacuum cleaners in Britain, by 1935 400,000 and by 1939 nearer a million. For some at least, a car made shopping easier and refrigerators meant that food did not have to be bought every day. But economic changes could not alter social expectations overnight – which accounts for the 'Nelly saga' running as an unbroken thread throughout Virginia Woolf's life. She could not manage entirely on her own but was weary of being dependent and having someone else dependent on her.

In Bloomsbury the domestic servants were not offered the servile status of the Victorian age, but neither had they the businesslike employer/employee relationship which can be established today between the 'daily' woman who 'helps' and the woman who is 'helped'. They were part of the household, in a sense a part of the family, but they were also independent human beings, equals with feelings to be respected. Ideally, hopefully, they were friends. But how many of one's friends are there whom one can see daily, who are dependent on one for a livelihood, who hold one's comforts in their hands, and with whom one is never bored or cross?[18]

E. M. Delafield, Enid Bagnold and others, who were not as 'advanced' as Bloomsbury, still tried to maintain the old patriarchal relationship with their servants, lacking the courage and the *savoir-faire* to turn it into something more in keeping with the post-war world. Many women felt that their social status necessitated servants, but could not tolerate their friendship. Others openly hated living a life with strangers perpetually watching them but, again, lacked the initiative to organise their domestic arrangements on different lines. Over and over again

104

in novels of this period one finds scenes of a couple lying in their twin beds as the light comes through the curtains. Gladys the maid either brings the tea late, or she forgets to run the bath, or she has quarrelled with cook and so there is an 'atmosphere'. Whether husband and wife are feeling argumentative or loving, the intrusion of someone whom they pay but who resents their payment can never have been a good start to the day.

In Martin Armstrong's *St Christopher's Day* (1928), the reader cannot but conclude that Christopher and Rosamund would have been happier together if only they had ever been alone and if she had had something to do all day. As it is, he is perpetually tense and can only relax on the bus journey to Lincoln's Inn Fields, while she neurotically builds up petty resentments and grudges with her mind empty of any real challenges. The novel covers the events of one day, which is Christopher's birthday.

> She was often angry with him for no reason, a blind, unreasoning resentment which she had long ceased to be able to control. But this morning she had a reason for her anger, though she was not aware of it as such. She was angry with him because it was his birthday and she knew she ought to wish him many happy returns. She ought to and she wanted to, but a sulky devil in her would not allow her, made it utterly impossible for her to speak pleasantly and kindly to him. And because she could not do so she felt resentful towards him.[19]

Because it is his special day Christopher makes a great effort. He leans across the table: ' "Rosamund . . . why do we go on like this? It's enough to break a man's heart." ' She replies in a 'cold, hard voice that chilled and wounded even herself: "My dear Christopher, what *are* you talking about?" '

Throughout the day they both brood: Rosamund because she has nothing else to do and Christopher because he is neglecting his legal practice.

> She had by now laid the dinner-table and arranged the fruit and flowers on it; the last details had been settled with the cook; the drawing-room was ready. There were still

four hours before the dinner-party, and the only matter that remained still unsettled was that of the wine.

She was sitting now in the little morning-room on the ground-floor, with her tea on a tray at her elbow. The preparations for the evening and this gnawing anxiety about Christopher had exhausted her, and she lay, with limbs and body relaxed, in a deep armchair, gazing into the fire.[20]

Rosamund, true to her middle-class background, uses her domestic circumstances to keep her husband at a distance, for the constant presence of servants often made it hard for members of the same family to be informal with each other. The quite unsurprising distance that could grow up between parent and child is illustrated by the following anecdote from the *Diaries* of Cynthia Asquith.

Eddie told a very good child story, about a dog called Paddy run over by motor and killed. Mother hardly dared break news to child. Did so during pudding. To her intense relief, after a second's pause, the child calmly continued pudding. Later mother heard crying, and found child with absolutely tear-congealed face. 'Oh Mummie, Paddy's killed.'

Mother: 'Yes, but I told you that at lunch, darling.'
Child: 'Oh, I thought you said it was Daddy!'[21]

For the child, his father was probably someone less loved and admired than the cook or butler, a state of affairs it would have occurred to few upper middle-class parents to change. Many preferred to keep their children at an emotional distance but became jealous if they became too fond of anyone else. The short-lived nanny in *Miss Linsey and Pa* (1936) by Stella Gibbons is told by her employer not to tell Tabiatha fairy stories. She should 'just leave her alone as much as possible to day-dream and make her own games . . . It's much better for the child than overheating her imagination with stories and complicated toys.' But after a weekend away

Perdita pushed open the door, which was ajar, and walked

in. The air of enchanted intimacy in the room struck her at once with a shock of jealousy. Tabiatha, her hair ragged-robin from sleep and her eyes reflecting the soft glow of a bedside lamp, sat on Miss Linsey's knee, looking up into her face, while Miss Linsey, gently stroking her little hand, gazed down at her with smiling love.[22]

So Miss Linsey goes, because though a child's mother may not love the child herself, she will not allow another to substitute for her. They are all victims of the prevailing argument that a middle-class woman must have help to be free to bring up her children properly.

'The servant problem' runs like a thread throughout the women's novels of this period. It is in a sense a parable of the changes taking place in England between 1914 and 1939. In the early part of the period it was to most middle-class women merely an unavoidable annoyance (as Vera Brittain had found on her fortnight's leave, 'the universal topics of maids and ration-cards now completely dominated the conversation') but one they were unsuited to deal with – Mrs Brittain demanded that her daughter Vera return from her nursing at the Front to help her because of the inefficiency of the domestic help then available. As time went on the shortage of domestic help became an accepted fact of life, although most middle-class women never really understood why young girls preferred to work in a factory. Many solutions were put forward: some even considered that the servant problem might be solved if middle-class homes swapped unmarried daughters amongst each other. A reviewer of *The Psychology of the Servant Problem* (1925) by Violet Firth suggested that 'Mary Ann' should go 'and the superfluous daughter of one middle-class home must supplement the labour of another middle-class home, thus solving the problem of assistance for one woman and maintenance for another'.[23]

In Lettice Cooper's *The New House* (1936), Mrs Powell has rather the same unthinking attitude to others as Mrs Brittain appeared to have. Her daughter Rhoda is, however, able to see the other point of view.

Rhoda came into the kitchen and stood just inside the

doorway, looking shy. She always felt shy when she pene-
trated to that downstairs world. The life lived so near to
them and so far apart from them was a dark continent, full
of unexplored mystery. It had distressed her lately to think
that cook and Ivy were managing somehow to do the work
of a house that had once been run by five maids. It had not
really distressed her mother. Mrs Powell would be very
kind to a servant who was ill or in trouble, but she could
never feel that they were independent human beings. It
astonished her that they should be unwilling to sacrifice an
afternoon out for her convenience. When they had
birthdays and were given presents of bath salts, powder-
puffs, and coloured beads, she commented on it to Rhoda
with surprise. What did they want with things like that?
Regarding them at the bottom of her heart as automata,
she handled them with assurance and precision, while
Rhoda was secretly afraid of asking too much, and got a far
more unwilling and inefficient service.[24]

To a less 'literary' writer there might have been material for a
novel in these two entries from Virginia Woolf's diaries.

I am sordidly debating within myself the question of Nelly;
the perennial question. It is an absurdity, how much time
L & I have wasted in talking about servants. And it can
never be done with because the fault lies in the system . . .
Here is a fine rubbish heap left by our parents to be swept[25]
. . . it is the freedom from servants that is the groundwork
& bedrock of all this expansion. After lunch we are alone
till Breakfast. I say, as I walk the downs, never again never
again. Cost what it may, I will never put my head into that
noose again.

I walk; I read; I write, without terrors and constrictions.
I make bread. I cook mushrooms. I wander in & out of the
kitchen. I have a resource besides reading.[26]

For the same reasons that 'Mrs Britain' could not have
described her life in a novel, so England's great army of servants
could not have described their lives. (Only in the 1970s have we

had books, written long after the event, like Margaret Powell's *Below Stairs* to evoke servants' lives from their own point of view, and to leave us marvelling at a way of life in which other people were employed to iron boot laces and pages of *The Times*.) But the servant problem was fast becoming the province of the women's magazines. Before the war the 'society' journals such as *The Lady* and *The Queen* would have written about domestic matters only incidentally. But during the twenties there was a great expansion in magazines aimed at the middle classes. These ranged from the shilling ones such as *Homes and Gardens* and *Ideal Home* which then, as now, described affluent surroundings for middle-class couples, to the sixpenny ones for the rather more penny-pinching woman such as *Modern Woman*, *Wife and Home* or *Mother*. They all carried the same message – a woman's place is in the home and any normal woman should find cooking, shopping, sewing and mothering of all-absorbing interest. It was economic forces that dictated the tone of the magazines – once so many women had been forced out of their jobs after the return of the men in 1918 it was important that they should stay contentedly at home and they therefore had to accept domestic responsibility as an entirely worthwhile occupation. The new 'women's pages' in the national newspapers and the magazines were all used to impress upon women that it would have been morally reprehensible for them to emerge from the confines of their home. (Some novels were also written on this theme, notably *This Freedom*, see page 73.)

Fashions became more 'feminine' again and there was much discussion of the best way to remain alluring to a husband. One magazine wrote:

> The tide of progress which leaves woman with the vote in her hand and scarcely any clothes upon her back is ebbing, and the sex is returning to the deep, very deep sea of femininity from which her newly-acquired power can be more effectively wielded.[27]

During the Depression, women's magazines of all types concentrated on budgeting hints and by the late thirties *The Lady* commented:

> It looks as though a good deal of suburban elegance will have to be abandoned, and simple household ways adopted. The luxury of an attendant almost constantly on duty will have to go the way of candlelight, open fires and other amenities now only possible to the rich.[28]

After the First World War, when housework should have been increasingly less of a burden because of better mechanical aids, women were encouraged to strive for such ridiculously high standards that they could have had little time to wonder whether their lives might have been better spent than in this endless round of domestic ritual. Here is part of a prize-winning entry to a competition run by *Our Homes and Gardens* in 1920. The brief ran: 'What we want readers to do is send us an account of how they run, or would run, a servantless house for a middle-class family.' The winner modestly admits her good fortune in living in a house built in 1912 'when already the domestic service problem was looming large, so there is no hearth-stoning to be done at the front entrance'. She owns a vacuum cleaner, cinder sifter and other appliances. She uses the patent mop daily and dusts pictures and skirtings, electric light and cupboard tops thoroughly once a week.

> After breakfast, while beds are airing, any root vegetables are prepared. These are put to boil while the washing-up is in progress, afterwards cooking themselves in the hay-box cooker without supervision . . . The meal-table crockery is washed and lifted from the sink to the rack. Here it stays to dry and polish itself while other tasks are done. Knives, forks and spoons must be dried at once. I find rubbing the forks and spoons with a damp cloth on which a cleaning powder is sprinkled removes the stains, and saves much plate polishing . . . After dinner the gas stove should be wiped with a hot dish cloth. A thin coating of oil on the outside obviates the use of black-lead.[29]

But the owner of the servantless house had a harder life than the other prizewinner, the owner of 'the daily-help house'. Every room is turned out once a week and this is the daily's typical Monday:

The daily-help arrives and washes up the breakfast dishes and the supper dishes from the evening before, then cleans the front door step, brasses and taps.

Then, on Monday, she washes the flannels, handker-chiefs, small white articles, blouses, towels and kitchen towels, while the mistress brushes and dusts the sitting-rooms. Then she rubs over the bedrooms with an O-Cedar mop (the rooms are covered with cork carpet), and brushes the stairs and hall, afterwards dusting them. The other member of the family, who is elderly, peels potatoes and makes a pudding. The 'help' cleans up the small scullery and kitchen. The mistress lays the table, and has dinner ready by 1 o'clock. The 'help' washes up, cleans saucepans, fills coal boxes and cleans knives. By then it is 3 o'clock.[30]

Yet all this seems effortless compared with the lot of the poor housewife who bought *How to Run Your Home without Help* published just after the Second World War. Although middle-class housewives had by this time adjusted to lower standards, yet the manuals and magazines obviously lagged behind. Merely to read the chapter on 'adapting the routine when baby comes' induces exhaustion and most modern readers would not know whether to laugh or cry when they read the end of the section on 'how to plan your day':

After the meal, given some willing help with the clearing away, you should be free of the kitchen between 8 and 8.30 pm.

And is the rest of the day yours? Well, don't forget the ironing, and mending or knitting. But you can sit down for these, and with a companion to talk to, or a good programme on the radio, that last hour or so won't seem too much like work.[31]

By the time this little book was published in 1949 it must already have seemed like a relic from a bygone age. But in the inter-war period, high standards still mattered to almost all middle-class women: very few women novelists mocked the conventions that held such a tight grip, even if some like E. M. Delafield railed at their tyranny. Rose Macaulay was an exception: in *Crewe Train* (1926) she describes a heroine who tries to flout convention but is, after a struggle, firmly crushed. After growing up abroad, Denham arrives in London, untamed and unconformist, believing 'that the thing was to be happy and comfortable in a nice place'. She dreams that 'one would be alone; one would have no standards' – but in vain, for she is gradually subdued and has to thrust aside her dreams of 'a very low-class, lazy, common life; it was better not to think about it while one was trying to be civilised and high-class'.

Denham tries hard to conform and her final submission after a fierce struggle is described by Rose Macaulay as a minor tragedy. The ending is far from any 'so they lived happily ever after' story; in order to appease society Denham has had to stifle her inner nature. The last scene of the book is particularly poignant, with Denham's mother-in-law proposing to arrange her life for her:

'Well, first, then, you should really make out a time-table for the maid's week's work. It's the only way of getting everything done in order. Monday morning, clean the silver, Tuesday the knives, Wednesday, the paint, Thursday, the taps – and so on through the week. No day without something cleaned. And one room thoroughly turned out each day, too – that's most important.'

'Turned out . . .' Denham repeated it vaguely.

'Yes, turned out. The things all taken out of the room and put back again, you know . . .

'And,' continued her mother-in-law kindly, 'it needn't only be the maids who have a time-table either. I'm quite sure it's a great help in one's life to have some kind of scheme mapped out for the day, to which one tries to keep. It's wonderful what a help it is to see it written down. One should begin it right after breakfast – 9.30–9.45: see the servants; 9.45–10: do the flowers; 10–11: read the papers and write one's letters; 11–1: serious reading; 1–1.30:

lunch (an early lunch is nice in winter, I think, it leaves a longer afternoon); 1.30–2.30: lie down; 2.30–4: exercise or gardening, either alone or with friends; 4–5: tea and see friends . . . And so on, do you see? It regularises the day so, and prevents one drifting and idling the time away, as one's often inclined to do . . .

'There needn't really be *any* empty moments in one's day, if it's properly schemed out. Think of that! Not one empty idle, useless, minute.'

Denham thought of it . . .[32]

And thus the novel ends, a depressing tribute to the triumph of domestic convention over free will.

Authors like Rose Macaulay and E. M. Delafield made their readers reassess the nature of their everyday lives. By laughing at domesticity, they made its iron laws less sacred and encouraged their readers to view their households with a wry if daring detachment. The heroine of *Diary of a Provincial Lady* by E. M. Delafield embodied a certain attitude: married women, like it or not, were the focus of their households but gaiety and good humour were the appropriate qualities, not stuffiness or an unseeing passion for convention. When, inevitably and continually, Robert grunts and retires behind *The Times*, the reader too smiles ruefully with only a hint of edginess, knowing that the Provincial Lady is calmly picking up her darning and planning tomorrow's lunch rather than casting herself in the role of a second Madame Bovary. Society was never overturned by women like these, nor, for them, did knights charge up the drive on a white horse: nowadays we tend to describe the provincial ladies of England as the kind of women who won the war, paying homage to their activites in the WVS, behind tea urns, cherishing evacuees or, cheerily, digging up the lawn for victory.

The reason for the *Diary*'s unique qualities is the tone in which the Provincial Lady writes in it. It is inimitable: wry, witty, observant, yet hinting at a more profound awareness. Without castigating her heroine's daily round, E. M. Delafield yet makes the reader horribly aware of the empty complacency of provincial life – but her *alter ego* is too generous and self-deprecating to do more than laugh at it. Much of the comedy of the wonderful diaries (commissioned as a serial in *Time and Tide*) lies in the heroine's continual and irrepressible fight for life and vigour, a fight which is always lost to superior forces.

> November 12th – Home yesterday and am struck, as so often before, by immense accumulation of domestic disasters that always await one after any absence. Trouble with kitchen range has resulted in no hot water, also Cook says the mutton has *gone*, and will I speak to the butcher, there being no excuse in weather like this. Vicky's cold, unlike the mutton, hasn't gone. Mademoiselle says, '*Ah, cette petite! Elle ne sera peut-être pas longtemps pour ce bas monde, madame.*' Hope that this is only her Latin way of dramatising the situation.
>
> Robert reads *The Times* after dinner, and goes to sleep.[33]

It is of course not coincidental that the other novel which captures a middle-class woman's everyday life to brilliant effect was also presented in an unconventional form, but in weekly articles rather than a diary. In 1938, Peter Fleming, an editor on *The Times*, commissioned a series of articles from Jan Struther about her family life. Her brief for her fifteen-hundred-word weekly episodes was to write 'about an ordinary woman – someone rather like yourself'. The atmosphere and activities described in what was to be the book *Mrs Miniver* (1939) are very similar to the Struther family life 'observed with tenderness, humour and astuteness, yet imbued with witticisms, family jokes and a deep knowledge of natural history'.[34] The chapters breathe the atmosphere of 1938–9 as lived by a middle-class Englishwoman not a stone's throw from Harrods whose greatest problems are domestic. The film *Mrs Miniver* (1942) displayed the same down-to-earth, sensible, liberal (and liberated) values as the book. Its effect on American audiences was to make them more pro-British – indeed Roosevelt said he was certain it inspired the Americans to help the British war effort, and Churchill said in the House of Commons that 'the film was more use to the war effort than a flotilla of destroyers'.

Some readers today may find books like *Mrs Miniver* impossibly dated and therefore uninteresting: others may dub it a period piece and find it absorbing. But the original readers of these articles would have been loyal to family, country and friends, in that order, and would have agreed with Mrs Miniver's musings as she lies in bed on Christmas morning listening to the children opening their stockings.

> This was one of the moments, thought Mrs Miniver, which paid off at a single stroke all the accumulations on the debit side of parenthood: the morning sickness and the quite astonishing pain; the pram in the passage, the cold mulish glint in the cook's eye; the holiday nurse who had been in the best families; the pungent white mice, the shrivelled caterpillars; the plasticine on the door-handles, the face-flannels in the bathroom . . . the shortened step, the tempered pace, the emotional compromises, the divided loyalties, the adventures continually foresworn.[35]

Like all the other home-centred heroines of the period, she is continually juggling private pleasures with family duties:

> As a rule she managed to keep household matters in what she considered their proper place. They should be no more, she felt, than a low unobtrusive humming in the background of consciousness; the mechanics of life should never be allowed to interfere with living. But every now and then some impish poltergeist seemed to throw a spanner into the works. Everything went wrong at once; chimneys smoked, pipes burst, vacuum-cleaners fused, china and glass fell to pieces, net curtains disintegrated in the wash. Nannie sprained her ankle, the cook got tonsilitis, the house-parlourmaid left to be married, and the butterfly nut off the mincing machine was nowhere to be found.[36]

The tone is rueful but uncomplaining. The unspoken moral is that in order 'to keep household matters in . . . their proper place' the mother who provides the bulwark between nursery and outside world must sacrifice thoughts of self – but the rewards are worthwhile and ultimately greater than those of money, fame or achievement. Elizabeth Cambridge took the title of her 1933 *Hostages to Fortune* from Francis Bacon: 'He that hath wife and children hath given hostages to fortune; for they are impediments to great enterprises, either of virtue or mischief'. For the heroine the rewards are a long time revealing themselves; most of the time, life with small children seems a harsh routine of meals, mending and fading boilers:

> Other women had managed to write novels and bring up families. Catherine wondered if they had all washed behind their children's ears and pushed them about in perambulators and swept under their beds and weeded the garden and picked the fruit and made their children's clothes and done the hundred and one odd jobs that fell to her share because William was always out and odd labour was ruinously dear. Perhaps they were so successful that they managed to pay for decorators and carpenters and sewing-maids and expensive reliable nannies.[37]

The children become people, Catherine is less consumed with weariness, the house becomes less bitterly cold. The novel's ending is optimistic. Catherine and a friend admit to themselves that they are thoroughly worn out by their years of domestic toil and they resolve to approach their lives with a new honesty:

> 'I'd be happier if everybody gave up pretending,' Catherine said. 'We've had such a lot of that . . . cheerful idiots yapping encouragement whilst we got on with the work. "Business as usual" in the War, the "good time" afterwards . . . wasn't it fantastic and wasn't it stale? . . . And this sickening constant cant about "personal freedom". Freedom! There isn't room in this world to get your elbows away from your sides.'[38]

The pessimism is muted by the verdict of the children – 'You see, you all expected such a lot.' But Catherine has no regrets, she would do it all over again.

> We've had hard times, we've been hungry, we've been starved for amusement and interest and friends. We've

been desperately tired. I've sat down again and again and howled with disappointment. I've made mistakes. I've been angry. I haven't often understood what I was doing for the children. But I've loved them. I've had a wonderful time.

Those who haven't had them can't understand. Fancy expecting your children to be grateful to you! I'm grateful to them. I used to think it would never be over . . . the bringing them up, the endless work . . . But all the time I was enjoying it.[39]

And she is sensible enough to realise that the time has come for her to sit back, out of the way, to stop caring about her children's happiness and to accept them in their own right. 'And with the loss of that, the last of her ambitions, she lay still, and was content.'

Elizabeth Cambridge's approach to motherhood might be called the realistic one. In Enid Bagnold's *The Squire* (1938) we are, however, shown a different kind of heroine. She is quite remote from the 'outside' world, living snugly rather like a knight's lady in her castle, impinged upon by very few practical details. With all domesticity off-stage, so to speak, 'the squire' (whose husband is away) is free to explore the emotional complexities both of her fifth pregnancy and of her four existing children. The novel is one of the few written by a woman which sets aside swollen ankles, heartburn or the question of 'to layette or not to layette' and preoccupies itself almost exclusively with the more philosophical aspects of motherhood.

Admittedly cook gives notice and the last hours of the squire's pregnancy are spent telephoning registry offices. But otherwise the novel is birth-centred: the whole household is in suspended animation. For a very short time, the squire manages to escape her role of queen bee and to concentrate on the baby who is about to be born. And by so doing, she is closer to death than at any other time in her life, as indeed she had anticipated in pregnancy, with her thoughts of 'walking in undergrowth, walking in a wood, sitting in a wood, sinking in a wood, buried in a wood, *gone* . . .' During labour, she would have seemed tortured, tossing, crying, muttering, grunting. She was not unconscious but she had left external life. She was blind and deaf to world surface. Every sense she had was down in Earth to which she belonged, fighting to maintain a hold on the pain, to keep pace with it, not to take an ounce of will from her assent to its passage.[40]

The squire, too, like so many other mothers in fiction, has surrendered what once she yearned for. Her gaze is fixed now on her family and her thoughts of self have evaporated.

How her ambitions had changed! How nature, almost without her consent, had set her horizon on the next generation! How short a time ago was it that she had cried, '*My* life! *My* life!' stretching her arms and her young body, fierce, alone, adventurous, – and now a mother five times![41]

All too soon, the already-grown children begin to devour her, she is rapidly 'tired and testy' and the midwife tries hard to protect her from the iniquity of the temporary, disastrous cook. 'Gentle life, with the little untroublesome companion. Any trouble was the midwife's; all the heaven was the squire's.' And so the days of lying-in, punctuated as they are by scenes of wonderfully tender and satisfying breast-feeding, draw to a close. The midwife would extend them, but for her patient 'the instrument of her household had so many keys; she longed to be back at her playing'.

The overall effect of this unique book is of unashamed, passionate devotion to the pleasures of the nursery. It is a panegyric to motherhood. Of course, the cynic might observe, who would not enjoy maternity with all domestic worries coped with by others and the mother granted so much harmony and contemplation that she has time to brood not on tomorrow's puddings but on the idyll of birth? And it is true, the squire lives in a world removed from the ordinary realities. To visit the house where it was set, Enid Bagnold's home at Rottingdean in Sussex, is to be aware that she did lead a charmed life and the pressures and the worries of most of her contemporaries were unknown to her.

Nevertheless 'the attempt to get servants at the last ditch of servanthood pierced my happiness and filtered through my sleep. They were a dying class. Mine too. Treacherous courtiers round a paper queen on a paper throne. (With exceptions.)'[42] Yet in *The Squire* Enid Bagnold achieved a work of art of outstanding quality. It is a memorable and original statement about the cutting of the umbilical cord; even though the squire knows that in Europe 'the tempest howled', she ignores it, immersed in her children and her responsibility for them.

The heroine of *The Brimming Cup* (1921) is less accepting. Dorothy Canfield's novel, set in America but widely read in England, was reviewed by Rebecca West; in her review she singled out Chapter XV, 'Home Life', as encapsulating all that is worst and best about the true daily round of a mother. Marise has three children and has suffered some soul-searching because the 'baby' has gone to school for the first time. She flirts with a neighbour and, eventually, is drawn closer to her husband when his trusting patience becomes apparent to her. In 'Home Life' she is finding it hard to cope with her household because her antennae are so unusually sensitive. Her children demand all her attention and she is exhausted.

> Oh, her very soul felt crumpled with all this pressure from the outside, never-ending!
>
> The worst was not the always recurring physical demands, the dressing and undressing the children, preparing their food and keeping them clean. The crushing part was the moral strain: to carry their lives always with you, incalculably different from each other and from your own. And not only their present lives, but the insoluble question of how their present lives were affecting their future. Never for a moment from the time they were born, to be free from them though, 'Where are they? What are they doing? Is that the best thing for them?' till every individual thought of your own was shattered, till your intelligence was atrophied, till your sensibilities to finer things were dulled and blunted.[43]

By the end of this severely moral book Marise has accepted

where her true affections have always been. But she still dreads her lover's presence: 'Would he come back to haunt her in those inevitable moments of flat ebb-tide in life, when what should be moist and living withered and crisped in the merciless drought of drudgery and routine?' Quite soon, however, he holds no more fears for her and her spirit returns with renewed affection to her husband. With an uncomfortable sugariness, Dorothy Canfield writes: 'The ineffable memory of all the priceless past, the ineffable certainty of the priceless future was in their kiss.' And once more they are a united family, cherishing their children, protecting them from the blows of the world, finding time among the domestic chores to listen and respond to them. The reader can take comfort in the knowledge that by being domestic, ordinary and maternal Marise is being both creative and life-giving; she embodies the lines Frances Cornford was to write a decade later:

> They must go free
> Like fishes in the sea
> Or starlings in the skies
> Whilst you remain
> The shore where casually they come again.[44]

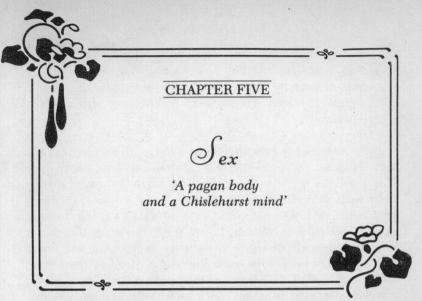

CHAPTER FIVE

$\mathcal{S}_{ex}$

'A pagan body
and a Chislehurst mind'

'She had thought of something, something about the body, about the passions which it was unfitting for her as a woman to say. Men, her reason told her, would be shocked. The consciousness of what men will say of a woman who speaks the truth about her passions had roused her from her artist's state of unconsciousness. She could write no more.'[1]

Virginia Woolf saw clearly that many prejudices would have to be overturned before women were free to write about those aspects of their existence which had for so long been ignored. For the Victorians sex was *the* great unmentionable. Sexual impulses, particularly in women, were feared and therefore denied. Male sexuality was seen as inevitable and therefore tolerated: women, pure creatures, were claimed to be free from the sexual instinct, as Acton noted so anxiously and so memorably:

I should say that the majority of women (happily for them) are not very much troubled with sexual feeling of any kind. What men are habitually, women are only exceptionally . . . The best mothers, wives, and managers of households, know little or nothing of sexual indulgences. Love of home, children, and domestic duties, are the only passions they feel.

121

As a general rule, a modest woman seldom desires any sexual gratification for herself. She submits to her husband, but only to please him; and, but for the desire of maternity, would far rather be relieved from his attentions.[2]

But, by the last two decades of the nineteenth century, women were beginning to challenge this suppression of their sexuality. The publicity given to the 1877 Bradlaugh–Besant trial over their birth control pamphlet *The Fruits of Knowledge* meant that many middle-class people were at least aware that it was now possible to prevent conception. With the recognition that it was no longer necessary to have large families, a few brave women began to look for other ways of controlling their lives, and a new kind of heroine began to appear in the 'New Woman' novels as well as in those of writers, such as Mrs Humphry Ward, who were opposed to some aspects of feminism, for example votes for women. And by the 1890s writers such as Thomas Hardy in *Tess of the D'Urbervilles* (1891) and *Jude the Obscure* (1895) and George Moore in *Esther Waters* (1894) were, too, describing women 'as complete human beings with individual and sexual rights'.[3]

It was not only in fiction that a change was evident. In English society at the time women were becoming less restricted: for example, the bicycle gave them a new mobility; the Rational Dress Society campaigned for clothes which gave some freedom of movement after the fearsome constriction of Victorian petticoats. In addition, the activities of the suffragettes and suffragists and the gradual growth of educational and job opportunities meant that women were beginning to break free from the restraints that had so deeply irked Florence Nightingale.

Yet the Victorian ethic of sexual purity held a tight enough grip: and Christabel Pankhurst's particular sexual purity campaign in 1913, though criticised by many women, was a reflection of the high incidence and overwhelming fear of venereal disease. During the Great War, moral standards began to be eroded and the pieties that had prevailed for so long began to crumble a little. By the 1920s, contraception had become a reality at least for the informed middle classes, and the work of the 'sexologists' (Krafft-Ebing and Havelock Ellis for example) and of Freud in particular, with his insistence on the existence of infantile sexuality, had played a part, too, in changing middle-class sexual attitudes. Popular books began to explain to the general reading public the importance of sexuality in normal life.

As a contemporary writer said, Freud 'attributed very many of the Neuroses which exist in modern civilized societies'[4] to the sex-repression so widespread in Western Europe. And by the 1920s, in certain strata of society, the Victorian strait-jacket had been set aside, for, as Winifred Holtby remarked, a woman had to learn to 'enjoy the full cycle of sex-experience, or she would become riddled with complexes like a rotting fruit'.[5]

Whether women had as yet found the method for speaking 'the truth about her passions' was, according to Virginia Woolf, extremely doubtful. Other writers believed themselves quite free of inhibitions – much to the disgust of Katharine Mansfield, who wrote in 1920:

> I don't know whether it's I that have 'fallen behind' in this procession but truly the books I read nowadays astound me. Female writers discovering a freedom, a frankness, a license, to speak their hearts reveal themselves as . . . sex maniacs. There's not a relationship between a man and woman that isn't the one sexual relationship – at its lowest.[6]

And a year later, extolling the charms of *Emma* to Lady Ottoline Morrell, she wrote:

> It's such an exquisite comfort to escape from the modern novels I have been forcibly reading. Wretched affairs! This fascinated pursuit of the sex adventure is beyond words boring! I am so bored by sex *qua* sex, by the gay dog sniffing round the prostitute's bedroom or by the ultra modern snigger – worse still – that I could die – at least.[7]

The majority of women writers were, at this period, taking

heed of the words of Lord Riddell who advised the popular novelist Ruby M. Ayres that writers of her type should 'take her heroines as far as the bedroom door and then leave them'.[8] There were two kinds of writers who tried to describe women in the throes of sexual passion. The first group inherited the mantle of such Edwardian novelists as Miss Braddon, Rhoda Broughton, Ouida and Marie Corelli, and were often blatantly erotic. Elinor Glyn and E. M. Hull (who are discussed in greater detail in Chapter Seven) are two examples of writers who wrote quite openly about sexuality but had various fail-safes to protect their work from the attentions of reviewers, police or other censorious bodies. To begin with, they often received little critical attention and could therefore afford to be more daring than the kind of novelist whose work was reviewed and discussed in intellectual circles and came to the attention of those responsible for directing good taste. In addition, they set their sexual adventures in remote surroundings, and used a vocabulary imbued with moral overtones.

The second kind of writer who tried to explore female sexuality was thus in a different category from the romantic novelist – but lacked a vocabulary and an approach to release her from her inhibitions. She had accepted that 'the majority of women are neither harlots nor courtesans',[9] and wanted to describe the ordinarily sensual woman without resorting to the methods of pulp fiction, or making publication impossible by being obscene. Yet there was a fatal self-consciousness where the erotic was concerned, and the undeniable association of fictional sensuality with either the perverse or the absurdly exotic. Ordinary love presented to these writers far greater problems than out-of-the-ordinary eroticism.

Virginia Woolf largely avoided the issue by writing about pre-sexual heroines (*The Voyage Out, Night and Day*), a firmly maternal one (*To the Lighthouse*) or heroines who have not achieved sexual happiness (*The Years*); while in *Orlando* she explored the nature of sexuality as an almost philosophical concept. Only in *Mrs Dalloway* does she tentatively explore her heroine's sexual self, and then by making it clear that her marriage is loveless. Clarissa Dalloway has rejected sexuality, unable to forget the exquisite moment in her life when Sally Seton kissed her, when 'the whole world might have turned upside down!' She no longer sleeps with her husband but in a narrow bed in the attic and 'she could not dispel a virginity preserved through childbirth which clung to her like a sheet'.

> She could see what she lacked. It was not beauty; it was not mind. It was something central which permeated; something warm which broke up surfaces and rippled the cold contact of man and woman, or of woman together. For *that* she could dimly perceive. She resented it, had a scruple picked up Heaven knows where, or, as she felt, sent by Nature (who is invariably wise); yet she could not resist sometimes yielding to the charm of a woman, not a girl, of a woman confessing, as to her they often did, some scrape, some folly. And whether it was pity, or their beauty, or that she was older, or some accident — like a faint scent, or a violin next door (so strange is the power of sound at certain moments), she did undoubtedly then feel what men felt.[10]

What men feel is the norm; what women feel is 'a tinge like a blush', an illumination quickly over — Mrs Dalloway has only the standard of men's feelings by which to measure her passion for Sally Seton; her own tenuous emotions are considered unreal, insubstantial. Although the vocabulary in this part of the narrative may be the thinking woman's equivalent of purple prose, nevertheless its overtones are heavily erotic ('a tinge like a blush which one tried to check and then, as it spread, one yielded to its expansion, and rushed to the farthest verge and there quivered and felt the world come closer, swollen with some astonishing significance, some pressure of rapture, which split its thin skin and gushed and poured with an extraordinary alleviation over the cracks and sores').[11]

Mrs Dalloway's asexuality is, however, implicit in the title of the book. She is a wife. And as such she is not an object of desire to her husband. This concept held sway not only in fiction but also in upper- and middle-class life. In Freud's 1912 paper 'The Most Prevalent Form of Degradation in Erotic Life', he argued that very few cultured people can achieve an ideal fusion of tenderness and sensuality, and that this manifests itself in a lack of sexual desire for women who inspire affection – in other words the well-brought-up wife.

The question of whether one woman can be all things to one man was raised often in women's fiction between the wars (though the corollary far less often). The marrying of the opposing sides of a woman's personality is perhaps the most crucial struggle in which twentieth-century woman is engaged, welding as she tries to do her erotic, intellectual, maternal, domestic and managerial qualities in a unity of undoubted but precarious magnificence. And novelists often used the themes of a man falling carelessly out of love with someone merely because she is his wife, the 'little woman', and of a man loving and needing two women at once. In *Third Act in Venice* (1936), for example, Sylvia Thompson describes one man's battle to shrug off his Profane love in favour of his Sacred one. But he cannot do it, and continues to love Adria for her mind and Josephine for her sexuality. Unfortunately, but unsurprisingly, the novel is written from his point of view, so we never fully understand why Adria was less erotic to her lover than her rival manages to be. The implication is that she is too 'nice', while Josephine is not at all averse to some Elinor Glyn erotics:

> Soon he stopped seeing with his eyes, and began to feel her looks in his nerves and in his body, the texture of her skin choking him in his throat, and the shape of her mouth making his head hot and aching, and her neck, the shape of her thigh under her tight dress making him feel sickish, and her ugly hands making his own hands shake stupidly . . . [Later] she hadn't more than a minute's passive nonsense, and then went ahead, with an adept alternation of ferocity and languor, of silences and half choked husky talk, that word by word, and gesture by hesitant experimental gesture, maddened instinct again and again to appetite.[12]

In Rosamond Lehmann's *The Weather in the Streets* (1936), Rollo accepts if not encourages his wife's delicacy in order to exonerate his guilt for wishing to be unfaithful to her. His mistress Olivia imagines her 'under a white satin quilted bed-spread with pink and apricot satin cushions, monogrammed, propping her head, and a blue satin and lace wrap on, being visited by assiduous doctors, exuding that restrained pervasive hygienic sex-appeal that is so telling'.[13] In Rollo's case, it is clearly the 'my-wife-doesn't-understand-me' (my wife won't do what I want in bed *and* understands me all too well) syndrome with which all women are only too familiar. As Margaret Lawrence wrote in 1937: 'does the question still have to be asked whether or not the cultivation of a woman decreases in some hidden way her erotic attractiveness, or does the whole matter go back to the man's hidden need of feeling superior to a woman?'[14]

Isabelle, in Rebecca West's *The Thinking Reed* (1936), defines a male type which must be excruciatingly familiar to many women but which no novelist, either male or female, had ever portrayed in fiction.

When he was her lover he was grave and reverent but too often there was afterwards this solemn clowning about sex, this midwife chatter about the bringing to birth of pleasure. Don Juan, it seemed, was a case of split person-ality; his other half was Mr Gamp. And he did what he could to draw her with him into the madhouse, for he tried to split her personality into two. It was suggested to her that her beauty and her capacity for passion were a separate entity, a kind of queen within her, and that it was to this that his loyalty was given, and that the rest of her was a humbler being, who ought to feel grateful that this superior part had caused her to be associated with such a grand gesture of chivalry. She, Isabelle, was supposed to be possessed by *la femme* as by a devil.[15]

Then there is the over-sexed man towards whom Stella Gibbons turned her malicious wit in *Cold Comfort Farm* (1932). Mr Mybug asks Flora, the sensible and good-humoured heroine, to go for a walk with him.

Flora was now in a dreadful fix, and earnestly wished that the dog-kennel would open and Amos, like a fiery angel, come to rescue her. For if she said that she adored walking, Mr Mybug would drag her for miles in the rain while he talked about sex, and if she said that she liked it only in moderation, he would make her sit on wet stiles, while he tried to kiss her. If, again, she parried his question and said that she loathed walking, he would either suspect that she suspected that he wanted to kiss her, or else he would make her sit in some dire tea-room while he talked more about sex and asked her what she felt about it.[16]

And yet, despite the clear female loathing of some of the male approaches to sexuality, many women have no choice but to bind themselves to them. For some it is uncomplicated love and affection, and this is the main theme of 'pulp' fiction. For others, it is a response to the world they live in, a kind of socialisation process dictated by habit and convenience. Isabelle in *The Thinking Reed* is portrayed as a woman who, given the chance, would probably be far happier leading an independent life. But she cannot imagine a life unconstrained by a male presence, and in any case society applauds the couple and still disapproves of the woman alone. She dislikes her lover in many ways (for his Mr Gamp qualities, for example) but

he had a hold on her for the simple reason that when he and she were linked by passion they formed a pattern which was not only aesthetically pleasing but was approved, and indeed almost enjoined, by everything in civilisation that was not priggish . . . She felt herself the victim of some form of public opinion, which was so firmly based on primitive physical considerations that the mind could not argue with it, and it operated powerfully even in the extremest privacy.[17]

This perceptive passage defines in a haunting way one woman's struggle to reconcile her warring emotions of conformism and independence. It is a far more subtle approach to sexuality than was usual; the more conventional novel described love with intermittent scenes of love-making, whereas Isabelle realises that society ensures that the success or failure of 'primitive, physical considerations' actually dictate life's more sophisticated aspects. The central question in *The Thinking Reed* is why does a sensible woman have to disrupt her life because of physical appetite? Why, indeed, cannot the sexual appetite be assuaged in the same way as other appetites (food, fresh air, music and so on) without the disruption of normal existence? Miss Clephane (see page 139) would have argued that it could, but Isabelle had the wrong group of friends for this kind of *insouciance*. And of course she was bound by the old morality which declared that a sexual male was potent and manly but a sexual woman was a nymphomaniac. As the heroine of Michael Arlen's *The Green Hat* (1924) put it, 'it is not good to have a pagan body and a Chislehurst mind, as I have'.[18]

The light-hearted abandon with which, in 1913, Enid Bagnold surrendered her virginity was clearly unusual. 'The great and terrible step was taken. What else could you expect from a girl so expectant? "Sex," said Frank Harris, "is the gateway to life." So I went through the gateway in an upper room in the Café Royal.'[19] And even after the war few unmarried women can have welcomed sexual experience with the same unabashed eagerness as Charlotte in *The Romantic* (1920) by May Sinclair:

> That evening in the office when he came to her — she could remember the feeling that shot up suddenly, and ran over her and shook her brain, making her want him to take her in his arms. It was that. It had never been anything but that. She *had* wanted him to take her; and he knew it.[20]

The old-fashioned morality was still widely prevalent in the homes of the great majority. A woman learnt to temper her sensuality with discretion and moderation — otherwise the fabric of society would disintegrate. In any case the whole sex-obsession was very much exaggerated. Beatrice Kean Seymour probably summed it up for many readers when she wrote in *The Romantic Tradition* (1925) of her

> own secret conviction that men and women weren't half so interested in sex as we novelists pretended. It wasn't even

that we recognised it as a little bit of life . . . the only little bit worth writing about! . . . but that we wrote of the part as if it were the whole. And all the time people were interested in so many other things. In horse-racing, politics and clothes, in dining and lunching out; in getting comfortable shoes and more money to spend; in taking holidays, assuaging thirsts and in seeing their friends; in doing odd jobs about the house; in fretwork, gardening and the price of food; in the interchange of ideas, in the theatre, in books, sight-seeing and in work.[21]

The American novelist Ellen Glasgow, writing in the *New York Herald Tribune* in 1928, was even harder-hitting. She puts paid to a 'favourite myth', that of woman as inspiration, seeing her instead as a hindrance to man's higher activities. 'Never, at least in fiction, has she impeded so successfully as in her latest literary aspect of nymphomaniac.' In her view a woman's search for sexual fulfilment fatally encroaches on 'man's exclusive right to the pursuit of liberty and happiness'.[22] She concludes her article by noting approvingly that May Sinclair tended to consign 'unfortunates' of this persuasion (nymphomaniac) to an asylum. Which is indeed true. In *The Allinghams* (1927), the heroine is shown as unstable from early childhood, jealous of her sister's lover and given to tantrums. Finally someone proposes to her and the engagement sees the real beginning of her 'queerness'.

As the days of her engagement went on, Margie's excitement increased. When she was with her lover she talked on with a strained intensity and emphasis; her high-pitched laughter rose on a trembling, unstable note, as if it would break into crying. And there was always a deep flush on her face . . . One day she was taking tea with him in his house . . . suddenly Margie began unhooking her bodice, which she took off and flung from her. She had slipped off her skirt and was unbuttoning her underbodice when he cried out, 'Margie, what on earth are you doing?'

She looked at him with glittering eyes, eyes of madness.

'I am going to take off all my clothes, so that you can see how beautiful I am.'

He was terrified. But he kept his head. He was calm and quiet. Margie was mad. He knew that mad people must be humoured.[23]

So poor, infinitely pathetic Margie is taken home, locked up and eventually carted off to the asylum. Her mother remarks poignantly 'the doctor told us she would be completely cured if she were married'. Yet the fashion for long, celibate engagements must have brought many women to a severe pitch of frustration or thrown them despairingly into frigidity. Ironically, Margie's sister, who has become pregnant by her lover, is welcomed back into the family fold by her family once she has had the baby. Margie had lacked the sophistication to be efficiently seductive and therefore had to be punished.

The theme of the unmarried mother was the exception to the sexual conservatism of the Victorian novel. If *The Allinghams* had been written thirty or forty years earlier, the illegitimate baby would not have been welcomed cheerfully into the bosom of the family; but then Margie, had she tried to undress for her lover, would have been portrayed to the reader as genuinely deranged rather than a victim of sexual repression. By the 1920s, it would be a relatively unsophisticated reader who was totally ignorant of Freudian theory and did not wonder whether repressed libido was perhaps an unfortunate liability.

Havelock Ellis was one of the most powerful influences on post-Victorian attitudes to sexuality. His work was banned in England when it first appeared in 1897 but a revised version was published in 1906 and the final version of *Studies in the Psychology of Sex* was published in 1910. Ellis, and Edward Carpenter, whose *Love's Coming of Age* appeared in 1906, both argued that women were not biologically condemned to be frigid but that sexual pleasure was a normal part of human existence. Their ideas gradually began to be widely read and understood. In 1914, the British Society for the Study of Sex and Psychology was formed, the works of Freud were beginning to be read in translation, and in 1918 Marie Stopes published

Married Love and then *Wise Parenthood*, which was more specific about birth control methods.

Stopes had written about Ellis's books that they had 'made me feel that *abnormalities* are for experts only, and that what the world needed was knowledge about the normal and how to handle it rightly'.[24] She was in part prompted by her own unhappy experiences. It had taken her a year to realise that her marriage was unusual in any way and, as her biographer Ruth Hall observes, 'Marie wanted children, but, incredible though it now seems, did not link their appearance with anything beyond botanical chit-chat in Liberty-printed drawing rooms and passionate, if inconclusive loveplay in her sweet-memoried bedroom.'[25] After two years of unconsummated marriage, she realised that something was wrong and 'in a very impersonal manner, she took up her own case as a piece of scientific research. She went to the British Museum and read pretty nearly every book on sex in English, French or German.'[26] As Ruth Hall points out, 'the lifelong justification for Marie Stopes in her campaign for sexual reform, her burning light on the way to Damascus, was the experience of her first marriage.'[27] On her divorce five years after her marriage, when she was thirty-six, Marie Stopes was still a virgin. Yet there was more to her zeal than personal frustration, for her interest in sexual reform began before she had any inkling of the problems that her marriage would bring.

In *Married Love*, Stopes insisted that sexual pleasure was a female as well as male prerogative. So lyrical were her descriptions of the orgasm that writers must have wondered who needed fiction when they had Marie Stopes? For example:

> The half-swooning sense of flux which overtakes the spirit in that eternal moment at the apex of rapture sweeps into its flaming tides the whole essence of the man and woman and, as it were, the heat of the contact vaporises their consciousness so that it fills the whole of cosmic space.[28]

In the book (which had sold a quarter of a million copies by the mid-1920s) she addressed herself to people like Mr LW, who in 1920 wrote to her:

Lately I have felt a sexual longing when sitting on the couch with my fiancée. I often get this feeling. It is as if, although both are fully dressed, I long to get near her. You probably understand better than I can explain.

Am I normal and natural to feel this sexual longing or am I abnormal? I suppose I should try and smother my sexual feeling?[29]

But she replied bracingly: 'From what you tell me you are quite normal. It is indeed the usual result of a long engagement.'

Thousands of others would clearly have benefited from her sensible advice – for example the young Enid Starkie who, in 1926 at the age of twenty-eight, had a shattering experience: she resisted yielding to a man but did so finally because she sensed

urgency in his voice and I thought it was pain. I was so ignorant and inexperienced that I imagined I might harm him physically by withdrawal then . . . I thought I had incurred obligations towards him. I knew nothing at all. Nothing of that scene has faded from my mind though it is many years ago now. It is burnt into me . . . Maybe you will think it is a small thing, but to me it was the most terrible thing in my life.[30]

In 1927 Jonathan Cape brought out Bernhard Bauer's *Woman*, a book published in Vienna in 1923 and translated into English by E. S. Jerdan and Norman Haire; by 1929 it was into its third edition. The book presumably escaped the attention of the law by announcing on the cover that it should 'be sold only to Members of the Medical and Learned Professions or to Adult Students of Psychology and Sociology'. Norman Haire, an eminent gynaecologist and an apostle for sexual freedom, wrote in his foreword:

The present volume, which has enjoyed enormous popular success in Austria and Germany, gives a clear presentation of the sexual anatomy and physiology of woman, deals with her psychology and love-life, and shows how sex dominates all her activities from the cradle to the grave. The appendix on prostitution is particularly valuable for the English reader, as so little is available on this subject elsewhere.[31]

Haire warns the reader that Bauer 'is diametrically opposed to the conception of the Victorian age, which invested woman with a halo'. The modern reader must agree that Bauer and his translators have indeed shrugged off all possible associations with prudery, inhibition or coyness. In the chapter on 'Touch' he describes various types of kisses:

> The fact must be frankly faced that the tongue kiss and the kiss last described play a great part in female eroticism. The woman wants her kisses to eroticise both the man and herself as highly as possible, and it is only her training which prevents her admitting this. There is no woman who does not really desire, and who would not willingly permit, these kisses. Even the woman who has been chaste all her life; even the woman who, in the very climax of passion, still pursues that phantom, modesty; even such women will easily be brought to the point where they cannot forgo the pleasure of these 'unchaste, unaesthetic' kisses, when once they have been fully and completely eroticised by means of them.[32]

In 1930 Helena Wright published *The Sex Factor in Marriage*, which was to be reprinted eleven times over the next twelve years. The first line informs the reader that 'sex is one of the most fundamentally important things in life' and the book is 'based on the knowledge that a healthy and satisfying sex-life is a beautiful and creative element, and should be in the possession of every married person'.[33] Helena Wright set out to help the reader enjoy her sex life through an understanding of herself: 'The attainment of complete sex-pleasure in a woman is the fine flowering of a healthy body.'[34] And she must have been one of the first writers in English to assert that 'the only purpose of the clitoris is to provide sensation; a full understanding of its capabilities and place in the sex-act is therefore of supreme importance'.[35]

For the middle classes, birth control had become a possibility and therefore sexual pleasure was beginning to be a practical proposition without the fear of pregnancy and with a decreasing risk of venereal disease. Yet economic causes were also an important factor in the fall in the birth rate (21 per cent between 1911 and 1931). 'The reasons for the decline in middle-class birth rates . . . include the so-called "emancipation" of women, the desire to improve the chances of life of those children who *are* born, and the desire of parents to maintain a high rate of consumption of goods and services.'[36] This section of the population was lucky enough, thanks to Marie Stopes and her followers, to be able to control their family size; but the upper middle classes did not have the same financial incentive for birth control as did the professional middle classes, and there was a strong feeling among those families who had lost male relations during the First World War that if they could afford to do so it was their duty to try and replace the flower of England's manhood with a new generation of sons.

Social historians have not written a great deal about contraceptive methods and opinions differ as to the methods actually used. A. J. P. Taylor guesses that 'in the eighteen eighties, when the decline in the birth rate appears statistically, the middle classes, who were the first to limit their families, simply abstained from sexual intercourse'. He notes the introduction of the sheath during the First World War and the invention of the diaphragm in 1919, but says that between the wars only one man in ten used a sheath regularly and that very few enlightened women in the upper middle classes used a diaphragm. (He ignores the use of the vinegar sponge, and the 'safe' period was not promoted as a method of birth control.[37]) Taylor asserts that 'interrupted intercourse was apparently the normal pattern in at least 70 per cent of marriages' and makes the rather astonishing observation that between 1880 (when limitation started) and 1940 (when the use of the sheath had become widespread) the British were 'a frustrated people': 'the restraint exercised in their private lives may well have contributed to their lack of enterprise elsewhere.'

Sadly, it seems that some middle-class women 'in the know' about birth control were secretive about it because they nurtured confused ideas that working-class women would become depraved if they too could practise it. And contraception was of course very expensive – in the early 1930s one sheath cost ten pence,[38] while a diaphragm, although cheaper because at 1s 3d it could be re-used far more often, demanded good washing facilities and privacy for its use to be tolerable. As Mrs Peel pointed out in 1933, while the middle classes 'discuss birth control with the same freedom as they discuss the latest novel . . . it is practised in all strata of Society, except, perhaps, in the one in which it is most needed, that is, amongst the poorest and most degraded of the community'.[39] And so, although middle-class women used diaphragms or their husbands used sheaths, working-class women had all too often to resort to abortion (called 'bringing on periods'), one of the degradations condemned by Leonora Eyles in her polemic novel *Margaret Protests* (1919):

> Her face was greenish white, her eyes dull and fish-like. I spoke to her, but she did not answer, and I was getting into a state of panicky indecision again, wondering whether to risk all and fetch a doctor, when there was a smothered, coughing moan, a few convulsive writhings and she clutched my hand with one of hers, tearing off the bed-clothes with the other, and throwing them on to the floor.
>
> I had to summon every shred of courage, then, to see the thing through. Not only was I disgusted and frightened but I was physically sick and faint, trying not to see what was happening, conscious that I *must* see, for her life, for a while, was in my hands. When it was all over, she lay back, white and still, her damp hair streaked over the greyish pillow, and I collapsed into the big chair . . .
>
> 'Thenk Gord it's all over safely,' she said, in heartfelt tones. 'Never no more. By Christ, I'll watch it – that I will. I shan't get out of the next as easy! Was it a girl or a boy?'
>
> 'A boy,' I whispered, looking across to the chipped enamelled basin over which I had laid a white cloth and a newspaper.
>
> 'Good job it never come to anything, then,' she said, with sudden vicious spite. 'One less man in the world to ruin some poor girl, and lead her wrong.'[40]

The lack of birth control is, by implication, at the heart of Margaret's protest throughout the novel, although her greatest hardship is due to the poverty she experiences when her husband dies. (The book, greeted with enthusiasm when it first came out and reprinted in the 1960s, is nevertheless too simply an impassioned plea for an improvement in women's circumstances for it to stand up as a work of fiction; it would have benefited from the mock-realism technique of *The Woman in the Little House*.)

For the working classes, as portrayed in the novels of the 1920s and 1930s, sexuality often had little to do with eroticism or happiness. In *Treasure in Heaven* (1937) by Rosalind Wade, the 'do-gooding' Fanny visits one of the mothers in the 'Dwellings'.

Mr Ruxton had been almost continually unemployed ever since the wedding, and there were five children to provide for. 'And that's just where the trouble comes in now,' Mrs Ruxton continued sadly; 'when the last little one was born I made up my mind that it wasn't right to bring any more into the world till Mr Ruxton finds regular work. He agrees with me in the day-time but when the evenings draw in, and we can't afford to burn the gas, all his reasoning and common sense flies out of the window and he's got one idea of passing the time, and one only. He don't care what it means to me to bear another child nor to the kid neither to grow up in a home like this. 'E'll satisfy his feelings, he says, or beat me till I give in, and, as I told you, miss, he's as good as 'is word. Lately, I've made 'im sleep in the chair or I've done so myself to keep him away from temptation: it seems 'e's nothing else to think about since he can't afford to go to the pictures, and I can't leave the kids to go out with him anywhere. But I've made up my mind, miss, to stick to what I think's right, no matter how much he knocks me about. I know I'm right, aren't I, miss?'

Fanny could not answer. Within her breast a horde of conflicting curiosities and repressions battled, while she tried to offer the wholesome, impartial advice expected of the social worker. Mrs Ruxton addressed her frankly, as one woman to another, ignoring the unsurmountable barrier of experience and inexperience which lay like a pall between them.[41]

Leonora Eyles, in an excellent chapter called 'The Sex Problem' in *The Woman in the Little House* discusses the issues evoked by Mrs Ruxton. She describes a Mrs Smith where she lodged complaining that she 'could put up with anything but the going to bed side of it'. And how

> when Smith came in for his tea, I looked at him curiously – a big, hefty sort of man, quite nice to look at, with horny hands and stooping back. I noticed how he loved his whippet, a little frail thing that sat between his legs as he ate, trembling with joy because she was so near to her beloved master; and he was infinitely kind to the girls when they were ill. I used to puzzle about the Smith problem for many years.[42]

Mrs Eyles goes on to deplore the lack of sex education and describes how pregnancy only adds to the burden of the working-class wife. She points out 'how disastrous for a woman is this male idea that continence is unhealthy, self-control a cheating of their rights; and most working-class men seem to think that the use of preventives is bad for them; the idea that it causes consumption is pretty general'. Finally she puts in a plea for 'wooing' and for an end to the 'queer ill-humour and nervous irritability' that seems to result from sexual desire. And she describes a typical evening.

> The man's work, in many cases, has tired his muscles, and he comes home to rest for the evening after a good meal; his muscles relax pleasantly during the evening until, at bed-time, he feels very well, very virile. His wife, on the other hand, has both tired muscles and nerves. Her muscles are tired with lifting heavy children, carrying coal, water, food – cleaning, cooking, washing, ironing, and running about in an enclosed space practically the whole day. Her nerves, because she is alone practically all day with only the children, have become frayed before her husband reaches home; she has not eaten very sensibly, and drunk

much strong tea; during the evening, while she is ironing, or mending, or nursing the baby, her husband has been resting; when bed-time comes, she feels light-headed, aching in every limb, a little hysterical; she would like to sit down and cry. It would not take much to make her jump clean through the window; a doctor examining her at that moment would tell her that she was in a state of nervous exhaustion produced by too long hours, too much monotony, too little wholesome food and fresh air, too much worrying about trifles. He would put her in a cool, quiet room, and give her a sedative. Instead, she unfastens her clothes and lets them drop off; and hears some disparaging remark about her unattractiveness; she dashes away a few tears, because she knows that if she cries she will cry and cry until she loses control completely; she drops into bed, hoping devoutly that the baby won't waken; she stretches herself carefully on the bed, afraid to move for the aching of her back, now that the support of her corsets has gone — and she prays devoutly that the man will go to sleep.[43]

Clearly it was only too true that 'sexual emancipation in the twenties and thirties remained confined to a narrow, privileged section of society'.[44] But there was nevertheless a franker attitude to sex and the Victorian horror of the naked body had diminished. By the time Irene Clephane published *Towards Sex Freedom* in 1935 it was less controversial to write that

sex is one of the fundamental elements of life, and without it no life is simple or normal. Fear of sex, fear of nakedness have poisoned life too long, and every experiment that helps to exorcise these twin fears from the human mind is to be praised.[45]

And Miss Clephane even declared that

the idea that physical infidelity means the end — even the desire for the end — of an established relationship is dying fast among women . . . A new love gives new colour to life, but, if the basic relationship is sound, it will appear the more valuable in its serene familiarity by contrast with the fire of the unfamiliar.[46]

She went so far as to recommend an affair to bring new life to an ailing marriage, believing that 'the ready acceptance of new loves, new loyalties in the life of husband, wife, or lover is an essential part of a revised sex ethic'.

Yet only a few women led this kind of emancipated life. In her autobiography Naomi Mitchison describes hers so clearly that one tends to forget that she was rather exceptional. She attributes the change in attitudes to marriage at this period almost entirely to effective contraception, although makes allowance for women's newly independent feelings after the First World War. Describing her and her husband's love-making after their wartime marriage, she wrote:

> We were both virgins, but you must remember that at this period that was not unusual for a young man in his early twenties . . . I got little or no pleasure except for the touch of a loved body and the knowledge that for a time he was out of the front line. The final act left me on edge and uncomfortable. Why was it so unlike Swinburne? Where were the raptures and roses? Was it going to be like this all my life? I began to run a temperature.[47]

But by the end of 1918 she was longing to visit her husband in France.

> I was all the more anxious to come because I had just read Marie Stopes's *Married Love* which seemed to me to have the answers to some of my own troubles if Dick too would read it and put some of it into practice. This was the first serious sex-instruction book for my generation and must have made an immense difference to the happiness and well-being of thousands of couples.[48]

Although Marie Stopes helped them a great deal ('Why had none of these elementary techniques occurred to either of us before?') their marriage was already bruised and some years later they both began to have affairs, albeit with dignity and control and great concern not to endanger their marriage: it was enriching and pleasurable and, even though guilt was unavoidable, going to bed with other people was obviously an accepted gloss on life for the Mitchisons and their friends. But the essential factor was contraception, usually a Dutch cap used with an ointment or pessary, provided either by a doctor or a clinic, at which middle-class women often helped with interviews and form-filling. Money-raising was another activity; for example, in 1924 there was a birth-control ball at the Hammersmith Palais. 'To show that it was a philoprogenitive movement, rather than otherwise, a leading woman novelist [Naomi Mitchison] attended it in an advanced stage of pregnancy.'[49]

Naomi Mitchison tried to describe in her fiction some of what she experienced in life, particularly in *We Have Been Warned* (1935), one of her few novels set in contemporary England (she is best known as a historical novelist). In her autobiography she relates in some detail the reluctance of publishers to print a novel that contained sentences like 'she had brought these contraceptive things for herself and Tom', 'she found a dirty shirt and smelt it tentatively; yes, this was how he smelt', or 'her hands were now on his trouser buttons – he couldn't let a woman do that!' As published (by Constable, finally), the novel contains some scenes that are more explicit sexually than anything that had as yet been written by a woman writer (and that was with many cuts made at the publisher's request).

After her difficulties with *We Have Been Warned*, Naomi Mitchison returned to writing historical fiction and commented in 1979, 'in some of the stories in *The Delicate Fire* (1933) there is, I would have thought, far more overt sex than in *We Have Been Warned*, but apparently it's all right when people wear wolfskins and togas'[50] (the convention exploited by Elinor Glyn and other romantic writers earlier in the century). And it is true that a modern reader of *The Delicate Fire* does feel some surprise that Jonathan Cape rejected the realism of *We Have Been Warned* in the same year that they printed scenes from the former novel such as that in which a man helps her to express breast milk into a cup:

I looked down and saw my breast lying in the cupped palm of his rather dirty hand; it was white and blue-veined, the veins standing out now that it was so full, and hard like a fruit, a great fruit. And his brown fingers worked at it gently and the milk spurted in four or five little jets, and the cup filled and Drako drank it up. And then Damis's fingers did the same thing for my right breast, easing me.[51]

Two years later, Pamela Hansford Johnson was 'sick with fear lest it [her novel *This Bed Thy Centre* (1935)] should become a subject for prosecution'.[52] The local (Battersea Rise) library refused to stock it and she received many obscene postcards. She meant merely to tell the truth about a group of young people in a London suburb, though Dylan Thomas's suggestion for the title undoubtedly did give the book 'an immediate shine of lubricity' very far from her intentions. But although the reviews used words like 'outspoken', 'fearless' and 'frank', the moral sentiments were perfectly 'pure' compared with those of non-fiction works like *Towards Sex Freedom*, or even Dora Russell's *Hypatia* (1925), which proclaimed women's right to sexual pleasure and liberty. These books gained licence from abstract argument while a novel is necessarily explicit, and could shock, even with a description like the following from *This Bed Thy Centre*:

Slipping his hands under the ribbing at the waist of her sweater, he felt for her breasts.
'Sweet.'
'Roly, darling, darling. Kiss me.'
Her mouth was as fresh as the grass. She locked her lips over his. They lay together on the ground, lost in their love and want. At last she drew his hands away.
'Why?'
'No.'
'But why? Don't we love each other?'
'Just because.'

Most readers would surely have found this scene less 'outspoken' than the breast-milk one in Naomi Mitchison's novel; or E. Arnot Robertson's references to periods (a more or

142

less taboo subject in fiction until even more recently) in *Ordinary Families* (1933) and in *Four Frightened People* (1931) in which the heroine, trekking through the jungle, is

> expecting the usual curse of my sex, which came to add another minor trouble to my lot the next day, and (as with most women) the turmoil in the blood beforehand and at the time inclined me to be unreasonable if I was subjected to any strain.[54]

This, I believe, is the first mention of 'the curse' in English fiction.

But no one objected to the heady atmosphere of sexuality of this novel, which makes it quite clear that Arnold and Judith fall in love with each other only after they have become lovers. 'Physical and mental impulses are too inseparable, at least sexually in women, for me to say that this love was of the flesh alone, but it was mainly physical.'[55]

> – Judith, my poor girl, I said inwardly, trying to ridicule myself out of this stupid state, you aren't becoming a nymphomaniac, are you? Surely it isn't natural to want two men so much in so short a time?
> – It is natural, in an atmosphere of death and imminent danger, answered another part of me soberly.
> – One love affair in twenty years is enough! More than enough, I think.
> – It makes no difference what I *think*. No man should have hands that look so strong and are so shapely.[56]

Clearly Arnold had been feeling something similar: ' "I touch nothing these days," he said, looking at me but not altering his normal, matter-of-fact tone, "that isn't your body, Judy." '

Yet, despite the efforts of Naomi Mitchison and E. Arnot Robertson, and the influence of Joyce, Lawrence, Freud, Ellis and so many others, the average middle-class reader in the period between the wars, going to her local library to get her weekly novel quota, would still have heartily echoed the words of Rose Macaulay's Mrs Potter when she remarked, ' "I hope I am as modern as any one . . . but I see no call to be indecent." '[57] They preferred their fiction not to threaten the *status quo* as they knew it, and still associated anything vaguely 'indecent' with 'rubber shops'. Society may have found a new freedom in the eyes of Dora Russell or Mrs Clephane, but for most women the shadow of the Victorian age still hovered. Not for them the pleasure of a lover to comfort a loveless marriage: the sacrifice of Laura and Alec in Noel Coward's play *Still Life* may have seemed quaint to some, but millions of women identified passionately with them when they agreed to part. (It was only after 1934 that the divorced mother guilty of adultery was allowed access to her children as of right.)

Laura meets Alec by chance and they fall in love. They become lovers, but two months later the furtiveness and deceit become too much for Laura, who declares that it is not only their love that matters – 'other things matter, too, self-respect matters, and decency – I can't go on any longer'. (It is interesting that in the 1935 stage version the couple become lovers but in the famous and much-loved 1945 film version, *Brief Encounter*, they never do.)

They agree to give each other up, Alec murmuring understandingly, 'The feeling of guilt – of doing wrong is a little too strong, isn't it?' When their final meeting comes (the one which is so memorably interrupted by the bustling intrusion of Dolly Messiter), Alec and Laura talk entirely in terms of renunciation and sacrifice. They agree not even to write:

Alec: Please know this – please know that you'll be with me for ages and ages yet – far away into the future. Time will wear down the agony of not seeing you, bit by bit the pain will go – but the loving you and the memory of you won't ever go – please know that.
Laura: I know it.
Alec: It's easier for me than for you. I do realise that, really I do. I at least will have different shapes to look at, and new work to do – you have to go on among familiar things – my heart aches for you so.[58]

There is nothing here of the pleasurably abandoned sex recommended in textbooks and some novels. The audience was meant to weep in sympathy, not to scoff, to admire their heroism and emulate it themselves. The distasteful aspect of the play is to be found in the parallel theme of the refreshment room waitress and her cheery flirtation with the porter. They do not really 'count', with their slap-and-tickle humour and their derisory references to the Romeo and Juliet who meet over tea and bath buns: there is an uncomfortable air of class warfare in the play which disappeared to some extent in the film *Brief Encounter* – here Myrtle (the tea-lady) and Albert (the ticket inspector) may provide light relief but they are not figures of fun. The hint, evident in the 1935 version, that they are feckless and sensually over-indulgent, was, sensitively, removed by 1945. In fact, the good humour and vigour of the station staff provide a rather marked contrast to the cerebral intensity of Alec and Laura. For those who looked beyond the intended moral, there was a parallel one that perhaps if they had made love with more passion and less soul-searching, thinking of pleasure more than duty, they might not have got into this mess.

Yet it is clear that, by the late 1930s, women were finding it hard to reach an equilibrium between the prudery of their mothers and grandmothers and the uninhibited attitude of a small minority of their contemporaries. Magazines were as divided as the reading public for which they catered: in 1938, *Good Housekeeping* deplored 'the obsession with sex which had prevailed now for some years', yet *Woman's Own* claimed that 'ignorance of the obligations, privileges and marvels of married life is as widespread today as it was in the darkest ages of the history of women'.[59] And if contemporary writers disagreed about the sexual habits of a group which was after all in some ways fairly homogeneous, it is hardly surprising that we, fifty years later, find it hard to draw convincing conclusions. There can be no firm generalisations as regards the interest or disinterest, pleasure or repugnance, with which the average middle-class woman viewed the sensual side of her nature. Safest, perhaps, to accept the point of view of Linda in *The Pursuit of Love*:

'I was forced to the conclusion,' she said, when telling me about this time, 'that neither Tony nor Christian had an inkling of what we used to call the facts of life. But I suppose all Englishmen are hopeless as lovers.'

'Not all,' I said, 'the trouble with most of them is that their minds are not on it, and it happens to require a very great deal of application. Alfred,' I told her, 'is wonderful.'

'Oh, good,' she said, but she sounded unconvinced, I thought.[60]

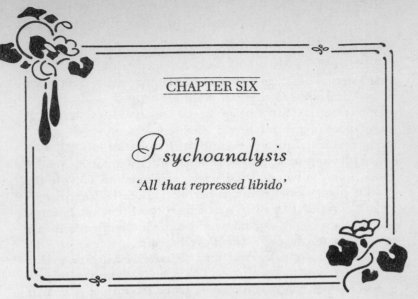

CHAPTER SIX

Psychoanalysis

'All that repressed libido'

'I fancy that there is some truth in the view that is being put forward nowadays that it is our less conscious thoughts and our less conscious actions which mainly mould our lives and the lives of those who spring from us.'[1] Samuel Butler wrote this in the early 1880s. He sensed a fresh current in the air and, had he been writing thirty years later, might have chosen to explore his characters' thoughts and feelings as they experienced them rather than as he, 'the all-wise' author, arranged them.

We have had sixty years to get used to Freud.

> To us he is no more a person
> Now but a whole climate of opinion[2]

wrote Auden after Freud's death – but in the 1920s he was still new and radical. Yet thoughts of the unconscious were much in the air. The reason was partly scientific – new discoveries in the field of neurophysiology – and partly philosophical and historical: and writers, reacting against the nineteenth century's firm repression of anything disagreeable, were becoming increasingly obsessed with the hidden side of people's natures. The individual began to be seen *as* an individual, and behaviour seen in the light of unconscious as well as conscious motives.

147

What is more, childhood experiences were seen to be crucial factors in adult life and this included children's sexual experiences – a radical and shocking notion to many. Previously secure ideas about behaviour were overturned, and ordinary everyday behaviour began to be analysed in terms of unconscious desires and needs, often severely repressed.

The first translation of Freud's work came out in 1909, with new works appearing almost annually after that. Soon popular books began to be published which explained his ideas to the general public; one such was Barbara Low's *Psycho-Analysis* (1920), sub-titled 'A Brief Account of the Freudian Theory', which is a succinct explanation meant for the literate reader rather than for the professional psychologist.

The author begins by explaining the relationship between the Unconscious and the Conscious. The latter is 'all the mental processes of which a person is aware', while the former is 'all that realm of mind which is unknown and cannot be spontaneously recalled by the subject, which is only made manifest (and only then in disguised form) in special states such as Dreams, Trances, Fantasies, Mania, etc.' She defines the Pleasure-Principle and the Reality-Principle and the Repressions in the Conscious Mind.

> Bit by bit a Censorship develops both from without (due to training, parental commands, education, etc.) and from within (due to its increasing 'civilization' and psychic development), and the primitive desires begin to be repressed – a prison-house is created for them – and as the forces of civilization close in around the individual, so does the barrier or Censorship between the Unconscious and the Conscious grow stronger in potency and more extended in its sphere.[3]

Barbara Low then explains that human beings have taken the path of Sublimation, 'a result of the creation of manifold moral, religious, and cultural taboos, which latter give rise to conflict with the primitive impulses pursuing the Pleasure-principle'. We are all involved in a continuous process of adjustment between the primitive and the more evolved; 'the need for Repression leads to the creation of Complexes' and it is these that cause mental illness. But 'the interpretation of dreams is the *Via Regia* to the knowledge of the Unconscious in mental life': they are of primary importance in psychoanalytic knowledge, the purpose of which 'is to set free the Unconscious with a view to the discovery and comprehension of the Patient's buried Complexes'. And the book's final chapter is a summary of the uses of psychoanalysis, particularly with reference to children.

Many writers have commented on the effect of Freudian theory upon their lives, of whom Dora Russell was one:

> It is still not easy to explain fully the liberating effect of Freud's theories when they first became known. There was a good deal of amateur psychoanalysing; doctors and others went through a long and arduous analysis at great financial expense, in order to understand and/or treat patients. People would urge their friends to get 'analysed' in order to recover from traumas of their childhood; it became the fashion at least to get rid of your inhibitions and persuade others to do likewise. A searchlight was turned on family life, and sex as a pervasive element within it; sons were deemed to be in love with their mothers, daughters with their fathers . . . Parental confidence in handling their children was shaken, through fear that they might harm them by excessive dominance, or by excessive love.[4]

In this period between the wars, a small group of novelists, greatly influenced by psychoanalysis, were writing fiction in which they explored the inner workings of their characters' minds at the expense of plot, action, description and direct statement. May Sinclair was one of the most important of the 'psychological' novelists. She, indeed, explored her characters' thoughts and behaviour in preference to their actions and sociability, and was so obsessed by the twin ogres of environment and heredity, and used psychoanalytical case-histories so blatantly, that parts of her novels have been criticised for their textbook tone.

'It is very nearly medical'[5] was Frank Swinnerton's comment upon *Harriett Frean*, while Katharine Mansfield had written fifteen years earlier about *The Romantic* that 'what we do deplore is that she has allowed her love of writing to suffer the eclipse of psycho-analysis'.[6] Virginia Woolf, too, complained in these terms. Heading a review 'Freudian Fiction', she observed spikily that 'a patient who has never heard a canary sing without falling down in a fit can now walk through an avenue of cages without a twinge of emotion since he has faced the fact that his mother kissed him in his cradle. The triumphs of science are beautifully positive'.[7] But for novelists it is a different matter and when 'all the characters have become cases', fiction suffers. May Sinclair did not agree, and combined her love of psychoanalysis with her love of novel writing. In 1913 she became a founding member of the Medico-Psychological Clinic of London and in 1916 she wrote her first article on psychoanalysis called 'A Clinical Lecture on Symbolism and Sublimation'. In all her later novels the theories of psychoanalysis are clearly visible for those familiar with them: occasionally the jargon overtakes the writer of fiction.

For May Sinclair was very much ahead of her times, her interest in abstract philosophy having impelled her to study at first hand the theories of the psychoanalysts. Her novel *Far End* (1926) is about a writer who explains his methods with clarity and insight. It is quite clear that the novelist hero and May Sinclair share a voice, since his opening reference to God Almighty echoes an interview she had given five years earlier to the *Pall Mall Gazette* when she had said much the same thing:

I'm eliminating God Almighty, the all-wise, all-seeing author . . . I don't display a superior understanding . . . There's no author running about arranging and analysing and explaining and representing. It's presentation, not representation, all the time. There's nothing but the stream of Peter's consciousness. The book *is* a stream of conscious-ness, going on and on; it's life itself going on and on. I don't draw Peter feeling and thinking. Peter feels and thinks and his thoughts and feelings are the actual stuff of the book. No reflected stuff. I just turn out the contents of Peter's mind . . .

I gain a unity which is a unity of form, and more than a unity of form, a unity of substance, an intense reality where no film or shadow of anything extraneous comes between. I present a world of one consciousness, undivided and undefiled, a world which is everybody's world. You can't stand outside of your own consciousness, and the nearer you get down to one consciousness the nearer you'll be to reality.[8]

The phrase 'stream of consciousness' had been used by May Sinclair in 1918, in an essay on Dorothy Richardson. She was echoing William James, who had written in 1890 that 'consciousness does not appear to itself chopped up in bits . . . It is nothing jointed; it flows . . . Let us call it the stream of thought, of consciousness, or of subjective life'.[9] May Sinclair pointed out that the basic subject matter of the thirteen-volume sequence *Pilgrimage* (1915–38) was the heroine's consciousness and she observed 'nothing happens. It is just life going on and on.'[10] And Virginia Woolf wrote a year later:

The reader is not provided with a story; he is invited to embed himself in Miriam Henderson's consciousness, to register one after another, and one on top of another, words, cries, shouts, notes of a violin, fragments of lectures, to follow these impressions as they flicker through Miriam's mind, waking incongruously other thoughts, and plaiting incessantly the many-coloured and innumerable threads of life.[11]

There are clear disadvantages involved in this paring down of the novel to the bare essential. If the reader is interested in the character whose mind is being exposed she will read on; if not, it will soon seem rather a tedious business to continue to participate in a long drawn-out exploration of Miriam's self. Frank Swinnerton wrote in 1935:

I find it excellent as impressionism – tones, looks, turns of speech all as they might, as they *must*, have been. But if I am asked whether I consider such impressionism anything more than a marvellous feat of memory, or reproduction, I must answer there comes a moment in which one wishes that Miriam had died young, or that she had moved through life at a less even and ample pace.[12]

As he so wittily pointed out, Miriam does not impose herself upon life, she suffers its effect and its humiliations; 'she does not act; she resents and records'.

There is also the problem of the form in which psychological novels should be written. Many critics had pointed out that this new subject-matter of the novel demanded a bold new form and most seemed to think that the 'stream of consciousness' technique served this purpose rather well. Virginia Woolf made the point most memorably:

> The writer seems constrained, not by his own free will but by some powerful and unscrupulous tyrant who has him in thrall, to provide a plot, to provide comedy, tragedy, love interest, and an air of probability embalming the whole . . . [but] life is not a series of gig-lamps symmetrically arranged; life is a luminous halo, a semi-transparent envelope surrounding us from the beginning of consciousness to the end.[13]

In other words, the traditional form of the novel would not really do. Something more fluid, less intent on a story-line was needed to replace the old-fashioned descriptive novel (Virginia Woolf's 'loose, baggy monster') with a firm beginning, middle and end. But such fiction was, by its very nature, difficult to mark, learn and inwardly digest and this drawback created an efficient censorship process which ensured that the proportion of psychological novels was small. Dorothy Richardson wrote out of a kind of obsessive *daemon* (she was distraught at the thought of ever finishing *Pilgrimage* and after her death was found to have been working on a fourteenth volume). Virginia Woolf sacrificed a great deal to technique and the admirers of her novels among the general public were never great in numbers. May Sinclair, although never so obsessed with the form of her novels, sacrificed some elements of action and characterisation to her interest in the scientific analysis of human nature.

Yet Dorothy Richardson in some respects set the pattern for the woman's novel in the twentieth century and her successors should not avoid paying her homage. In her use of language, she anticipated the work of Joyce and Woolf. She was the first (as she wrote years later) to 'attempt to produce a feminine equivalent of the current masculine realism'.[14] By exploring Miriam Henderson's mental processes, she was seeking the truth behind the material, male-dominated world defined by Virginia Woolf as one of 'rents and freeholds and copyholds and fines'.[15] Miriam is inward looking; her kind of feminism is a private one because she has freed herself from the male version of reality, and she is one of the first women in fiction to be shown *other* than in relation to a man.

This is the major stumbling block for most readers: in the traditional novel action is paramount, while in the psychological novel so little tends to *happen*. Indeed, it was often what did *not* happen to a character that mattered far more than what did. As so many people have pointed out, the tragedies in Dorothy Richardson, May Sinclair, Virginia Woolf or Rosamond Lehmann are all tragedies of wish-fulfilment rather than of mistakes decisively made. For the characters to be more assertive, to go out into the world and fight for themselves, the all-important unconscious perception would have to defer to conscious thrust and action, which would result in a quite different kind of fiction. Hence Miriam's lack of active feminism: she may perceive that woman consistently play second fiddle, but she is too bound up in her own self-awareness to consider righting the wrongs she sees around her. Campaigning feminism and self-absorption are impossible bedfellows since the former can only have an influence if it is articulated; if suppressed, it is futile and deteriorates into a general sense of grievance. And where relationships with men are concerned, it is impossible for Miriam's lovers to be intuitive enough, clever enough, manly enough, because if they displayed all the vital qualities, they would have to be given the key to her heart, and this her self-interest would forbid.

As a portrait, Miriam is a superb creation. At the same time it is rather heartening for the reader to be able to make her own judgements, to imagine her own settings, without God Almighty in the shape of the novelist continually stepping in and doing so for her. When Miriam decides, for example, to break from yet another would-be suitor, the author does not need to give us explanations, we can draw conclusions for ourselves by reading Miriam's thoughts:

> *He* had never for a moment shared her sense of endlessness. More sociably minded than she, but not more sociable, more quickly impatient of the cessations made by social occasions, *he* had no visions of waiting people. His personal life was centred on her completely. But the things she threw out to screen her incommunicable blissfulnesses, or to shelter her vacuous intervals from the unendurable sound of his perpetual circling round his set of ideas, no longer reached him. She could silence and awaken him only in those rare moments when she was lifted out of her growing fatigues to where she could grasp and state in all its parts any view of life that was different from his own. Since she could not hold him to these shifting visions, nor drop them and accept his world, they had no longer anything to exchange.
>
> At the best they were like long-married people, living alone, side by side; meeting only in relation to outside things.[16]

'Incommunicable blissfulnesses' are perhaps the first things that would have to go were Miriam to become generous enough to love and be loved. But Dorothy Richardson does not have to tell us this, and in this respect her fictional technique is very much warts and all, it cannot edit or hide but has to reveal the reality of a mind in all its light and shade. And when it succeeds, when the central character endears herself to the reader, then the novel can be far more moving than the 'old-fashioned' outside-in novel, for the reader has *been* the heroine, has shared her consciousness, throughout the book. *Mrs Dalloway* nearly succeeds in this respect, but there is something about her character that ensures that we are moved, tinged with some of her sadness, but remain ultimately detached, caring but not distraught.

The same could not be said of Rosamond Lehmann's *The Weather in the Streets* (1936), a superb novel which uses some of the methods of Dorothy Richardson, May Sinclair and Virginia Woolf but moulds them into the form of 'a woman's novel' in the sense in which the phrase is used as the sub-title of this book. For it is a novel which draws on established literary techniques but handles them without obscurity or evasiveness to create a whole which manages to be readable and moving without being trite or self-indulgent. The novel avoids the stodginess of *Pilgrimage* because it interweaves the thoughts of Olivia, the heroine, with dialogue. Also, although courting disaster by gravitating towards 'impossible' men, Olivia is not as serenely passive as Miriam. She endures unhappiness in the name of love rather than as by-product of a form of long-suffering hostility. Her sexuality is her undoing, whereas in Miriam's case it is her asexuality, and few readers have any doubts as to which they would rather read about.

For *The Weather in the Streets* is one of those rare novels which enters into a woman's mind fully and intimately without being obscure. Olivia appeals to anyone who has ever loved foolishly and recklessly; and, apart from Kay Boyle's *Plagued by the Nightingale* (1931), is the only novel in English describing pregnancy sickness, an agony which for some women far exceeds that of labour and delivery. How innovative both writers were can be judged by the fact that Rose Macaulay was attacked by Patrick Braybrooke for her 'extreme frankness' in writing in *Crewe Train* (1926) 'Denham felt, and often was, sick in the mornings.' He wrote the next year that the author's 'realism is tinged with an obvious pandering to the disgusting license that certain women novelists take such a pernicious delight in exhibiting'.[17]

When I am pregnant I gain some modicum of comfort from re-reading *The Weather in the Streets*. I identified with it particularly during my first pregnancy, when I wandered the streets of New York, spinning out the minutes until I could retreat yet again to 'Choc Full O' Nuts' for a creamcheese-and-walnut on toasted brown, the shiny red leather top of the stool sticking to my thighs, my stomach heaving yet imperious for food. And then the climb up the stone stairs to the eighth floor of a brownstone, my body so weak that I eventually crawled through the door towards the floor cushions. Things were not very different for Olivia:

> Sluggishly, reluctantly, the days ranged themselves one after the other into a routine. Morning: wake heavy from heavy sleep, get up, one must be sick, go back to bed; nibble a biscuit, doze, half-stupefied till midday; force oneself then to dress, each item of the toilet laborious, distasteful, the body a hateful burden. Tidy the bedroom more or less, dust a bit in the sitting-room, let in what air there was: for Mrs Banks was on holiday, there was no one to keep one up to the mark, no sharp eye and sharper tongue to brace one or contend against. Prepare to go out for lunch. Rouge, lipstick, powder . . . do what one might, it wasn't one's own face, it wasn't a face at all, it was a shoddy construction, a bad disguise. Walk down two side streets to the Bird Cage: morning coffee, light lunches, dainty teas, controlled by gentlewomen; blue tables, orange chairs.
>
> She maintained in one compartment of her handbag a supply of salted almonds and these she chewed on the way . . . She kept on at them steadily till the mob-capped lady waitress set before her the first delicacy of her two-shilling three-course ladies' lunch. At least there was no particular smell in the Bird Cage, nobody smoked much or drank anything stronger than orangeade. There was nothing to remind one of men. The china was sweet and the menus came out of *Woman's World*.[18]

It is also a novel about love, about the near-impossibility of two individuals creating a domestic, harmonious unit, and about the love that embraces more than the individual lover. Olivia says to Lady Spencer, her lover's mother, that she was more than fond of her and her family and thinks that she was 'in love with the whole lot of them'. Yet recognition of this difficult kind of love (Charles Ryder embroils himself in similar difficulties in *Brideshead Revisited*) does not allow her to exorcise it, to seek out something more lasting and comfortable. Indeed, some streak in her personality had earlier impelled her to reject her comfortable husband. When he comes temporarily to her rescue after the abortion, she has no regrets, yet appreciates his qualities:

> Off he trotted, delighted: a midnight spread! . . . He's awfully willing and domesticated. He'd be happy if he could live like this always: with some one or other for company — some one just in practical control but shelved as an exacting aggressive individual — some one being agreeable, not picking on him. He'd be a treasure to a lady invalid with cultured tastes. He'd push her chair round and round the garden, and take an interest in the bulbs, and they'd have hot scones for tea.[19]

If Rosamond Lehmann had been more interested in expounding her psychological insights as a fictional technique she would have explained what it was in Olivia's upbringing that had made her exacting and aggressive, determined to reject the ordinary domestic bliss that her sister Kate had embraced so wholeheartedly. But Olivia is such flesh-and-blood, so palpably a creature of motive, complex, libido and repression that we *need* no jargon to explain her. Nor, indeed, would the novel be what it is, for it would have needed an omniscient author to step in and explain things. Rosamond Lehmann's method was similar to that of Virginia Woolf, which was to allow Olivia's consciousness to unfold, the author responding rather than masterfully creating. Olivia *is*. She is neither case history nor pointed moral; and as such she lives.

Rosamond Lehmann was herself conscious that her role as novelist was receptive as much as manipulative. She wrote in 1946, when describing how a novel germinates:

> When the moment comes (it cannot be predicted, but it can be helped on by the right kind of passivity) these images will start to become pregnant, to illuminate one another,

to condense and form hitherto unsuspected relationships. The characters will begin to emerge, to announce their names and reveal their faces, voices, purposes, and destinies. The author does not 'invent' his characters or know about them from the outset. They reveal themselves gradually to him in and through that state of doubtful conviction which I have mentioned before. Characters must make plot or action; never the other way around.[20]

And six years later she observed in a similar vein:

Yet when I come to think harder, it seems truer to say that the creator is *acted upon*: that what one really feels at the outset of the enterprise is: 'This has started *to be done to me*.' And that what is necessary is to remain as it were actively passive, with mind and senses at full stretch, incorporating, selecting, discarding; in fact abandoned — not to sanctimonious looseness — but to every unbargained-for, yet acceptable, inevitable possibility of fertilization.[21]

From this it is clear that Rosamond Lehmann tried to allow her characters to behave and develop in a way that was true to their inner natures. She would not have 'worked out' what they were going to do next, she allowed them to behave through instinct and intuition rather than through rhyme and reason. In this she was very different from her mentor May Sinclair.

Nevertheless, Katharine Mansfield noted, at the time she was reviewing *The Romantic*:

I am amazed at the sudden 'mushroom growth' of cheap psycho-analysis everywhere. *Five* novels one after the other are based on it: it's in everything. And I want to prove it won't do — it's turning Life into a *case*. And yet, of course, I do believe one ought to be able to — not ought — one's novel if it's a good one will be capable of being *proved* scientifically correct. Here — the thing that's happening now is — *the impulse to write is a different impulse*. With an artist — one has to allow — Oh tremendously — for the sub-conscious element in his work. He writes he knows not what — he's *possessed*. I don't mean, of course, always, but when he's *inspired* – as a sort of divine flower to all his terrific hard gardening there comes this sub-conscious . . . wisdom. Now these people who are nuts on analysis seem to me to have *no* sub-conscious at all. They write to *prove* – not to tell the truth. Oh, I am so dull aren't I? I'll stop. I wish they'd stop, tho'! It's such gross impertinence.[22]

Some would disagree with Katharine Mansfield. In *Mary Olivier* (1919), May Sinclair was much more subtle than the short-story writer Ethel Colburn Mayne who, in 'Light', makes a mother explain her adolescent daughter's feelings to her.

'Daughters sometimes don't love mothers very much, Athene. It would take too long to tell you why, but there's a reason, and it's no one's fault. Daughters love their fathers so much better that sometimes they don't want their mothers there at all. You would have liked *me* to be gone away from you for ever, but you couldn't bear to feel that, so you held me tight and cried, and all the while that other part of you was trying to get on the top . . . Next time you will know what's happened, and you'll find it stops much sooner, for you'll know the way to stop it. You will say: "I love my Daddy best, but I love Mummy all I can, and Mummy knows I do." You see, you'll have control of that part of you, for it won't be shut away. It's always trying to get out, and when we don't know *what* it is that's trying to get out, we're like blind people fighting something they can't see. But if we know, and give it room in us, and let it *breathe* . . . well, then it won't torment us half so much.'[23]

In May Sinclair's novels the characters are often shown to be so completely lacking in self-knowledge or any wish for happiness that, unlike Rosamond Lehmann's characters, they become implausible. Yet one might expostulate – 'but none of May Sinclair's people *want* to be happy' and she would have answered perhaps that that was just the point – she is showing the reader what it was in their environment (their childhood in particular) that made them deny themselves pleasure and fulfilment.

For the fundamental theme running through her novels, one which her reading of psychoanalysis was to confirm, was that infantile traumas and childhood frustrations can damage a person irrevocably. This is why many of her novels start with childhood, for it is here that the seeds are sown. It also makes her novels more interesting, for the reader can have far more empathy for a character known virtually from birth. The girls in *The Three Sisters* (1914) react in different ways to the paternal domination that has been their fate since childhood. And it is her mother's shameful treatment of her as a child that makes the heroine of *Mary Olivier* come to life; if we had merely seen her as an unhappy adult we would care less. It was perhaps with justification that G. B. Stern wrote to May Sinclair that 'of course the reason why she's so infinitely more wonderful than anything Dorothy Richardson has done is that Mary herself matters, and Miriam didn't – Heavens, how Miriam bored me!'[24] While Rebecca West concluded that, in *Mary Olivier*, May Sinclair was showing Dorothy Richardson how to do what, throughout *Pilgrimage*, she was trying to achieve.

Despite the difficulties of language (how to achieve Virginia Woolf's sentence 'which we might call the psychological sentence of the feminine gender'[25]), the form of *Mary Olivier* is relatively straightforward. It combines a 'stream of consciousness' style with a brevity and nimbleness of structure which is what endears the novel to those who cannot get along with Dorothy Richardson's slow-paced volumes. Katharine Mansfield disagreed and wrote in her review:

> It is too late in the day for this new form, and Miss Sinclair's skilful handling of it serves but to make its failure the more apparent. She has divided her history of Mary Olivier into five periods, infancy, childhood, adolescence, maturity and middle-age, but these divisions are negligible. In the beginning Mary is two, but at the end she is still two – and forty-seven – and so it is throughout. At any moment, whatever her real age may be she is two – or forty-seven – either, both.[26]

But many readers point to the fluidity of the time-scale as one of the novel's great achievements, and so might Katharine Mansfield if she had read the work of Proust (which had begun to be published in France in 1913 and in English translation in 1922). When Mary Olivier is a child the seeds of adulthood are sown but when she is an adult she is still a child. It is not for nothing that she remarks ' "I shall go on growing younger and younger till it's all over" '; she is mature, but she has not managed, in adult life, to transcend her infancy, during which her mother thwarted her at every turn from developing into a self-contained, confident personality. Mary's tragedy is that she does not hate her mother. She longs for her to love her and bows to her domination. She only accepts fully that her mother's jealousy derives from her own frustration when it is much too late: by then she is middle-aged, heart-whole and clear-sighted — but too good a person to desert the mother whom, in spite of all, she still loves. She tells her brother who has got away:

> 'It's different for you,' she said. 'Ever since I began to grow up I felt there was something about Mamma that would kill me if I let it. I've had to fight for every single thing I've ever wanted. It's awful fighting her, when she's so sweet and gentle. But it's either that or go under . . . She doesn't *know* she hates me. She never knows that awful sort of thing. And of course she loved me when I was little. She'd love me now if I stayed little, so that she could do what she liked with me; if I'd sit in a corner and think as she thinks, and feel as she feels and do what she does . . . I *should* be lying then, the whole time. Hiding my real self and crushing it. It's your *real* self she hates — the thing she can't see and touch and get at — the thing that makes you different. Even when I was little she hated it and tried to crush it.'[27]

For Mary Olivier, self-sacrifice is ecstasy, or rather, it has a real spiritual meaning for her: it is, in its own way, its own reward. Indeed, in almost all her novels May Sinclair sounds out that 'feminine note' in literature that E. M. Forster defined in 1910 as 'a preoccupation with relative worthiness. The characters in a woman's novel try not so much to be good, to measure up to some impersonal standard, as to be worthy of one of the other characters'.[28] This is truer of no one than of Harriett in May Sinclair's *Life and Death of Harriett Frean* (1922). She has been taught by her mother that 'it's better to go without than to take from other people' and thus when she grows up she gives up the only man she loves in order not to take him from her friend Priscilla. But this novel is about far more than one girl and her personal, pernicious self-sacrifice. It is about a whole way of life, a whole breed of people, embodied by the word Victorian. The renunciation, sacrifice and martyrdom which they thought so crucial and so fulfilling is here by implication shown as sterile and life-denying — even selfish; a whole way of life was founded on these principles and it is one of the most far-reaching effects of the fresh air that blew in with the twentieth century that new ideals came with it. The novel is putting into fictional form some of the ideas thrown out by Virginia Woolf when she wrote that

> in or about December, 1910, human character changed . . . In life one can see the change, if I may use a homely illustration, in the character of one's cook. The Victorian cook lived like a leviathan in the lower depths, formidable, silent, obscure, inscrutable; the Georgian cook is a creature of sunshine and fresh air; in and out of the drawing-room, now to borrow the *Daily Herald*, now to ask advice about a hat . . . All human relations have shifted — those between masters and servants, husbands and wives, parents and children.[29]

But Harriett Frean, because of her early conditioning, represses her true needs and feelings, thereby sacrificing her happiness. Her parents have, blindly and ineptly, failed to nudge her into the twentieth century, because they too fail to acknowledge that personal self-fulfilment and happiness matter more than some 'notion of duty'. Psychoanalysis represented more than a method of dealing with neuroses — it signified a new and passionate concern for the individual and her personal welfare. At the same time it symbolised a sloughing off of some of the old ideas, customs and conventions. As Virginia Woolf said, the modern woman was born 'in or about December 1910' because she began to develop a sense of what it was to act freely and for herself: Harriett Frean was already an anachronism, symbolic of something dead and gone.

I always think of my mother when I read this novel. Born in 1907, she was brought up by a nanny who was so exceptionally repressive, and presumably cruel, that she affected my mother for the rest of her life. She did all the usual things that ogre-like nannies did (do they still?). But she went even further; for example, she used to tell her two charges that if they always walked along the street with their eyes down they would eventually see enough pins for it to be unnecessary to buy any. I used to laugh at this; yet, as May Sinclair realised, if these ideas are impressed on someone from an early enough age, even an intelligent woman may never slough them off. But the nanny's more enduring legacy to my mother was her rigid denial of the pleasure-principle. 'We are in this world to do good, not to be happy,' my mother used to exhort us three children and I really believe that she meant it. (It has taken me most of my life to learn how to seek pleasure guiltlessly, but I am learning slowly; thankfully I have no trouble buying pins.)

When Harriett Frean tells a young girl about her renunciation years ago, the girl's response is firm. She unhesitatingly declares that Harriett had thought purely of herself, 'of her own moral beauty' rather than of others, that her self-sacrifice was egocentric rather than genuinely giving. And Harriett realises that 'the beauty of that unique act no longer appeared to her as it once was, uplifting, consoling, incorruptible'. (Here again one is reminded of the theme of *Still Life*, where some might conclude that there is an element of cowardice in Laura's heroic renunciation of Alec. It is one of the most important questions engendered by romantic love which fails to run smooth – is it braver to wound the discarded first love and go to the second or to renounce happiness and thereby blight one's own life?)

In all her novels May Sinclair manages, with varying degrees of success, to combine her insight into the individual consciousness with her art as a novelist. *The Romantic*, for example, is only flawed as a novel because of the way the ends are tied: a psychotherapist is brought in to explain the truth of the matter to Charlotte, the heroine. Other novelists kill people off, or find them a priest or a lover to explain their plight; but they have a private language in the same way that scientists do. The explanation given by the doctor to Charlotte is, certainly, not one that would have graced the pages of the traditional novel, but the jargon used is very much of its time (1920).

> Conway was an out and out degenerate. He couldn't help *that*. He suffered from some physical disability. It went through everything. It made him so that he couldn't live a man's life. He was afraid to enter a profession. He was afraid of women . . . The balance had to be righted somehow. His whole life must have been a struggle to right it. Unconscious, of course. Instinctive. His platonics were just a glorifying of his disability. All that romancing was a gorgeous transformation of his funk . . . So that his very lying was a sort of truth. I mean it was part of the whole desperate effort after completion. He jumped at everything that helped him to get compensation, to get power. He jumped at your feeling for him because it gave him power. He sucked manhood out of you. He sucked it out of everything – out of blood and wound.[30]

Happily, this explanation of her dead lover's impotence and cruelty is a tonic to Charlotte. The doctor has helped her to exorcise her lover, she is able to feel compassion for the dead man and is cleansed and ready should love come her way again. Had the doctor not explained the truth to her, she might have remained obsessed, either full of hatred or unable to forget, but in any case with her mind deeply troubled. It was, in Rebecca West's view, 'from a technical point of view, unfortunate' that the novel was rounded off in this way: but presumably from the heroine's it was a happy release.

And, after all, Rebecca West herself had used a device not so altogether different in her own novel published two years earlier, *The Return of the Soldier* (1918). This too is a novel which allows the central character to 'come through' because of someone's insight into the unconscious, but in this case it is a warm, intuitive woman who makes the cure while the doctor stands by approvingly. It is not primarily a novel about war, for the war is only the device which causes Chris to lose his memory because of the trauma of shell-shock. But Rebecca West had read about doctors who, in treating those suffering from shell- shock, used Freud's theories to try and discover what fears their patients were suppressing. The only direct reference to the fighting is right at the end when, in a memorable passage, Rebecca West points to the irony that only when a man is 'cured' is he considered fit enough to face death again. (It is the same ghastly paradox as the condemned man being denied the means of suicide because he must be kept alive and ready for his execu- tioner.) At the end Chris walks back across the lawn 'with his back turned on this fading happiness'.

> He wore a dreadful decent smile; I knew how his voice would resolutely lift in greeting us. He walked not loose- limbed like a boy, as he had done that very afternoon, but with the soldier's hard tread upon the heel. It recalled to me that, bad as we were, we were yet not the worst circum- stances of his return. When we had lifted the yoke of our embraces from his shoulders he would go back to that flooded trench in Flanders under that sky more full of flying death than clouds, to that No Man's Land where bullets fall like rain on the rotting faces of the dead.[31]

The central impetus to the novel is the new, twentieth- century insight into the unconscious. Chris is 'cured', or rather is forced to face up to reality again, because the sight of his dead son's jersey involuntarily jerks him into remembrance of the life of which his son had been part and which he had been obliterat- ing from his mind. But it was not a conscious obliteration, and he could not cure himself even if his conscious self had wished to do so: the doctor is quite sure of this:

> 'A complete case of amnesia,' he was saying . . . 'His unconscious self is refusing to let him resume his relations with his normal life, and so we get this loss of memory.'
>   'I've always said,' declared Kitty, with an air of good sense, 'that if he would make an effort . . .'
>   'Effort!' He jerked his round head about. 'The mental

life that can be controlled by effort isn't the mental life that matters. You've been stuffed up when you were young with talk about a thing called self-control — a sort of barmaid of the soul that says, "Time's up, gentlemen," and "Here, you've had enough." There's no such thing. There's a deep self in one, the essential self, that has its wishes. And if those wishes are suppressed by the superficial self — the self that makes, as you say, efforts and usually makes them with the sole idea of putting up a good show before the neighbours — it takes its revenge. Into the house of conduct erected by the superficial self it sends an obsession.'[32]

Despite these wise words, the doctor is obviously something of a radical, for he declares, 'It's my profession to bring people from various outlying districts of the mind to the normal. There seems to be a general feeling it's the place where they ought to be. Sometimes I don't see the urgency myself.' He concludes that Chris has forgotten his life with his wife because he was 'discontented' with it. And the ending is doubly poignant, for not only will a 'cured' man have to be returned to the trenches but he will have to face up to reality, 'make an effort' and recognise that the tender, innocent love that he once had for Margaret has gone for ever except in his dreams. He has to face the truth, emerge from a fantasy world and face up to cold reality.

'Reality' and 'psychoanalysis' were, by the 1920s, linked words in many people's minds, and even the most middlebrow writer would have expected her readers to know something of what she was talking about when they were mentioned. Laura, in *The Way Things Are* (1927) by E. M. Delafield, is kept up to the mark by her sister.

'Well,' said Christine kindly, 'I can't say that I believe you. And any decent analyst would tell you that you're doing yourself a great deal of harm by this constant pretence. It's bound to create the most frightful repressions. What sort of dreams do you have?'

But Laura, even though she did live in the country, knew all about Herr Freud and his theories, and declined to commit herself in any way upon the subject of dreams.[33]

Indeed, by the 1930s Freudian ideas about memory and repression had become near-clichés of popular fiction and drama. They were certainly a good way of rounding things off, as May Sinclair and Rebecca West had demonstrated. In Rosalind Wade's *Treasure in Heaven* (1937), the explanations of the analyst are used to bring the novel to a calm, generally optimistic conclusion rather as if he were vicar or nanny or other *savant*. Fanny, the middle-aged heroine, is left desolate because all her attempts at helpfulness and charity in the slums of the East End have come to nothing – worse, her efforts have so misfired that she has been forbidden any more contact with her 'cases' or her fellow workers. She tells the 'very young man' about her misery and humiliation, and he reassures her. He tells her that she is suffering from a sense of failure but that if she comes to understand her true motives then she will understand herself and be at peace.

> Sometimes she winced, for he did not spare her feelings. He suggested, in no uncertain terms, that her interest in Mr Waters, her devotion to Neil and her passionate enthusiasm for the work at Maylie Street had been nothing more or less than a repression and sublimation of the sex impulse. Because life denied her husband and children she had instinctively found substitutes.
>
> 'But I haven't really regretted that,' she whispered, 'not for years, anyway. I have Janet's children, you see, and I was always so busy – there wasn't time to mope.'
>
> That was just the trouble, he explained. She had forced her natural wishes so severely into the background that the necessity for 'compensation' was redoubled . . .
>
> 'Oh, you're so cruel,' she told him, 'you leave me no pretences, no illusions, nothing. And what do you suggest? That every woman who hasn't got a husband must go about miserable and degraded because life's cheated her?'[34]

Poor Fanny has to admit that 'she had wanted love, her own home, protection and babies'. She asks herself whether it was not too late, but catching a glimpse in the mirror of 'her round face lined and tear-stained, the unpretentious felt hat pushed from her forehead, she knew, unquestionably, that it was too late . . . She had missed something that could never now be claimed on this side of death'. And the truth *is* comforting: Fanny has no illusions any longer and is grateful and, finally, optimistic.

This was understandably a rather unsuitable theme for the lending libraries. But the analyst is a useful prop to de-fuse an otherwise emotional scene. In her short story 'The Salt of the Earth', written in 1935, Rebecca West allows no such easy way out. The heroine, Alice, is unshakeable in her conviction that she is always right, sensitive to others and admired by everyone for her good sense. She cannot allow herself to go behind the screen that stands between her and reality, since to do this would be to destroy all her illusions and thus the very fabric of her life. Even when her busband finally, desperately, tries to make her see the truth, she will not even begin to accept it. Yet it is as if she cannot help her behaviour and therefore cannot control it. As she explains to her husband, in her nightmares something awful comes nearer and nearer which she knows is eventually going to destroy her. But, as she says, 'the funny thing is . . . I could perfectly well stop this awful horror coming at me. Only for some reason I can't. I have to go on doing the very thing that brings it nearer.'

Clearly, Alice's conscious self prevents her from controlling her unconscious self, even though her dreams are showing her the way out. But because there was no doctor or other perceptive person to help her to understand her 'true' self, there is no solution apart from stalemate or violence; and Rebecca West would have spoilt the shape of her story if she had sought for explanations, though she does hint that Alice has a paranoid personality by making her say plaintively, 'people have always loved being nasty to me all my life'. But deeper than this she does not go.

Her acuteness as a critic must have rendered Rebecca West's task as a novelist rather more difficult, since she was so aware of the difficulties. And she was sometimes guilty of shortcomings which she had pointed out in the work of others. For example, in an essay written in 1926 she observed very wittily that

Henry James and Mrs Wharton and Miss Sedgwick were responsible for an entire school of fiction writers who invariably ended their stories with an elliptical remark on the part of their principal figure: 'Oh, but you see,' he said humbly, 'I never really did,' and rounded them off with a brief passage ecstatically ascribing to him reduced circumstances and spiritual radiance. These are the glycerine tears of fiction.[35]

So indeed they may be, but tears that were not entirely unknown to Rebecca West herself. Nor was a rather simplistic view of Freudian theory unknown to her. In *The Judge* (1922), the reader cannot but wish that she had followed more faithfully the methods of Henry James and Edith Wharton and made the things that are *not* said count for more than the things that are. It is rather heavy-handed when the mother cries out as if with the full force of a revelation: ' "Of course! Of course! He cannot love Ellen because he loves me too much! He has nothing left to love her with!" ' And because she wants him to be happy she tries to syphon off some of his love for her towards Ellen. But the ending is melodrama and there must be many readers who would have opted for something more 'glycerine', less over-stated if they had had the choice.

Although many writers of this period must have been familiar with Freud's precepts, few would have read him at first hand. Virginia Woolf wrote in 1932 that 'I have not studied Dr Freud or any psychoanalyst – indeed I think I have never read any of their books; my knowledge is merely from superficial talk . . . any use of their methods must be instinctive.'[36] Certainly it is possible that she had never read Freud, although unlikely since the Woolfs' Hogarth Press had been publishing the translations of his work since 1924. Yet her understanding of the subconscious could plausibly have evolved without any knowledge of his work at first hand merely because simplified versions of his ideas were so much 'in the air'. And in some ways they were too much in the air for comfort, for writers like Virginia Woolf were pursuing their careers at a difficult time as far as women were concerned. Winifred Holtby pointed out with some acuteness that at the very moment when an artist might have climbed out of the traditional limitations of domestic obligation by claiming to be a human being, she was thrust back into them by the authority of the psychologist. A woman, she was told, must enjoy the full cycle of sex-experience, or she would become riddled with complexes like a rotting fruit . . . All the doubts and repudiations of those who reacted against the Edwardian tradition were hers, combined with all the tumult of the conflict surging round Mrs Fawcett and the Pankhursts. The full weight of the Freudian revelation fell upon her head.[37]

Cynics might reply that if it hadn't been the Freudian apple falling upon her head it would have been another variety and that all women, and men, consider themselves to have been born into a difficult period. This theme was a particular favourite of Rose Macaulay's. It is a pity that this writer, once so popular, perhaps because she was writing for an England more classbound than now, is now out of fashion: certainly it is hard to admire the way she dandles her characters rather like puppets, contemplates their follies and asks the reader to laugh at their dear, funny ways. There is something spiteful about the novels; one is reminded of the child's guilty delight in cutting a worm in half or impaling an insect on a pin; there is little of the tenderness of the mature writer or observer.

In *Dangerous Ages* (1921) the women all imagine that they are at a difficult stage in their lives, and the moral is, rather obviously, that no age is easy until we are so old that we have the wisdom, finally, to perceive this. Mrs Hilary embraces psychoanalysis rather as she might have welcomed a confessor. 'To pour it all out – what comfort! To feel that some one was interested, even though it might only be as in a case.' And at first the doctor comes up to her expectations. When she confesses to depression, to feeling useless, he says to her:

If you are perfectly frank, you can be cured. You can be adjusted to life. Every age in human life has had its own adjustments to make, its own relation to its environment to establish. All that repressed libido must be released and

diverted . . . You have some bad complexes, which must
be sublimated.

It sounded awful, the firm way he said it, like teeth or
appendixes which must be extracted. But Mrs Hilary knew
it wouldn't be like that really but delightful and luxurious,
more like a Turkish bath.[38]

She enjoys her treatment very much, explaining her 'troubles
with the maids' as well as more profound worries. Not that she
exactly welcomes the truth about her dreams (she perceives 'that
terrible Unconscious' rather as if it 'were a sewer, sunk beneath
an inadequate grating'). Nevertheless she faces up to it and is not
even wounded when her analyst tells her that her gratitude to
him merely means 'that your ego is at present in what is called
the state of infantile dependence or tutelage'. But it cannot, of
course, last, and by the final chapter Mrs Hilary is to be found
'worse than before'.

She was like a drunkard deprived suddenly of stimulants;
she had nothing to turn to, no one who took an interest in
her soul. She missed Mr Cradock and that bi-weekly hour;
she was like a creeper wrenched loose from its support and
flung flat on the ground.[39]

Rose Macaulay wishes the reader to adopt her own brisk and
breezy attitude to analysis, which is that it passes the time
pleasurably enough but is no better a solution than any other
time-filling device. She is not, as a novelist, especially interested
in her characters and it is hardly surprising that her creations are
usually cardboard cut-outs who cease to exist in the reader's
imagination the moment they have put down the book. (*The
Towers of Trebizond* is an exception, where she uses her wit and
malice to excellent effect.) Whereas writers who managed to
absorb the methods of psychoanalysis to genuine purpose used
them to create characters of flesh and blood and spirit, characters whose subconscious behaviour was both *felt* and understood
by the novelist.

Some writers managed on their own, in blissful ignorance of
'the full weight of the Freudian revelation'. 'George Egerton'
wrote in 1932, long after she had finished writing novels:

Unless one is androgynous, one is bound to look at life through the eyes of one's sex, to toe the limitations imposed on one by its individual physiological functions. I came too soon. If I did not know the technical jargon current to-day of Freud and the psycho-analysts, I did know something of complexes and inhibitions, repressions and the subconscious impulses that determine actions and reactions. I used them in my stories. I recognised that in the main, woman was the ever-untamed, unchanging, adapting herself as far as it suited her ends to male expectations; even if repression was altering her subtly. I would use situations or conflicts as I saw them with a total disregard of man's opinions. I would unlock a closed door with a key of my own fashioning.[40]

CHAPTER SEVEN

Romance

'Came the Dawn'

The novels which Laura Jesson or Mrs Miniver or the Provincial Lady borrowed once a week from Boots were firmly middle-brow. No woman with intellectual pretensions (the 'professional' woman or the university-educated) would have read them, preferring Huxley and Virginia Woolf and, at a pinch, Rosamond Lehmann and Elizabeth Bowen. Only with detective fiction (Dorothy Sayers and Agatha Christie) would their tastes have overlapped – here middlebrow and highbrow would have presented a concerted front in opposition to romantic or 'Came the Dawn' novels. Luckily (and unsurprisingly in a class-dominated society) there were libraries especially for the lowbrows.

There is a photograph on my desk taken in about 1923, of G. Stevens, Newsagents and Lending Library, 25 Church Street, Basingstoke, Hampshire. The manager, his wife and the shop assistants are to be seen standing outside: it is they who served their daily customers with their newspapers, magazines and library books and it is the novels stocked by this 'twopenny library' that are the subject of this chapter. G. Stevens's customers would have been less well-off than the customers of his rival library, Boots or W. H. Smith in the High Street; they would have been about half male and half female, whereas at

Boots only one-quarter of the library customers were male. Stevens's shop would have stocked between two hundred and three hundred titles, divided roughly as follows: Mysteries (45 per cent), Westerns (15 per cent), Romances (30 per cent) and 'Other' (10 per cent). (Whereas at W. H. Smith about half were romance, a quarter were adventure stories and a quarter crime.) The big names in thriller and western writers were Nat Gould, Edgar Wallace, 'Sapper', Sax Rohmer, Zane Grey and William Le Queux, and then there were the detective novelists. The most popular romantic novelists were Ruby M. Ayres and Ethel M. Dell, although at least a dozen other writers of romance such as Margaret Pedlar and Denise Robins made a good showing.

It cost twopence or sometimes threepence to borrow a book from a small lending library and there was no danger of being unable to find a new book since the small shopkeeper rented his library stock from a wholesale library which generally held about 2,500 books. And since over two hundred new titles were published in Britain every week the wholesaler too had no trouble in turning over his stock. The women who came in to choose their novels off the two or three shelves at the back of Stevens's shop were part of the new leisured class who needed to while away a good deal of time and the twopenny library was a vital part of their lives.

The sugary, unreal qualities of the inter-war romance and thriller fiction would seem to some modern readers both delightfully harmless and infinitely preferable to the wares on offer at any airport bookstall. Yet there was then rather more disapproval of the 'pulp' qualities of light fiction than there is nowadays, when most people seem to take for granted the crudity of many of the novels published. Few today would write with the vehemence of Rebecca West when she said, with reference to *Charles Rex*, one of Ethel M. Dell's heroes:

And in every line that is written about him one hears the thudding, thundering hooves of a certain steed at full gallop; of the true Tosh-horse. For even as one cannot walk on one's own trudging diligent feet if one desires to attain to the height of poetry, but must mount Pegasus, so one

cannot reach the goal of best selling by earnest pedestrian-
ism, but must ride thither on the Tosh-horse. No one can
write a best-seller by taking thought.[1]

But, then as now, it was the thoughtlessness, the predict-
ability, of romance that provided its main appeal. Mr Stevens
knew what he had on offer and his customers knew what they
were getting. They wanted exactly what Storm Jameson wished
they did not want when she wrote in 1939:

> You can see how dangerous the novelist is, because the
> medium in which he works is not words but it is your mind.
> He plays on it to make you laugh and cry . . . There are
> novelists who make a great deal of money by playing over
> and over *All That I Want is Somebody to Love Me . . .*
> And when we want to wear grief or joy we take down some
> shabby ill-made garment belonging to Miss So-and-so, the
> popular novelist, and muffle our foolish heads in it . . .
>
> A novelist who is merely clever or merely witty or
> merely, as we say of children, very noticing, may write
> novels which amuse or excite or soothe us, but at least he is
> only helping us to pass our time. At worst he is unfitting us
> for life by giving us weak or distorted or foolish notions
> about it.[2]

Storm Jameson wrote her attack on popular fiction, of which
this is part, in 1932, the same year that Queenie Leavis published
her full-length study, *Fiction and the Reading Public*. They
were both preoccupied with lowbrow fiction as a force for good
or evil and were both secure in their belief that its influence was
corrupting. Mrs Leavis's oft-quoted stricture was that popular
novels 'actually get in the way of genuine feeling and responsible
thinking by creating cheap mechanical responses and by
throwing their weight on the side of social, national and herd
prejudices'.[3]
Ever since the character in Jane Austen's *Northanger Abbey*
(1818) confessed to reading 'only a novel', and the French
censors of the late 1850s declared that Flaubert's *Madame
Bovary* was corrupting because it showed a married woman led

astray by an over-rich diet of light fiction, this argument has refused to go away. Mary McCarthy even managed rather subtly to extend the corrupting influence as far as the library itself.

> Emma [Bovary] and Léon agree that membership in a circulating library is a necessity if you have to live in the provinces and they are both wholly dependent on this typical bourgeois institution. The lending library is a central metaphor of *Madame Bovary* because it is the inexhaustible source of *idées reçues* – borrowed ideas and stock sentiments which circulate tritely among the population . . . the lending library is an image of civilization itself. Ideas and feelings as well get more and more soiled and grubby, like library books, as they pass from hand to hand.[4]

At some private circulating libraries subscribers could pay extra for the privilege of borrowing new books – perhaps they did this not merely to avoid germs but also to give the sentiments they proposed to imbibe a better chance of being unspoilt by the common touch.

But light fiction had millions of supporters, as sales and borrowing figures demonstrated. The publisher Michael Joseph wrote in *The Commercial Side of Literature* (1925) that

> the demand for fiction on such a wholesale scale must be due to the artificial complexities of a civilised state. Men and women, especially women, seek in the vicarious realm of fiction the wider range of human experiences which a complex and narrowed life denies them. Having neither time nor opportunity in this crowded, hustled existence to taste the joys and sorrows, the vicissitudes and triumphs of a more elemental experience, they turn to fiction to satisfy their natural craving . . . for emotional satisfaction, civilisation-hampered people turn to fiction.[5]

He pointed out that people read fiction for entertainment, escape, instruction, enlargement of their range of experience, to enjoy observing and criticising and, fundamentally, to enjoy the illusions which real life fails to sustain. (Realists refuse to hand the reader a pair of rose-coloured spectacles and have, therefore, to cater for a more discriminating public.) And he defined the best-seller as needing sincerity, a good story, strong and sustained human interest, a happy ending *after* great troubles and tribulations, and an outstanding theme or moral. Readers were generally prejudiced against the psychological and morbid novel and the types of story that would be difficult to 'place' included historical romances, stories with a religious or spiritual bias, stories with a very strong moral flavour and 'pre-war' stories. Short stories were also disliked, the ideal length for a novel being one that could be read at a sitting (i.e. in an afternoon or evening).

The comparative excitement of 'the times in which we live' was Michael Joseph's explanation for why the historical novel was.then out of favour. But by the middle of the 1920s, writers like Anya Seton and Georgette Heyer were just beginning long writing careers which were to last for fifty years. In the latter's novels, historical trappings are combined with the basic Jane Eyre plot of the socially underprivileged girl falling in love with a superior man who does not notice. A variation on the theme was the heroine proudly refusing to admit her love, as in *Regency Buck* (1935), in which Judith fights with her handsome guardian for three hundred pages before they are finally reconciled.

'Nonsensical child! I have been in love with you almost from the first moment of setting eyes on you.'

'Oh, this is dreadful!' said Miss Taberner, shaken by remorse. 'I disliked you amazingly for weeks!'

The Earl kissed her again. 'You are wholly adorable,' he said.

'No, I am not,' replied Miss Taverner, as soon as she was able. 'I am as disagreeable as you are. You would like to beat me. You said you would once, and I believe you meant it!'

'If I only said it once I am astonished at my own forbearance. I have wanted to beat you at least a dozen times, and came very near doing it once . . . But I still think you adorable. Give me your hand.'[6]

Michael Joseph's distinction between 'pulp' fiction and the rest is clear. One is escapist, the other enlarges the reader's experience, one is widely read and the other minimally, one is not reviewed in newspapers and magazines, the other is. It is a situation which persists today and only very occasionally are the barriers breached, as in the case of *Jane Eyre*, *Rebecca* and *Gone with the Wind*. (Although I can think of one or two women of my mother's generation who profess to intellectual and social awareness but still managed to ignore an outstanding work of fiction like *Rebecca*. Of couse, a small minority censors good novels on the grounds *alone* of mass appeal, being loath to associate itself in any way with Mrs Leavis's 'herd prejudices'. But it has always mystified me that someone can have political, often socialist, feelings without wanting even occasionally to share in a mass imaginative experience – people were reading *Rebecca* at the time of the 'phoney war'; any good historian of the period should read it in tandem with contemporary newspapers.)

The stock of twopenny libraries stayed firmly on one side of the barrier, avoiding any possible pretensions to literary quality and these libraries provided their customers precisely with what they asked for, a good light romantic novel which would not make them feel 'uncomfortable', preferably on the theme of 'All That I Want is Somebody to Love Me'. The basic storyline should be boy meeting girl, various seemingly insuperable difficulties coming between them and, finally, the revelation of their true and hitherto suppressed feelings. The arch-exponent of this theme was Ethel M. Dell, and she established her reputation with her first novel *The Way of an Eagle* (1912), a novel which was to set the pattern for pulp fiction for the next seventy years at least. Complaining about the lazily eulogistic reviewer who corruptly praises everything he reads, George Orwell described him

sinking his standards to a depth at which, say, Ethel M. Dell's *Way of an Eagle* is a fairly good book. But on a scale of values which makes *The Way of an Eagle* a good book, *The Constant Nymph* is a superb book, and *The Man of*

Property is – what? A palpitating tale of passion, a terrific soul-shattering masterpiece, an unforgettable epic which will last as long as the English language and so on and so forth. (As for any *really* good book it would burst the thermometer.)[7]

The Way of an Eagle had been rejected by more than eight publishers before Fisher Unwin accepted it for their First Novel Library on condition that it was cut from 300,000 to 90,000 words. Published in January 1912, the novel was an instant success, being reprinted twenty-seven times in the next three years alone. Its author was a recluse, refusing to be photographed and knitting her own clothes rather than having to face the publicity of a department store changing room. Although she married when she was forty, she remained by temperament extremely virginal and had no direct experience either of India (where so many of her novels are set) or of the physical violence which runs as an exotic, titillating thread throughout her work.

Most modern readers will greatly enjoy *The Way of an Eagle*, for it remains the best kind of read for anyone wishing to curl up in an armchair, flu-bound and lackadaisical, and wallow unashamedly in a book that is entirely timeless, oblivious of realities and predictions – even if it is written by an author who is part of what George Orwell called that 'huge tribe of Barries and Deepings and Dells who simply don't notice what is happening'.[8] There is also something undeniably cheering in reading and enjoying a novel that has given pleasure to so many for so long; I love to imagine my mother and grandmother sobbing over books like this.

The Way of an Engle opens dramatically with the final days of a siege at a British-held North-west Frontier fort. Muriel, the Brigadier's daughter, is under great strain from the prolonged bombardment and tension and 'there came a time when Muriel Roscoè, driven to extremity, sought relief in a remedy from which in her normal senses she would have turned in disgust' (opium). As the crisis nears, her father chooses Nick Ratcliffe to look after her. Muriel does not care for him.

'Only the other day I heard him laugh at something that

was terrible – something it makes me sick to think of.
Indeed, Daddy, I would far rather have Captain Grange to
take care of me. Don't you think he would if you asked
him? He is so much bigger and stronger, and – and
kinder.'

'Ah! I know,' her father said. 'He seems so to you. But it
is nerve that your protector will need, child; and Ratcliffe
possesses more nerve than all the rest of the garrison put
together.'[9]

This passage holds the clues to the rest of the novel. Nick is
sexual yet frightening – he is not tender like Grange. But Muriel
dislikes him for reasons she would rather not admit (he is
unashamedly sensual and intolerant of convention). Eventually,
however, the two will be lovers, but the reader settles
comfortably into her chair knowing there are 350 pages of
difficulties before the happy climax. Their escape from the fort is
dramatic but they reach the haven of Simla unscathed. Muriel
agrees to marry Nick, who is described as too careless of propriety to bother about a courtship. But she cannot shake off the
frightening memory she has of Nick in the desert

bent to destroy like an eagle above his prey, merciless, full
of strength, terrible – saw the man beneath him, writh-
ing, convulsed, tortured – saw his upturned face, and
starting eyes – saw the sudden downward swoop of Nick's
right hand – the flash of the descending steel.[10]

She may have been bred to be the wife of a fearless soldier, but a
killing in cold-blood was going too far and something that, she
imagined, the scrupulous Grange would not have undertaken.
So whenever Nick even takes her hand 'once more her old
aversion to this man swept over her in a nauseating wave'.

A few days later Muriel overhears a conversation in which her
shallow, small-minded English hostess makes it clear that the
English community assume that the couple are only marrying
because he has fatally compromised her on their trek through the
desert. She breaks off her engagement, in a scene which places
Nick firmly in the line of irresistible, incorrigible heroes

stretching from Mr Rochester to Rhett Butler; and goes home. Here she becomes engaged to Grange, the smooth, polite but clearly sexually inept officer from the days at the garrison. Nick too comes home on leave and, after various dramas, Muriel has to recognise the truth.

She knew now! She knew now! He had forced her to realize it. He had captured her, had kindled within her − by what magic she knew not − the undying flame. Against her will, in spite of her utmost resistance, he had done this thing. Above and beyond and through her fiercest hatred, he had conquered her quivering heart. He had let her go again, but not till he had blasted her happiness for ever. None other could ever dominate her as this man dominated. None other could ever kindle in her − or ever quench − the torch that this man's hand had lighted.

And this was Love − this hunger that could never be satisfied, this craving which would not be stifled or ignored − Love triumphant, invincible, immortal − the thing she had striven to slay at its birth, but which had lived on in spite of her, growing, spreading, enveloping, till she was lost, till she was suffocated, in its immensity. There could never be any escape for her again. She was fettered hand and foot. It was useless any longer to strive. She stood and faced the truth.

She did not ask herself how it was she had ever come to care. She only numbly realized that she had always cared. And she knew now that to no woman is it given to so hate as she had hated without the spur of Love goading her thereto. Ah, but Love was cruel! Love was merciless! For she had never known − nor ever could know now − the ecstasy of Love. Truly it conquered; but it left its prisoners to perish of starvation in the wilderness.[11]

But there is still Pride and matters remain unresolved when Muriel and Nick both, separately, go back to India.

Life was a horrible emptiness to her in those days. She was weary beyond expression, and had no heart for the gaieties in which she was plunged. Idle compliments had never attracted her, and flirtations were an abomination to her. She looked through and beyond them with the eyes of a sphinx. But there were very few who suspected the intolerable ache that throbbed unceasingly behind her impassivity – the loneliness of spirit that oppressed her like a crushing, physical weight.[12]

Nick has seemingly disappeared and it is rumoured he has entered a monastery in Tibet. When he reappears it transpires that he has disguised himself as a beggar in order to remain undetected near her, and is well placed from his customary begging posture at the foot of the Residency steps to foil an assassination attempt on Muriel's host. But Muriel still has to find the words to tell him of her change of heart.

The tumult of her emotions swelled to sudden uproar, thunderous, all-possessing, overwhelming, so that she gasped and gasped again for breath. And then all in a moment she knew that the conflict was over. She was as a diver, hurling with headlong velocity from dizzy height into deep waters, and she rejoiced – she exulted – in that mad rush into depth.

With a quivering laugh she moved. She loosened her convulsive clasp upon his hand, turned it upwards, and stooping low, she pressed her lips closely, passionately, lingeringly, upon his open palm. She had found a way.[13]

Nick is as masterful as Muriel or any reader could have wished.

'I warn you, Muriel, you are putting yourself irrevocably in my power, and you will never break away again. You may come to loathe me with your whole soul, but I shall never let you go. Have you realized that? If I take you now, I take you for all time.'

He spoke almost with violence, and, having spoken, drew back from her abruptly, as though he could not wholly trust himself.

But nothing could dismay her now. She had fought her last battle, had made the final surrender. Her fear was dead. She stretched out her hands to him with unfaltering confidence.

'Take me then, Nick,' she said.[14]

Ethel M. Dell was a pleasure-giver pure and simple. She seems to have felt no need for heart-searching about her merit or her role as a writer, but after her initial success, continued to write novels on the same lines, aimed at the same kind of audience and guaranteed to give the same kind of enjoyment. Contemporary critics had no trouble in pinning her down:

> Her books are unpretentious contributions to the literature of escape: that is, they enable the weary and bored and depressed to transfer themselves temporarily to another sphere of life . . . Those below a certain standard of literary culture desire, in their imaginative exercises, to move in a world as different from their own as any world can be. Girls who travel on crowded tramcars and Underground trains among hordes of plain young men, or who live in kitchens and are visited by few save plain young butchers and plain young bakers, are likely to be responsive to the emotions of a heroine carried long distances through strange romantic country by a Nick Ratcliffe; or to those of another heroine attracted by the magnetic personality of a Charles Rex in the supposed romantic atmosphere of a liner.[15]

Mr Ward then retreats into what one might call the Madame Bovary argument and speculates whether 'fiction-fed minds may become in time permanently depressed and disgruntled by the conviction that life has not allowed them a fair deal'.

Books like *The Way of an Eagle* are superbly good at telling stories of drama and intricacy in which everything turns out all right in the end. The hero and heroine endure tests of endurance which would crush ordinary mortals, but the reader has the satisfaction of knowing that they will come through with flying colours. Herein lies one of the main counter-agruments to the Madame Bovary question – no shop girl, factory girl, skivvy or housewife could see the merest glimmer of a parallel between her life and those of Dell's heroines. Nor would she probably wish her daily existence to imitate the dramas that she is reading about. The only point at which she would certainly have liked life to imitate art was with respect to male sexuality. Dell's heroes may be proud, aloof, withdrawn and in need of taming. But at the same time they are passionate, loyal, forceful and (usually) moneyed enough to find no practical hindrance should they wish to follow their women to the ends of the earth. A. P. Herbert wrote about this problem in *The Water Gipsies* (1930) and also in this song:

> Jack loves me well enough, I know,
> But does he ever bite his lip,
> And does he chew his cheek to show
> That Passion's got him in a grip?
> An' does his gun go pop-pop-pop –
> When fellers get familiar? No.
> He just says, ' 'Op it!' and they 'op –
> It may be life, but ain't it slow?[16]

There is a serious issue here that is crucial to the next chapter. If men and women are to conform to the romantic ideal which, in the twentieth century, demands that domestic harmony should partner romantic love, how are they to achieve this if their imaginations are feeding on quite different fantasies? Poor Jack in A. P. Herbert's poem had probably never read a novel by Ethel M. Dell and would not have known Nick Ratcliffe, the most famous of her heroes, had he met him. But then should his wife have been secretly resentful that he was not more Ratcliffe-like? And again one thinks of Emma Bovary, privately in despair with Charles because he was so unlike a romantic hero. Who can say whether women should read less romantic fiction and demand less of their only-too-everyday men or whether men should read their fiction and try in private at least to live up more to the Dell-ideal? – an ideal which recognises sexuality as a vital part of intimacy. But if one reads the imaginary but horribly plausible description of 'Mrs Britain's' typical bedtime routine or that of Norah in Rosamond Lehmann's *A Note in Music* it is hardly surprising that they should seek oblivion in a romantic novel.

The heroes of romantic novels behave in a romantic way. They are also far more obviously sensual than the heroes of 'well-written' novels. In 1910, Arnold Bennett wondered why Elinor Glyn's 'magnificently sexual novel' (*His Hour*) had not been banned by the Library Censorship Committee, while Rebecca West commented in her inimitable way on the absurd double standards at work when she wrote, 'how true it is that there are those who may not look at a horse over a hedge; and there are those who may lead it out through the gate'. And she referred to the serious writer's wistfulness with which 'he gazes across the esplanade of any watering-place and looks at the old ladies reading their Ethel Dells. Truly we are a strange nation.'[17]

Already in the early years of the century Elinor Glyn had made it quite clear that women experience sexual desire and that this is something both usual and admirable. Yet she sidestepped the censor by ensuring that some form of retribution invariably struck, and by using language which gave an air of purity to her work. Mrs Leavis was the first to point out that many bestselling novels 'make play with the key words of the emotional vocabulary which provoke the vague warm surges of feeling associated with religion and religion substitutes – e.g. life, death, love, good, evil, sin, home, mother, noble, gallant, purity, honour'.[18] And it is true that when an Elinor Glyn hero finally seduces or is conquered there is always a mention of heaven, worship or eternity, as if religious allusions add the necessary moral tone.

But when one looks beyond the various disguises provided by religion, Nemesis or generally exalted implications, it is quite clear that the true goal for her heroines is sexual pleasure. Yet her grandson claimed that she personally 'was not much interested in sex; she thought it unromantic, animal, earthy. She was interested in love, in the romantic disguise which enveloped more material thoughts, and feelings, and the maintenance of which was the great ideal of her life.'[19] (And Barbara Cartland has declared: 'All my heroines are virgins – I don't think sleeping together is romantic.'[20]) Elinor Glyn nevertheless invented the word 'it' as shorthand for sex appeal; and few could seriously claim that *Three Weeks* (1907), her most famous novel, which had sold five million copies by the early thirties, was popular because of its emphasis on the merely spiritual qualities of love.

In this silly but very readable novel a young Englishman on holiday in Switzerland meets a mysterious and beautiful young woman who uses his gift of a tiger skin as a bed on which to teach him all there is to know about sexual pleasure.

> At the first glow of dawn, he awoke, a strange sensation, almost of strangling and suffocation, upon him. There, bending over, framed in a mist of blue-black waves, he saw his lady's face. Its milky whiteness lit by her strange eyes — green as [a] cat's they seemed, and blazing with the fiercest passion of love — while twisted round his throat he felt a great strand of her splendid hair. The wildest thrill as yet his life had known then came to Paul, he clasped her in his arms with a frenzy of mad, passionate joy.[21]

For three weeks the idyll continues, with Paul's mistress, who naturally turns out to be a queen, instructing him in all the ways of love, which includes the stress on masochism which was such an important element in popular erotic fiction:

> You see, Paul, a man can always keep a woman loving him if he kisses her enough, and make her feel that there is no use struggling because he is too strong to resist. A woman will stand almost anything from a passionate lover. He may beat her and pain her soft flesh; he may shut her up and deprive her of all other friends — while the motive is raging love and interest in herself on his part, it only makes her love him the more.[22]

Paul loses his queen but remembers something more practical she had once told him in between her coos and flutters (they are in a gondola by now): ' "You must not just drift, my Paul, like so many of your countrymen do. You must help to stem the tide of your nation's decadence, and be a strong man." '[23] This he does, becoming an important diplomat but forever mourning his queen, unable to marry anyone else, because, after all, what would an English girl know about love?' ' "The women of your country are sweet and soft, but they know not the passion I know, my Paul – the fierceness and madness of love – ." ' Erotic love was all right in Ruritania or in a gondola with its suitably honeymoon overtones, but the Library Censorship Committee could not condone it when it was associated with the kind of girls they might invite to their tennis parties. As Mr Justice Younger said in 1915 of the 'grossly immoral' *Three Weeks*, at a hearing when Elinor Glyn was suing for infringement of copyright, 'stripped of its trappings which are mere accident, it is nothing more nor less than a sensual, adulterous intrigue'.[24]

Thus sexual bliss in the fiction written in the afterglow of Victorianism had to take place somewhere far away and exotic, otherwise the circulating libraries would not be able to continue with their comfortable equation of distance equalling decency. If distance was impractical, then the surroundings had to be very unusual, as in Elinor Glyn's *Six Days* (1924), where the couple's honeymoon actually takes place in a makeshift church. David and Laline ('all that a really lovely American heiress should be') arrange to tour the battlefields together -- a popular pastime in the early 1920s. A priest shows them round a dug-out, there is a landslide and the priest's dying gesture is to marry the happy couple who spend their honeymoon alternately making love and scrabbling to get out. (Once rescued, David rapidly disappears on a secret mission; Laline is about to marry his best friend for the sake of the coming child when David arrives on a horse, declaring memorably, ' "I forbid this marriage to go on." ') The sexuality is, however, rather less obvious in this novel, partly because the couple are married and partly because a dug-out had unromantic if not morbid associations for most readers.

Another fictional method of bowing to the dictates of propriety was that of treating sexuality medically, rather as if the woman was a 'case' history. The heroine of *Anna Lombard* (1901) by 'Victoria Cross' is an English girl newly arrived in India who has a reputation for seriousness. She soon becomes engaged to Gerald, the narrator, but they cannot marry because of her secret and shameful passion for a native.

In the day she never saw him or sent for him except in his capacity as servant, and he was in no way favoured in money, dress or quarters above the other servants . . . In the day Anna was entirely with me, and if slander could have touched her at all it would have connected her name with mine and none other. Yet, even so, it seemed to me as if the whole matter must rise to the light in some way, and I waited in dread for the hour of discovery.

The more I studied Anna, the more incomprehensible and terrible this strange dual passion of hers became for me. But, also, I became more and more convinced I had decided rightly in not abandoning her to herself. Neither would she have deserved my desertion. For this miserable love that had overtaken her she was no more to be held responsible than she would have been for any physical malady she might have been stricken with. She loved me with the same faithful, tender devotion she had given me from the first, and it seemed, when we were alone together, impossible to me that she could be living the life she was. But, indeed, her love for Gaida seemed to have no sort of influence upon her love for, and her relations with, me. It was a thing utterly separate and apart from that self which she gave to me. Within her the two loves, the higher and the lower, seemed to exist together without touching or disturbing the other, just as in a river sometimes one sees two streams, one muddy, the other clear, flowing side by side without mixing.[25]

Sexuality at some distance and sexuality as 'physical malady' were both acceptable, but neither of them were such best-selling ingredients as sexuality as sadism. Until the mid-1920s, sexual pleasure for women was closely linked with cruelty; writers like E. M. Hull and Ethel M. Dell took firmly to heart Elinor Glyn's observation that 'a woman will stand almost anything from a passionate lover'. The most famous personification of a male brute was 'the sheik', in the novel of that name published in 1919 by Edith Maud Hull. She was the most unlikely kind of author for a novel which is the nearest thing to pornography written by any of the inter-war female novelists. Married to a pig-farmer, she lived quietly in the country. *The Bookman* wrote:

> One of the most popular of present-day novelists is Mrs E. M. Hull who is seldom to be met with in literary circles, for she spends a good deal of her time in travelling, and, when at home, prefers a country life in Derbyshire, and is keen on all manner of games and sports. She wrote her first novel *The Sheik* with no idea of publishing it, but as a means of personal distraction during the war when she had to be very much alone. When it was finished she decided to let it try its fortune with a publisher, and its prompt and unexpected success encouraged her to write a second book, *The Shadow of the East.*[26]

The Sheik is the story of a cold, cool English girl who is kidnapped in the desert by an Arabian sheik, endures rape for months and finally realises that she loves him. The novel relies neither on veiled erotic description nor on religious imagery, but on uninhibited sado-masochism.

> The flaming light of desire burning in his eyes turned her sick and faint. Her body throbbed with the consciousness of a knowledge that appalled her. She understood his purpose with a horror that made each separate nerve in her system shrink against the understanding that had come to her under the consuming fire of his ardent gaze, and in the fierce embrace that was drawing her shaking limbs closer and closer against the man's own pulsating body.[27]

By Chapter Three she is marginally less horror-struck by it all for she is 'resisting him dumbly with tight-locked lips till he held her palpitating in his arms . . . "Oh, you brute! You brute!" she wailed, until his kisses silenced her.' By Chapter Five, halfway through the novel, brutality has won the day for 'Love had come to her at last who had scorned it so fiercely'. From now on Diana is all submission — even to an Arab whom 'Aubrey would indiscriminately class as a "damned nigger" . . . She did not care . . . Oriental though he was, might he not be capable of a deep and lasting affection?' (Luckily the sheik turns out to be a decent English chap by birth.)

Other writers too used sadism as a perfectly acceptable substitute for eroticism. Ruth, in Vita Sackville-West's *Heritage* (1919), says, 'he cringes to me, and then I bully him; or else he bullies me, and then I cringe to him. But quarrel as we may, we always come together again.' But in another of her novels, *Challenge* (1923), which was only published in America, the love-making of Eve and Julian, modelled on the author and her lover Violet Trefusis, is described as a clash of personalities rather than a harmony of souls for 'they had no tenderness for one another . . . Violence was never very far out of sight.' And Ethel M. Dell used pain to excite her readers, presumably knowing that sensuality would be deplored by them but that sadism was perfectly acceptable. Rebecca West was among those dismayed by this paradox; reviewing *Charles Rex* (1922), in which an elderly roué takes a page on board his yacht and, discovering that he has rescued a girl in disguise, continues to treat her as a page-boy, she wrote:

> For five chapters the story titillates us (us includes, one amazedly estimates, the mass of the population of Surbiton, Bournemouth, and Cheltenham) with a description of the peculiar intercourse that takes place between them in these circumstances. There is a specially pleasing incident when they are playing cards and the girl-boy cheats, and Lord Saltash beats her with a riding-switch. We afterwards learn that she had cheated on purpose that she might have this delicious revelation of the gentleman's quality.[28]

It is one of the most mysterious aspects of the barriers and restraints a society chooses to impose upon itself that, in England in the 1920s, respectable middle-class readers cheerfully devoured the 'pleasing incidents' of E. M. Hull and Ethel M. Dell while denying themselves *Lady Chatterley's Lover*, *The Well of Loneliness* or *Sleeveless Errand*, all of which were banned. Yet *Sleeveless Errand* by Norah James, which came out in 1929, was banned merely because it accepted sensuality as an integral part of life and contained remarks like ' "we're bored with people who aren't bawdy. We call them prigs and prudes if they don't want to talk about copulation at lunchtime and buggery at dinner." '[29] It also offended because its characters were unrestrained on topics where restraint was more usual (' "For Christ's sake give me a drink" ') without the author appearing to disapprove. Similarly H. G. Wells had, in *Ann Veronica*, violated the prevailing moral code by condoning his heroine's behaviour. He and Norah James were attacking prevailing pieties while the middlebrow female novelists stayed firmly on the side of good manners. Anna Lombard's lover dies, she murders her dusky baby and endures a year's exile before being pronounced cured. Paul and his queen have only three weeks together, while the sheik turns out to have been ill-treated by his English father (which excuses many faults in his character).

The British legal system also took exception to the tenderness and lesbian love displayed by the two women Stephen and Mary in *The Well of Loneliness*, of whom we are told, finally, after many emotional vicissitudes, 'and that night they were not divided'. But their love was far more distasteful to the majority of readers than any amount of flogging or brutality. The reason for this hypocrisy was well understood by Elinor Glyn. Sensuality was acceptable in a far-off country, lesbianism, like 'rudeness', would taint and threaten the ordered respectability of the middle-class home and family. But no one nice was really going to step off the Metropolitan Line from Baker Street to Pinner and have to imitate Doctor Carew in E. M. Hull's *The Desert Healer* (1923):

A piercing shriek rang through the silent house. A shriek that was followed by others so terrible, so frenzied, that for a moment he reeled under the horror of them. And with the agonising screams was mingled the sound of a man's raving and other more pregnant sounds that drove Carew to the verge of madness . . .

Laying her on the bed he stripped the blood-wet silken rags from her lacerated shoulders, wincing in agony as they clung to the delicate broken flesh his trembling lips covered with passionate kisses. But he was doctor as well as lover and, forcing his shaking fingers to steadiness, he bathed the cruel wounds with tender skill.[30]

Had Carew been merely lover, Mrs Hull would not have been able to write about him kissing flesh or stripping off rags; but in the context of violence it was perfectly acceptable. Perhaps if Stephen in *The Well of Loneliness* had had a penchant for beating her fellow sex the book would not have been banned. But, of course, Radclyffe Hall overstepped another mark – she was being realistic and the reader was not to be offered the anodyne of a romantic finale. What most readers of women's novels wanted was a story that, after various vicissitudes, comes all right in the end. This point was well understood by a reviewer in *The Bookman*, who wrote in June 1923 (*The Desert Healer* having recently been published but not reviewed):

Those weary of realism – more or less real – provided so lavishly in the novels of the day, turn with relief to writers like Margaret Peterson [popular novelist, author of *The Scent of the Rose*]. The tale is full of trouble and misunderstandings, certainly, but we know from the beginning all will be all right in the end, so we regard these stoically . . . It is a pity Mrs Peterson has followed the revolting example of another popular woman novelist by introducing flogging on a grand scale. One writer with that idiosyncrasy is one too many.[31]

In his book on *Woman* (1927), Bauer argues that women are erotically stimulated by reading, far more so than men. He explained the censorship prevalent in highbrow and middlebrow novels by suggesting that their female readers kept their sensuality under better control.

Where is the flapper who has not secretly read at least one of the novels of Zola? Or the woman who has not read some chapter or other of the Decameron? Where is the woman of the lower classes who does not give up much of her free time to the reading of appalling 'love-stories'? Why are women the greatest purchasers of 'realistic' novels? Why is it that women spend all their time reading sensational novels, while their menfolk devote their studies to the more serious sorts of literature? Weininger insists in *Sex and Character* that there is something of the procuress in every woman, which finds a certain satisfaction in the union of lovers even in a novel or on the stage.[32]

What Bauer failed to point out is that male values are peculiar neither to highbrow nor to lowbrow novels, though they dominate less in the middlebrow 'woman's novel'. There is only a difference in tone and style between the forcefulness of Nick Ratcliffe and the domination of Mellors in *Lady Chatterley's Lover* (1928). Connie Chatterley, like Muriel, has a choice: she can either remain mentally aloof and self-contained or she can surrender herself body and soul to the demands of her man. To begin with she does the former:

> And a woman had to yield. A man was like a child with his appetites. A woman had to yield him what he wanted, or like a child he would probably turn nasty and flounce away and spoil what was a very pleasant connexion. But a woman could yield to a man without yielding her inner free self . . . she could use this sex thing to have power over him.[33]

But once Mellors has brought her to orgasm she swiftly capitulates. Having been waiting, separate, watchful, 'now in her heart the queer wonder of him was awakened' and she concedes her sexuality, she yields. And while Mellors is shown as kind and potent and sensual, Connie's body is depersonalised, it is erotic only in so far as it arouses desire in the man.

Lawrence takes the same stance as a romantic novelist, which is to show the woman's initial repulsion ('surely the man was intensely ridiculous in this posture and this act!'[34]) swiftly removed by the orgasm her lover is kind enough to bestow. The main focus of his interest is in the life-affirming, energy-releasing qualities of Mellor's potency, but apart from the mere fact of Connie's capitulation and subsequent pleasure very little more of her character is explained to us. And it is the same with Muriel – she concedes to Nick, she is full of joy, but we still only know about her with reference to her lover: the male fights and wins, the female receives pleasure and submits.

Lawrence's novels were banned because, while sharing the attitudes of many of his contemporary writers, his language was uncomfortably explicit; whereas writers like Ethel M. Dell used a kind of shorthand vocabulary – 'tumult', 'thunderous', 'gasping', 'conflict', 'rush' and so on – to hint not at actual but at potential orgasmic fulfilment. Lawrence also offended because he did not disguise matters with religious imagery, which is often heavily in evidence in Ethel M. Dell's reconciliation scene, to take the gloss off the sexual overtones. And he chose settings for most of his novels which were rather too close to home.

Ethel M. Dell and her imitators used settings far enough away to have a romantic, intense quality but which were at the same time plausible enough to make the reader identify with them. The choice of India and the Far East was a tradition initiated by Flora Annie Steel and continued by writers like Maud Diver, 'Sydney C. Grier' and Alice Perrin; in their novels they often explored the theme of the initially doomed but ultimately triumphant love of a pure English girl for a man who often displays distressing Eastern leanings but thankfully turns out to be an Englishman after all. Sometimes it was the other way round, as in *Anna Lombard*, in which Gerald marries Anna, but full atonement is only made when the poor dusky baby is smothered by its mother who, after a long period of mourning and heart-searching, finally comes to her husband cleansed of her passion and ready to be a demure English bride. It is a different pattern from the conventional 'Indian' romance in which the trimmings were North-west Frontier but the tone definitely Cheltenham, and in which the English are usually described as cold-blooded but civilised and the Indians as torrid but socially impossible.

India was a favourite setting when a firm moral line was required. Passion exiled to India meant that the Anglo-Indian sensibility, for example, which was promoted as upright, sensible, pukka sahib, could be contrasted with that of the sensual, feckless and inscrutable Indian. Forster took the opposite stance in *A Passage to India* (1924) when he disparagingly contrasted the passionless, socialised, constrained behaviour of the English with the warmer, more loving, more life-giving and spiritual qualities of the Indian.

When romantic novels no longer had to display quite such an upright moral tone, passion could take place closer to hand; and so during the late 1920s, writers like Berta Ruck, Ruby M. Ayres and Denise Robins began to make millinery shops, advertising agencies or tennis courts almost as torrid as any hill-station or bazaar. What remained constant was the vital necessity for the heroine to be well bred ('silly novels by lady novelists rarely introduce us into any other than very lofty and fashionable society,'[35] observed George Eliot). Just as the sheik turned out to be an English aristocrat, so the heroine of a romantic novel had to be one rung up the social ladder. This was not merely for reasons of snobbery; it was part of a pattern of wish-fulfilment, the assumption being that all readers of light novels would prefer to be a little better off, a little better connected than they in fact are. Those who borrowed books from the twopenny library wanted to sure that they *were* clamping the proverbial rose-coloured spectacles on to their noses. As Berta Ruck wrote in her autobiography:

> I think it is very wrong to give Youth the impression that it is unalterably doomed to disappointment. *'C'est en croyant aux roses'*, says a French proverb, *'qu'on les fait éclorer.'* It is by believing in roses that one brings them into bloom . . .
>
> It is my creed that the world was created to be merry as a marriage-bell and for the whole human race to be healthy, wealthy and wise enough to be happy on all cylinders.[36]

After the Great War this belief was still firmly held by romantic novelists, but a shade more realism was introduced into their work. The settings were more often home-based and the heroines often had some kind of job or occupation (which they would of course discontinue at Cupid's bidding). The adventure aspect of the pulp novel began to wane, the plots became more timid and the psychological machinations began to take on a greater importance; writers began to perceive adventures rather more in the mind than on the slopes of the Himalayas or the desert dunes.

Partly this was due to the prevalent interest in the inner workings of the human heart, partly because the drama of the war years had left the reading public with a distaste for the harrowing tragedies of which previously they had been fond. The settings of romantic novels became, during the 1920s, those with which the reader could identify; the hat or dress shop was a particular favourite, as the heroine of Angela Thirkell's *High Rising* (1933) discovers. Left a widow, realising that she had somehow to support herself and her sons, Laura Morland

> had considered the question carefully, and decided that, next to racing, murder and sport, the great reading public of England (female section) like to read about clothes. With real industry she got introductions, went over big department stores, visited smart dressmaking friends, talked to girls she knew who had become buyers or high-brow window-dressers, and settled down to write best-sellers. Her prevision was justified, and she now had a large, steady reading public, who apparently could not hear too much about the mysteries of the wholesale and retail clothes business.[37]

And indeed there were many writers, like Laura Morland, who turned out innumerable novels using just this formula: the poor little shop-girl theme appears over and over again during the next two decades – the editorial précis for a story in *My Weekly* being typical of countless others:

> Once upon a time there was a milliner, young, beautiful and attractive and her name was Peggy. She sold wonderful model hats to old, plain dowagers and pretty young girls; but none of her wealthy customers could boast of the beauty and charm which Peggy possessed, though she had not a penny to her name. Then one sunny morning, Romance stepped right across Peggy's path with such allurement and witchery that it well-nigh turned Peggy's

head. For it led her right away from the hat-shop and the drabness which had made up her life, and introduced her to an absolutely new world, where wealth made life easy and love paved the way to happiness.[38]

Whatever the gloss given to the romantic novel by the jazz age, there was nothing to beat the old formula. When the lecturer teaching Boots First Literary Course for librarians reached the love story, he defined it in the following terms – and in a sense nothing more needs to be said. The essential was a 'strong and silent' hero, the strength applying to his physique and the silence to a rather dour temperament. He usually comes from a good family but owing to some misunderstanding has cut himself off from society to brood about it in the outposts of Empire. The heroine is very well bred, with a distant ethereal sort of beauty. Delicately nurtured, it is therefore imperative to find someone to lean on. The two opposites meet. At first she is repulsed by the brute but gradually her delicate charm brings forth a softer side to his nature – and the story ends with a fervent embrace.[39]

CHAPTER EIGHT

ℒove

' "Oh, dulling," said my mother sadly.
"One always thinks that.
Every, every time." '

The Pursuit of Love (1945) by Nancy Mitford is the apotheosis of the woman's novel about love. In some ways it rounds off everything that was written on this topic during the inter-war period, mingling tenderness and wit into an unsentimental but deeply emotional whole. There are few novels which explore with such insight women's real natures, and critics who condemn Nancy Mitford as catering entirely for a snob-public are sadly missing the point.

What she is saying, as she steers Linda Radlett through three marriages, is that whatever society may pretend to the contrary women are, or ought to be, moved primarily by their passions. Economic and domestic necessity, as well as the lack of a suitable lover, conspire together to ensure that we place most stress on marriage, achievement, financial rewards, the breeding of children or a large circle of friends. But in our heart of hearts most of us are no different from the readers of pulp fiction: given the chance, we would sacrifice everything else to romantic love. Other happinesses are second best: yet they come first in most lives because a sensible upbringing or the pulls of propriety or the dictates of money push themselves to the foreground.

Linda marries the first time for reasons of money and status, and the second out of misplaced idealism. When, in the classic and unforgettable scene on the Gare du Nord, she meets Fabrice, there are few women who would not long to emulate her. The following scene is the sophisticated epitome of female fantasy.

She became aware that somebody was standing beside her, not an old lady, but a short, stocky, very dark Frenchman in a black Homburg hat. He was laughing. Linda took no notice, but went on crying. The more she cried the more he laughed. Her tears were tears of rage now, no longer of self-pity.

At last she said, in a voice which was meant to be angrily impressive, but which squeaked and shook through her handkerchief:

'*Allez-vous en.*'

For answer he took her hand and pulled her to her feet.

'*Bonjour, bonjour,*' he said.

'*Voulez-vous vous en aller?*' said Linda, rather more doubtfully, here at least was a human being who showed signs of taking some interest in her. Then she thought of South America.

'*Il faut expliquer que je ne suis pas,*' she said, '*une esclave blanche. Je suis la fille d'un très important lord anglais.*'

The Frenchman gave a great bellow of laughter.

'One does not,' he said in the nearly perfect English of somebody who has spoken it from a child, 'have to be Sherlock Holmes to guess that.'[1]

Fabrice and Linda have lunch together.

So this silly conversation went on and on, but it was only froth on the surface. Linda was feeling, what she had never so far felt for any man, an overwhelming physical attraction. It made her quite giddy, it terrified her. She could see that Fabrice was perfectly certain of the outcome, so was she perfectly certain, and that was what frightened her. How could she, Linda, with the horror and contempt she had always felt for casual affairs, allow herself to be picked up by any stray foreigner and, having seen him for only an hour, long and long and long to be in bed with him? He was not even good-looking, he was exactly like dozens of other dark men in Homburgs that can be seen in the streets of any French town. But there was something about the way he looked at her which seemed to be depriving her of all balance. She was profoundly shocked, and at the same time, intensely excited.[2]

Fabrice is out of line with heroes from Rochester, through Nick Ratcliffe to Rhett Butler and Max de Winter, because he is a gossip. He is not merely sensual, and unhesitatingly so, he can chatter and likes nothing better: which doubles his attraction for Linda. He is described in such a way that, for two generations of women, a small dark man in a Homburg is sex appeal personified. And his tenderness, his insight and his sensuality are combined with an understated heroism – Fabrice dies fighting for the French resistance at about the same time as Linda dies in childbirth. To Fanny, the narrator, their love was clearly unique: but her mother (who has run off with so many men in her life that she has become known as the Bolter) thinks otherwise.

'But Fanny, don't you think perhaps it's just as well? The lives of women like Linda and me are not so much fun when one begins to grow older.'

I didn't want to hurt my mother's feelings by protesting that Linda was not that sort of woman.

'But I think she would have been happy with Fabrice,' I said. 'He was the great love of her life, you know.'

'Oh, dulling,' said my mother sadly. 'One always thinks that. Every, every time.'[3]

There is no novel in English which ends on such a memorable note. It is *the* great ending, comparable in emotional effect to the opening of *Rebecca* (1938): 'Last night I dreamt I went to Manderley again.' The Bolter defines the resigned acceptance and the passionate romanticism which belong, inevitably, one to another: it is the continual and tortuous juggling of romance and reality which is the touchstone of most women's lives – even if, like Fanny, they have, sensibly but not bitterly, given up on the former. When Linda tells her about her happiness, Fanny reflects:

Alfred and I are happy, as happy as married people can be. We are in love, we are intellectually and physically suited in every possible way, we rejoice in each other's company, we have no money troubles and three delightful children. And yet when I consider my life, day by day, hour by hour, it seems to be composed of a series of pin-pricks. Nannies, cooks, the endless drudgery of housekeeping, the nerve-racking noise and boring repetitive conversation of small children (boring in the sense that it bores into one's very brain), their absolute incapacity to amuse themselves, their sudden and terrifying illnesses, Alfred's not infrequent bouts of moodiness, his invariable complaints at meals about the pudding, the way he will always use my tooth-paste and will always squeeze the tube in the middle. These are the components of marriage, the wholemeal bread of life, rough, ordinary, but sustaining; Linda had been feeding upon honey-dew, and that is an incomparable diet.[4]

Fanny is here summing up one of the 'pre-assumptions' (as defined on page 4) crucial to the world of *A Very Great Profession*. Marriage and passion are irreconcilable – society has organised itself in such a way that the depth of emotion prompting a couple to join together for life is invariably diffused by the demands of this life. Only the very rich or the very lucky or the very calculating can continue to feast upon honey-dew when the daily round is so relentlessly wholemeal. No novelist during the inter-war period, or perhaps ever, has described the raptures of married love, and with good reason – the placid joy of marriage is so unhistrionic, so self-satisfied even, that in fiction it would appear downright dull. There is no interest in sex that always goes well or in quarrels that vanish without sulks or bitterness. Nor is there the *frisson* of the forbidden or the transient, only the smugness of the condoned and the certain. So, in life and in fiction, passion is assumed to be the prerogative of the unmarried or the adulterous. Whether this is the flattering effect of domesticity or whether it is the need to separate lover from spouse is not at all clear – but as a pre-assumption it is undeniable.

This chapter explores a few of the novels by women which go beyond the 'and so they lived happily ever after' stereotype of 'Came the Dawn' novels; and which also reject as tedious the deep, deep peace of the double bed. Rather, they are about the romantic ideal of being 'in love', and they have one crucial factor in common: they end unhappily. If the trappings of romantic love cannot adapt themselves to domestic use, then the lovers must be thwarted by fate, family circumstance or death. Pulp novelists might describe the mildly-interrupted courtship followed by the clinch but novelists writing about love have simultaneously to introduce disaster. For, true to the conventions of courtly love, marriage and passion are ill-suited companions and hence true love must either be thwarted or come to fruition only after endless and stormy tribulations. Fabrice and Linda *have* to die to keep their love on an ideal plane: they are immortalised, and neither the passing of the years nor the obligations of domesticity can overshadow their romance. In the same way Vera Brittain created a memorial in *Testament of Youth* not only to Roland Leighton but to a whole generation of potential lovers, a memorial that she recreated three years later in her novel *Honourable Estate* (1936).

The ostensible theme of this book is 'how the women's revolution – one of the greatest in all history – united with the struggle for other democratic ideals and the cataclysm of the War to alter the private destinies of individuals'.[5] But the most powerful part of the six-hundred-page novel is the eighty or so pages which describe the love affair between Ruth, a nurse in France in 1917, and an American soldier named Eugene. She is so stirred by the grief of a fellow-nurse whose fiancé has been killed in action ('if only I'd had 'im! If I'd had 'im just the once, I wouldn't tyke on so, I swear!')[6] that, on the night before Eugene has to return to the front line, they make love:

Will he think me abandoned, disreputable, unworthy of his respect, because I offered myself to him in that way?

Does he understand what I really meant – that I wished him, before he goes back to face death, to have the whole and not just an incomplete knowledge of love? Does he realise how much I wanted to abandon, for him, all the cautions and calculations with which my life has been hedged, to give all I had to give and hold back nothing for lack of gallantry and generosity? . . . Suppose his love for me turns to contempt, because I let him take me so easily? Well, let him despise and humiliate me afterwards if he must! I'll accept even humiliation at his hands, rather than let him risk going to his death without all the experience of love that I can give him.[7]

An important factor helping Ruth overcome her scruples is the knowledge she has picked up about the contraceptive uses of quinine tablets. But when Eugene is killed she is bitterly regretful, knowing

with the blinding force of full understanding that in all the gigantic desolation of earth and sky there remained no breath of his life – not even in her body, where alone it might have achieved continuation.

Lying with her arms outstretched on the sand-dunes in the bitter October wind, she cried aloud.

'Oh, why was I so afraid of consequences – such a coward, such a coward! Why did I fear my family, my upbringing, my traditions! . . . Because their hold on me was so strong in spite of everything, I sacrificed the existence of Eugene's child. Whatever they did and said I could have faced it, lived it down, and at the end of it all something of him would have been left. Now there's nothing – nothing – nothing!'[8]

But there are memories – and even when Ruth marries someone else she allots a place in her heart to the sacred remembrance of her dead lover; death has immortalised her love in a splendid and final way, bestowing a romantic glory with which mere separation cannot quite compete. And if the heroine of Edith Wharton's *The Age of Innocence* (1920) had died, the hero could have cherished his memories of her for ever; but faced with a meeting years after their affair, he is forced to accept that his love has become stagnant, that he would rather not have to face the ravages of time but would prefer to keep his ideal intact.

The reading public of the 1920s and 1930s was judged to have had its fill of death, and so enforced separation was the impediment more frequently used to keep lovers apart. In addition, whereas death has an implacable finality, parting raises all kinds of everyday and shared questions. One of the most poignant themes is that of the lover who is already married to someone else. Tolstoy used it to memorable effect in *Anna Karenina* (1875) and he has had many imitators, for example Noel Coward in *Brief Encounter*.

Both writers upheld the established moral code, Tolstoy by making his heroine pay for her conduct with her life and Coward by making his sacrifice her passion and remain a staunch bastion of such middle-class values as family loyalty and self-sacrifice. James Agate wrote in a review of *Brief Encounter* that when he associated the film with the best of woman's magazine fiction he did not intend a backhanded compliment. 'For it seems to me that few writers of supposedly more serious talent ever undertake themes as simple and important any more: so that, relatively dinky and sentimental as it is – a sort of vanity-sized *Anna Karenina – Brief Encounter* is to be thoroughly respected.'[9]

Anna and Laura are both victims of a double standard that encourages women's romantic fantasies at the same time as it rigorously crushes them with notions of duty, deference and sacrifice. The only thing the middle-class housewife is allowed is a mild form of self-congratulation. She can hug compliments to her (while vigorously denying their truth) even if she is forbidden to hug her lover. This again is a leftover from the conventions of courtly love – the woman is expected to retain a certain mystery and aloofness, to be fickle and reserved, to receive homage. 'Hole-in-the-corner' stuff is not quite what she wants. Thus Laura is clearly doubtful when Alec explains to her:

Everything's against us – all the circumstances of our lives

– those have got to go on unaltered. We're nice people, you and I, and we've got to go on being nice. Let's enclose this love of ours with real strength, and let that strength be that no one is hurt by it except ourselves.

Laura: Must we be hurt by it?

Alec: Yes – when the time comes.

Laura: Very well.

Alec: All the furtiveness and the secrecy and the hole-in-corner cheapness can be justified if only we're strong enough – strong enough to keep it to ourselves, clean and untouched by anybody else's knowledge or even suspicion – something of our own for ever – to be remembered –

Laura: Very well.[10]

Depending on their sympathies, the audience for *Brief Encounter* may see it as a tragedy of true love, or may condemn either Alec for disrupting a previously secure existence or Laura for foolishly allowing herself to be placed at risk. The romantic would rest content with the this-thing-is-bigger-than-both-of-us theory – that the lovers were thrown together by the hand of fate but are denied happiness by the conventions of society. E. M. Delafield uses this convention twice, once to show her heroine sensibly giving up her lover and counting her blessings and once to show her deprived both of her lover and of family happiness. In *The Way Things Are* (1927), Laura is rewarded at the end, because of her sacrifice, with a kind of low-key optimism. She is an 'ordinary domesticated female' who falls in love with a man with the improbable name of Duke Ayland. He is not actually portrayed as a rotter but the name makes the reader doubtful and in any case he makes love to Laura on her home ground (whereas Coward's Alec and Laura at least meet in the anonymous surroundings of Milford Junction). He pretty soon wants to bring things to some sort of conclusion:

'I'm not going on like this.'

'But, Duke –'

'Darling, you can see for yourself that it's impossible. I'm madly in love with you, and I can neither marry you, nor take you away with me. And to meet as we do at present is more than I can stand.'

'You don't mean that you'd rather we didn't see one another any more?'

'Honestly, Laura, dear, there are times when I feel that might almost be easier than – this sort of thing.' Ayland glanced round the semi-deserted picture-gallery, in the middle of which, on a long red plush seat, he sat with Laura.

'You've told me that there's no hope whatever of my having you altogether, because of your children.'

'And because of my husband, too,' Laura pointed out, with ill-judged honesty. 'I'm fond of Alfred.'

Duke winced slightly. [11]

When Laura gives Duke up she 'at last admitted to herself that she and Duke Ayland, in common with the vast majority of their fellow-beings, were incapable of the ideal, imperishable, love for which the world was said to be well lost'. She is regretful but realistic, and is in the rational if miserable frame of mind that the film-goer presumes Coward's Laura to be in when she sits down in her usual chair opposite her husband and lets the events of the previous weeks unroll in her thoughts. In a sense, neither Laura has lost that much since they have the satisfaction of knowing that they can be something other than mere wife and mother; Coward's Laura will obviously take far longer to 'get over it', but E. M. Delafield's Laura was in fact done something of a service by Duke Ayland. A 'lovely, lovely lover' may be the complete answer to the syndrome of the nearing-forty, bored housewife and, in this Laura's case, she is shown by the end of the book to have gained a new, cheerier outlook on life.

This can hardly be said for the heroine of E. M. Delafield's novella *We Meant to Be Happy* (published in *Three Marriages*, 1939). It is the story of Cathleen who marries late and unexpectedly and is so grateful to have a husband and children that 'never, never would Cathleen get used to the miracle, not only of having children of her very own, but of being able to give them all the things that she herself had never had'. But she falls in

love with the doctor and after an afternoon of radiant joy she lies
awake that night

> alternating between her bliss and a dreadful sense of
> uncertainty.
>
> What would happen?
>
> She hardly wondered at all whether she and Kavanagh
> would become lovers. It seemed probable that they would,
> but Cathleen felt, with absolute certainty, that this would
> make her infidelity to her husband no greater than it was
> already. She was, at that very minute, being completely
> unfaithful to him, and she told herself so without hesitation
> or circumlocution.
>
> The thing that really puzzled her was whether she was,
> as she supposed most people would undoubtedly say that
> she was, a very wicked woman. If so, wickedness had taken
> possession of her without any volition of her own. An over-
> whelming force had driven her towards Maurice, and
> Maurice towards her. Supposing, she thought, she could
> just go to Philip and tell him the truth and say that she was
> just as fond of him as she had ever been, and ask him to tell
> her what would hurt him least, and what they had better
> do?[12]

But Philip reacts with outrage, has a heart attack and uses the
children and Cathleen's financial dependence to dominate her.
By the last page it is clear that her life is in ruins because she has
neither lover nor her husband's respect and affection. Yet the
culprit is the 'overwhelming force' rather than the lovers – the
moral is that the most serene, orderly existence can unexpectedly
be destroyed if fate steps in unopposed. For Cathleen's marriage
was not unhappy – she does not resent the unexacting
companionship of her husband and is not deceiving herself when
she thinks that 'she knew a lot about affection and kindness, and
in her opinion they counted for most when it came to living one's
life'. But because she allowed fate to take a hand, she has
surrendered her happiness, doubly so because she was honest
and confessed her infidelity. Only those women who can hug
their love to themselves can be allowed to continue, outwardly,

as they were before – those who have been found out or declared their love cannot expect the *status quo* to continue.

The clear message is that if a woman does have the good luck/misfortune to fall adulterously in love she must not let her husband know, for then she will be able to return to her marriage refreshed and renewed, indeed virtuous. Ann Bridge shows Rose in *Four-Part Setting* (1939) doing just this, although her sacrifice is even more noble because her husband Charles is unashamedly unfaithful – in fact some readers would probably condemn her behaviour as pointless martyrdom, since she considers her own virtue rather than her lover's happiness. But during a concert at the Queen's Hall, Rose has a kind of vision of the truth of civilisation, of 'something beyond love . . . beyond the agonies and passions . . . more born of effort and a sort of faithfulness'; and

> her part in it became clear . . . To go back, and then to go straight on; to give Charles his life, and to give it without grudging or counting; to relinquish the joyful thought of Antony, and join her life, all there was of it, to Charles; and to do this, not with sad eyes and a set mouth, like the resigned women with the impossible husbands, but with interest and curiousity and gaiety and zest.[13]

No such joyful self-sacrifice is allowed for the heroine of Kate O'Brien's novel *Mary Lavalle* (1936), in which a girl chooses to leave her suitable and devoted fiancé behind in Ireland and go to Spain as a governess. Here she falls in love with the married son of the house; the love scenes are written with unusual skill and tenderness and are far removed from the cliché-laden prose of a pulp novel. As Mary sits desolate in the train carrying her away from her lover, the reader accepts her emotions as a reality, for Kate O'Brien gives two deft twists to a novel otherwise straightforwardly about a love affair. She makes it clear that there is a roving side to Mary's nature which made her want to come to Spain in the first place, even though her fiancé begged her to stay submissively at home. And she leaves the reader in some doubt as to whether Mary is going to 'tell' her love or hug it to her in the years to come 'like patience on a monument'.

Some readers presumably believe in the primeval compulsiveness of Mary's passion, others, more cynically, assume that she has the fatal female penchant for the wrong man. In novels about love, it is on the whole essential that the reader believes in the this-thing-is-bigger-than-both-of-us concept, in other words that she sustains the romantic ideal; there would be no point in reading *Mary Lavalle* if one part of one's mind was grumbling that the heroine had a perfectly good man at home and should have kept her gaze off another. One must believe wholeheartedly in the overpowering Force of Love if any of these novels are to be a good read or to make their point. For example, in *The Weather in the Streets* (1936), Olivia nurtures no illusions that Rollo will give up his wife for her, she is pleased when he says reflectively, ' "I don't believe you'd ever make a scene." ' On the other hand she wants to keep their affair on the level of a *grand amour*.

> Driving back he'd say: 'Is there *nowhere* we can go?' . . .
> He suggested a hotel, and I wouldn't. Then he said couldn't
> we take a room, why didn't I let him rent a flat for me or
> something. But no, I said, no . . . In his heart of hearts I
> don't believe he wanted to either. I didn't want even the
> shadow of a situation the world recognises and tolerates as
> long as it's *sub rosa*, decent, discreet; that means a word in
> the ear, a wink, an eye at a keyhole . . . My idea being we
> were too fine for the world, our love should have no
> dealings whatsoever with its coarseness, I'd spurn the least
> foothold.[14]

Yet it is hardly surprising when Rollo admits that he is always interested in other women's 'figures', or when he is spellbound by a dancer called Thalassa (for Olivia, 'the worst feeling of my life'). She is expecting to be wounded, her masochistic streak needs to be fed, even the pain of the abortion is a kind of pleasure. Her inherently self-deprecating quality has, in fact, been anticipated in the earlier *Invitation to the Waltz* (1932) when, after Kate has been asked without her to the hunt ball, she thinks, 'I'm left behind, but I don't care.' She expects to fail and in her resigned acceptance of life's blows she is a clear successor to May Sinclair's heroines. When she is grown up, she chooses the 'hopeless' Ivor, she succumbs to the married, charming but selfish Rollo, and she has her negative expectations about life and love confirmed when things fail to work out. Similarly, the heroine of Rosamond Lehmann's first novel *Dusty Answer* (1927) luxuriates in her apartness, expecting to be disappointed. When, at the end, she realises that her friend Jennifer was not going to keep their appointment she thinks:

> Farewell to Cambridge, to whom she was less than nothing . . . She was going home again to be alone. She smiled, thinking suddenly that she might be considered an object for pity, so complete was her loneliness.
> One by one they had all gone from her . . . She was rid at last of the weakness, the futile obsession of dependence on other people. She had nobody now except herself; and that was best.[15]

In a brilliantly perceptive essay written in 1963, Simon Raven analysed the qualities shared by all Rosamond Lehmann's heroines and pointed out that, for them, love is vocation. Judith, Norah, Olivia and the others all embrace the ethic of romanticism without cavil, seeing their love as something sacred, unencumbered by the triviality of happiness or self-fulfilment.

> It is not, for them, a question of fun, of good value for money and effort, *because what has happened was in any case inevitable.* It was a solemn duty to obey the heart, which may not be denied. Love, indeed any personal relationship, is a matter of dedication. Given Olivia's love for Rollo, she must follow it up, live it out, take what comes for better or worse and never commit the blasphemy of counting the cost. She can do no other; and when it is all over, her only resource must be a Stoic withdrawal and the knowledge that she has submitted, with dignity and self-abnegation, to her allotted fate.[16]

Rosamond Lehmann, like Nancy Mitford, is intensely in favour of women sacrificing everything to love. A new generation of readers was moved recently to hear her bringing a radio interview to an end by declaring that she would rather have had the joy of a lastingly happy marriage than have been a writer; echoing a contemporary novelist, Denise Robins, who asserts in her autobiography that 'the only thing a woman truly needs is to love and be loved, and that nothing can be emptier than the golden bowl of success'. Yet, sadly, since there is something of every novelist in her heroines, I would conclude that Rosamond Lehmann herself loved men who could not return her love with the same intensity and that her novels are in a sense an elegy to this fatality. Yet they convey the intense, if different, feeling that comes with loss, the rediscovery of self that comes with love.

Dusty Answer, like Alain-Fournier's *Le Grand Meaulnes* and Evelyn Waugh's *Brideshead Revisited*, is best read when young because the intensity and mournfulness of their central characters can prove rather unremitting for the older reader. The over-sensitive, naked mind of the immature reader enjoys misery in a way which makes the more world-weary impatient; but *Dusty Answer*'s unhappiness probably inflicts irrevocable bruising on the spirit of the impressionable adolescent. The eighteen year-old reader is left with the conviction that life deals blows to the romantic nature − she will *expect* to be stood up in the Copper Kettle, expect her man to throw her over − it is the fate of those who love.

In this sense the nameless heroine of *Rebecca*, Daphne du Maurier's 1938 bestseller, *is* the young reader: she is professionally downtrodden, constitutionally crushed, and would never venture to do more than expect the worst of life and love. She is gratified when Max de Winter, having failed to make his intentions crystal-clear, declares rudely, 'I am asking you to marry me, you little fool', and so insecure are her feelings that when he tells her that he had murdered Rebecca her first emotion is not one of shock-horror but of delight: 'My heart was light like a feather floating in the air. He had never loved Rebecca.'

Similarly, the heroine of Elizabeth von Arnim's *Vera* (1921) resolutely ignores the truth about Vera, her husband's first wife. Lucy meets Wemyss at a vulnerable moment, on the day her father has died; but his wife had died the previous week and so the 'two stricken ones' are drawn together. He appears to her immensely kind and responsible and when he kisses her she is in turmoil.

> Death all round them, death pervading every corner of their lives, death in its blackest shape brooding over him, and — kisses. Her mind, if anything so gentle could be said to be in anything that sounded so loud, was in an uproar. She had the complete, guileless trust in him of a child for a tender and sympathetic friend . . .
> These kisses — and his wife just dead — and dead so terribly — how long would she have to stand there with this going on . . .[17]

But his grief succeeds in arousing her maternal instinct and so, unspokenly, they become engaged, although 'what the faces of his so-called friends would look like if he, before Vera had been dead a fortnight, should approach them with the news of his engagement even Wemyss, a person not greatly imaginative, could picture'.[18] Eventually he wins through and Lucy, brushing off rumours about Vera's death, or doubts about Wemyss himself, becomes his wife. The relationship continues deeply maternal, Lucy the assuager, Wemyss the assuaged.

> Yes, he was a baby, a dear, high-spirited baby, but a baby now at very close quarters and one that went on all the time. You couldn't put him in a cot and give him a bottle and say, 'There now,' and then sit down quietly to a little sewing; you didn't have Sundays out; you were never, day or night, an instant off duty. Lucy couldn't count the number of times a day she had to answer the question, 'Who's my own little wife?'[19]

In fact, Wemyss proves not merely an egoist, not merely a bully, but a sadistic brute who deluded the affectionate, innocent Lucy into marrying him because he has exploited her deep-rooted desire to give and to cherish and to be worthy. The clear moral is that if women like Lucy were taught as children *not* rigorously to put others first, *not* to take the leg of the chicken, *not* to sit in a draught, they would be learning how to crush their incipient masochism and therefore have some chance of happiness. It is the same with Grace in Rosamond Lehmann's *A Note in Music* (1932). She allows herself to marry Tom even though she knows it is a 'shame'; her depression contains the joy of martyrdom. When she tentatively declares her love to Hugh she replies to his muttered regrets:

'It's all right,' she said, smiling radiantly. 'It doesn't matter. You mustn't be sorry for me. I can't bear to be pitied.' (Really, he thought, she was extraordinarily nice.) 'I can stand *anything*. I'm very tough.'

And she thought: there was something in her that was not herself; something that seemed to prevail even beyond her own resources – an inheritance of strength, of endurance, of a religion that had no faith or hope.[20]

And when he has finally run down the front steps she exults in the integrity she has held on to so firmly. 'It could not have been better, she told herself . . . feeling her agony rise . . . it could not have been a more satisfactory parting.' Here the exultant joy with which Grace renounces passionate feelings again echoes the heroines of May Sinclair, so many of whom find strength through sacrifice.

If Grace had had children, she might have sublimated her emotional frustration in them. The tragedy of Margaret Kennedy's excellent *Together and Apart* (1936) is that the heroine sacrifices her husband *and* her children to her boredom. It is the other side of the coin from *A Long Time Ago* (1932), in which Margaret Kennedy describes a happily married man's passionate affair with a summer guest; his wife never finds out about his infidelity since her family and friends conspire together to keep her ignorant of the realities of her husband's friendship. The moral is that it was far nobler for the husband to have loved and lost than never to have loved at all but that it was doubly noble not to have jeopardised his family's happiness.

But in *Together and Apart* the theme is re-cast, with a soul-destroying description of a perfectly contented couple who needlessly destroy their own marriage. The blame lies partly with the 'interfering' mothers-in-law and partly with the immature selfishness of the heroine Besty.

It's not fair, she thought.

It never had been. All her life the essential unfairness of things had oppressed her. As a child she had complained of it loudly, it had seemed so monstrous that no impartial scheme of justice, no natural law, existed which should ensure that Betsy Hewitt got her rights. She still felt it to be monstrous, though she had learnt to keep the sentiment to herself. Not Alec, not her mother, not anybody in particular, but life had betrayed her. Now she was thirty-seven and she had never known real happiness. She had been cheated. Life had left her always hungry, always craving for something and unable to put a name to it . . .

Still, she did not know what she wanted, unless it was to go out and lie in the sun instead of being so busy. Nobody else had such a burden to bear. Alec was happy, and the children, and the maids. They did not have to think and plan and order a car to meet the London train that afternoon. Only she, upon whom they all depended, must be kept so active and so restless that now she was thirty-seven, would soon be forty, would soon be dead, without ever getting her rights.[21]

A woman in this frame of mind has five options open to her: she can either move house, have another baby, get a job, acquire a lover or leave home. Betsy determines to risk her marriage merely because she imagines 'the future' might be more fun.

Very much happier was how she imagined it. And not lonely at all. Of course she would marry again some time. And the other man, whoever he was, would love her better than Alec ever had, would worship and cherish her. She was experienced now; she knew how to make herself prized. She would not throw everything away a second time, giving all she had to give with both hands, as she had done when she was a girl. The other man should never be too sure of her, never take her for granted.[22]

In reality Betsy has no intention of destroying the fabric of her life, she is merely consumed with *ennui* and a natural human longing for some excitement. When the mechanism of divorce does grind into action she goes along with it because she thinks it is what she wants, and it is only when it is too late, when Alec has dutifully married someone else, that she regrets her impetuous behaviour. Like Anna Karenina, she is a victim of society's rules, but in her case she was allowed, even encouraged, to have her own way, with disastrous results for the rest of her family. Only when it is all too late, when she and Alec catch an unexpected glimpse of each other as they pass on escalators in the underground, does the reader fully realise what has been destroyed – for Alec could have given Betsy all she craved for, if the restraints of domesticity had not destroyed their love. (As Helena Wright observed in *The Sex Factor in Marriage*: 'At the present day much thought is given to household matters – food, servants, clothes, and so on – and little or none to the far more vital question of how to preserved the ardour and freshness of the honeymoon into old age.')[23]

Betsy, after all, had experienced boredom, but emotions any deeper and longer-lasting were outside the limited range of her experience. She had not known a lover die, nor was she forced by her husband to give anyone up. In fact she had no inkling of any of the misfortunes that can overcome women when they fall in love. For example, although Alec flirted with other women, he was still faithful to her and gave her no real cause for jealousy. But one of the most poignant themes running through women's fiction of this period is that of the woman who longs for the man to love her but is thwarted of that delight: for example, Mrs Britling in *Mr Britling Sees It Through* (1916) by H. G. Wells

went through life, outwardly serene and dignified, one of a great company of rather fastidious, rather unenterprising women who have turned for their happiness to secondary things, to those fair inanimate things of household and garden which do not turn again and rend one, to aestheticisms and delicacies, to order and seemliness. Moreover she found great satisfaction in the health and welfare, the growth and animation of her own two little boys. And no one knew, and perhaps even she had contrived to forget, the phases of astonishment and disillusionment, of doubt and bitterness and secret tears, that spread out through the years in which she had slowly realised that this strange, fitful, animated man who had come to her, vowing himself hers, asking for her so urgently and persuasively, was ceasing, had ceased, to love her, that his heart had escaped her, that she had missed it; she never dreamt that she had hurt it, and that after its first urgent, tumultuous, incomprehensible search for her it had hidden itself bitterly away.[24]

Oddly enough, there are very few novels of the inter-war period about jealousy – indeed, overall there are far fewer novels than one might expect on this subject and, at the one time in my life when I suffered acute agonies from this emotion, I found only *Othello* and Proust to turn to for comfort. Of course, Proust did write at great length about jealousy but his long novel suggests a possible reason why other novelists have generally ignored it as a topic – an inward-looking, obsessive emotion is, ultimately, cloying and in the same unfortunate way that the depressed are depressing, there is something negative and uninteresting about jealousy which, unless it is happening to you, often has a fatal lack of vitality. But one novelist, E. B. C. Jones, managed to describe this emotion without making it seem dull, partly because the heroine of *Quiet Interior* (1920) comes so clearly to life. Katharine Mansfield summed her up with some insight:

Claire Norris is not a simple character. She is one of those who are 'precious – but not generally prized'. Her feeling for life is exquisite; she is capable of rare appreciations, rare intensities – but for some mysterious reason life withholds its gifts from her. They go to lesser people who deserve them less and do not so greatly care. Why should this be? What has she done that she, who could cherish so beautifully, should be left empty-handed?[25]

The action of *Quiet Interior* brings these questions into sharp focus. Claire falls in love with Clement, but he prefers her sister Pauline who is livelier and prettier than she is; and Claire suffers.

> The strain of the past weeks was beginning to affect her – the continuous effort to appear normally cheerful, the perpetual dissembling of her pain and her emotion at Clement's proximity, her almost shuddering distaste at being left alone with him and Pauline, and her simultaneous unwillingness amounting to inability to leave them alone together. She had begun to wonder how long she could hold out. She spent more and more time with her father, more and more time alone; and, bitterest thought of all, she was not missed.[26]

She does not, as she could so easily have done, sink into despair; she rises above the pettiness of resentment and self-pity and takes comfort in her own strength of character, remembering that 'though simply to be herself seemed now a forlorn, small destiny, stripped of beauty and promise, it had seemed (once) a splendid responsibility'. Again, as in Rosamond Lehmann, there is the familiar feminine rejoicing in giving something up, and the determination to overcome the crushing dependence on others. Claire, by losing her lover, can anticipate the joys of independence and rely enough on her own intelligence not to become embittered. Clearly she will not allow her sorrow to take precedence in her life but will firmly and sensibly repress the emotions defined by one of the characters in Ethel Mannin's *Hunger of the Sea* (1924):

> This jealousy business . . . all the unhappiness it brought. It was the fierce unreasoning passion for possession, the property instinct. People were selfish, egotistical. Each individual was a free agent – yet all the time there was someone trying to chain up the individual, so that nobody was free to give either their bodies or their spirits where they willed . . . People weren't content to take a part; they must have a whole; nothing less would satisfy them; but why should one give the whole of oneself to one person to

the exclusion of all others? Didn't a thousand hands of life tear at one? Yet one was forbidden to respond because someone or other wanted the whole of you.[27]

E. Arnot Robertson was preoccupied in all her novels with the theme of jealousy and possessiveness. In *Cullum* (1928), she described a woman in love with a philanderer. In *Ordinary Families* (1933), a rather straightforward saga of boating and romance is given a sinister twist at the end. Lallie, the heroine who narrates the story, has a sister who is more disturbingly beautiful, more obvious than she is: but clearly the charm Margaret exerts over Lallie's new husband is almost involuntary, it is what is often called an 'animal magnetism' that she is barely aware of:

> He greeted Margaret friendlily. I was conscious of the difference between us, I, tired and dishevelled after the long drive in the shaky little car, and she radiant and with that fine, hard, new polish about her which made even her present untidiness seem too perfect to be uncalculated – but he did not appear to be. 'Lord, what a beautiful family I've married!' he said. 'Staggering when one sees it in bulk,' and fussed over getting us both some tea.
> I went into the bedroom to take off my things.
> They had not moved when I came back. Margaret was in our worn armchair, and he was bending over the gas-ring by the fire, but they were tense and still – unnaturally stilled for me by the sudden stopping of Time as I stood in the doorway – and looking at one another with the expression I knew, having seen it once before.
> Even this she must have, in all but face at least. Even this.[28]

And with a kind of vague obeisance to optimism, the novel ends, the reader disquieted and definitely cheated of a happy ending.

Jealousy and indifference, possession and surrender are opposed states which cannot possibly be compromised where love is concerned; they become particularly important when the love in question is of a kind frowned upon by society. Death, family ties, self-sacrifice, indifference and jealousy are some of the obstacles in the path of true love, but no less important are the incompatibility of sex and age. If a woman in fiction loves another woman the novel will inevitably end unhappily, for it is difficult for a lesbian couple to dwindle into contented domesticity or embrace on a and-so-they-lived-happily-ever-after note. In Radclyffe Hall's notorious novel *The Well of Loneliness* (1928), the reader is aware by the fifth page that Stephen is not going to grow into a conventional young woman, for her mother 'hated the way Stephen moved or stood still, hated a certain largeness about her, a certain crude lack of grace in her movements, a certain unconscious defiance'. The plot revolves around Stephen's attempt to love and be loved by another woman. When, finally, she is fulfilled (Mary cries out 'what do I care for the world's opinion? What do I care for anything but you . . .') she has three years of happiness with her lover. But when a man falls in love with Mary, Stephen finds the courage to give her up – and her future is bleak and desolate.

Some readers are moved by *The Well of Loneliness*, others cannot stifle a giggle when faced with its intense, overblown prose. Stella Gibbons was obviously in the latter category, for in *Miss Linsey and Pa* (1936) she cheerfully satirised a lesbian couple who are coming to blows over a man. As a gesture of protest Dorothy munches aspirins and threatens to do it again.

'I mean it. I swear before God I mean it. You're all I've got in the world; you're life; and I'd sooner die than let him have you. You know I'm not afraid to do it now, don't you? – as I've got so far. And it's easy to get stuff. Unless you swear a solemn oath, on all you hold sacred – on Beauty, on your Work – not to see him again, I'll do it, E. V. I swear I will.'[29]

But once the engagement is official, Dorothy, pausing only to burn her ex-lover's manuscript, rings up a close friend.

'Elizabeth, E. V.'s left me. She's gone to him.'
'My dear. What can I say?'
'There's nothing anyone can say – now. Only . . . I was wondering . . . it's so ghastly here alone.'
'I'll come at once. I'll be with you in fifteen minutes.'

'Elizabeth, what about Tim? Won't he . . .?
'He'll *have* to understand. He's working late, but I'll leave him a note.'
'It's pretty Christian of you, Elizabeth. I'm not quite sane, I think.'
'My dear . . . you know how I feel. I can't say things over the instrument. In fifteen minutes, then.'[30]

Lesbian love is frowned upon by society; so too are certain age differences. *Love* (1925) by Elizabeth von Arnim and *Family History* (1932) by Vita Sackville-West are both about women in love with men much younger than themselves. Both raise some of the same issues, though in the one the man's love is something of an adoring homage which the woman is, finally, grateful to accept, while in the other the lovers are spiritual equals but divided by their years. *Family History* also continues some of the themes of Vita Sackville-West's earlier and best novel *The Edwardians* (1930), particularly the importance of not being found out and the inadvisability of crossing the class barriers.

The Edwardians is about pre-war aristocrats who have been bred to 'take their place in a world where pleasure fell like a ripened peach for the outstretching of a hand'.[31] It is a world where unfaithfulness after marriage is condoned by all as long as the lovers do not make the cardinal error of being found out, a world where tradition reigns supreme. The true theme of the novel is class – the petty snobbishnesses revealed when the upper class comes into contact with the middle class. Sebastian (the heir to Chevron, a barely disguised Knole, the home of Vita Sackville-West's family) 'takes up' first with an exotic contemporary of his mother's and then with a doctor's wife. She visits Chevron for Christmas. Here

all her standards were revolutionised; instead of the petty economies and 'managings' of her life she contemplated his thoughtless extravagance; instead of her envious interest in the great, the notorious, or the socially eminent, she beheld his bored and casual familiarity; instead of the careful restrictions of middle-class codes and manners, she breathed the larger air of a laxer ease; instead of any rare little departure from the monotony of every day being regarded as an event, she came into contact with one to whom such diversions were no more exciting than a bit of bread.[32]

But when Sebastian tries to impress his moral code on Teresa, and casually to make love to her, she is genuinely shocked and tries stutteringly to explain how much she loves her husband and how her relations would never speak to her again if she was unfaithful to him. It is the clash of two worlds, since Sebastian genuinely cannot understand that the unfaithfulness would matter or that anyone would care as long as they were discreet about it. And Sebastian reflects angrily, 'love was one thing; middle-class virtue was another'.

Love and virtue have, in the novels described in this chapter, been accepted as two stark opposites, the soberness of marriage being assumed to be irreconcilable with the all-consuming passion felt by lovers. An additional pre-assumption is woman's unarguable dependence on her lover — there are no novels by women which chart the course of a love affair during which the female retains her previous autonomy. Women are shown, inevitably and shockingly, as subject to their lovers' demands, for example Isabelle in *The Thinking Reed* (1936) by Rebecca West:

> She had never been able to live according to her own soul, to describe her own course through life as her intellect would have been able to plan it. She had progressed erratically, dizzily, often losing sight of her goal, by repercussion after repercussion with men travelling at violent rates of speed on paths chosen for no other motive than the opportunities they gave for violence . . . In terror she thought, 'All men are my enemies, what am I doing with any of them?' But then it flashed into her mind, 'That is why making love is important, it is a reconciliation between all such enemies.'[33]

Only occasionally does one come across a portrait of a woman who accepts the differences between men and women not only cheerfully but gladly, who also rejoices in marriage's subsumptive effect on passion. One such is Una in Kate O'Brien's *Pray for the Wanderer* (1938). She sacrifices her being on the altar of maternity rather as does the heroine of *The Squire* (which was published in the same year). It is a type of love experienced by rather few women and which brings rewards unimaginable to those with their gaze on more worldly achievements – unimaginable too to men, for the saintliness of women like Una is definitely unsexual.

She loved her husband and, deriving from him, her children, with an unheeding, unaware strength of generosity such as Matt had never before observed in an adult. He had never before met in normal worldly life someone who quite precisely lived for others. Una did that – as naturally as she drank tea. He concluded, watching her, that here was a woman who actually never stared at her own face in the mirror and said 'Oh, God, I'm tired of this effort, I'm tired, I'm tired!' Or 'I'm so good to that man – Heaven, I'm much too good to everyone!' Or 'I wish, I wish – what do I wish?' If Una was tired, she said so to Will, not to her mirror, and she rested until she felt better. She was no one's martyr and had no idea that there was need for a martyr in the cause of domestic happiness. If the children plagued her too much, she shooed them off without pious pleadings. She lost her mild temper with them sometimes, and finding it again apologised as easily as if she were one of themselves. She respected their rights of liberty and secrecy without having to think of doing so. She was completely subservient to Will without once remembering that so she had vowed to be at the altar. She was occupied in one way or another for her household all day, but her blue eyes remained unflurried and it was clear that, were self-regarding in her nature, she would regard herself as a free creature, a self-directed and normally selfish woman. And Matt would have wagered a good deal that she was without a fantasy life, without a day-dream. All of her was in the here-and-now; she was complete. Without thinking of such a thing for a second, without self-consciousness or piety or even a breath of wonder, she was fulfilled. Will and the children used her up, and in so doing vitalised her.[34]

Una's life 'rose from the accident of perfect mating'. In other words, her love for her husband inspires her serenity – 'she was no one's martyr' – and she finds her life deeply fulfilling. She is the embodiment of married love, and although the portrait of her is rather flat-faced (since we never really see into her mind) she remains an unforgettable image, a symbol of a perfect wife and mother. She represents one ideal of love, a love which transcends passion to find itself in domestic bliss.

One of the key ideas in most novels about love is summed up by the two words 'if only' – it is the impediments to fulfilment that tug at the reader's heart-strings, turning love and disillusion into essential partners. 'Those damned romantic novels of romantically damned love'[35] is how a modern critic referred to Jean Rhys's work, but his definition could well apply to many of the novelists who were her contemporaries. Nor are the trappings of romance necessary to the subject of romantically damned love. Mary in *The Rector's Daughter* is far from the conventional ideal of a romantic heroine and in this has something in common with Charlotte Brontë's Lucy Snow and Jane Eyre. The reader is given few glimpses of the pulsating soul beneath the commonplace exterior – Mary's daily round is crushingly dull and it is hard to imagine passion burgeoning in her 'insignificant village'. But the smallest hint is enough to give the reader an idea of the depth of feeling that is being so rigorously and efficiently repressed.

'To love and be loved,' said Mary musingly. 'Did you feel it like a key, Dora, to let you out of prison and open a treasure-house to you?'

'Is that a pretty bit out of your writings?' said Dora with a kindness that would have checked the flow, but Mary was not listening. 'I have *longed* for it,' she went on.

She spoke with an intensity that startled Dora. She

turned round . . . Mary's eyes burnt . . . with a fire which made Dora uncomfortable. She turned away, and wondered when they would get back again to the dear, quiet Mary she knew.

'I have sometimes thought – ' Mary said with feeling, 'the kisses – '[36]

Epilogue

'Things she would never know again'

'Where, then, lay the truth? Henry by the compulsion of love had cheated her of her chosen life, yet had given her another life, an ample life, a life in touch with the greater world, if that took her fancy; or a life, alternatively, pressed close up against her own nursery. For a life of her own, he had substituted his life with its interests, or the lives of her children with their potentialities. He assumed that she might sink herself in either, if not in both, with equal joy. It had never occurred to him that she might prefer simply to be herself.'[1]

This is Lady Slane in Vita Sackville-West's *All Passion Spent*, looking back, after her eminent husband's death, at a long life spent servicing him; only in extreme old age does she have the chance to do what she wants, 'to be herself'. For her this chance has come almost, but not quite, too late: for her great-granddaughter it has come in her youth and the reader has no doubt that in terms of 'self-fulfilment' the younger generation will be far better off. Lady Slane is too generous a person to contemplate begrudging Deborah's freedom of choice, but dies content because she knows that some of the entrenched attitudes that bedevilled her life are being subtly sabotaged.

If I as author or you as reader were to venture to draw any overall conclusions from the eight chapters of *A Very Great*

Profession, these musings of Lady Slane would symbolise the most important. Whatever aspect of women's lives is being described – domesticity, psychoanalysis, love – it is clear that the woman of 1939 had far more autonomy than her mother had in 1914. Deliberately, throughout the book, I have avoided making comparisons with the present day, leaving the reader to mutter to herself '*plus ça change, plus c'est la même chose*'. But I cannot avoid pointing out how similar the middle-class woman of the 1930s is to her 1980s descendant. This is particularly obvious in the chapter on feminism, in which it is apparent that women had broken many of the barriers debarring them from a working life but had the identical difficulties when it came to reconciling a career with children. During the 1920s, it became less and less remarkable for a middle-class married woman to work outside the home – at the same time as it became more and more difficult for her to organise her domestic commitments. And by the 1930s, my mother's cheery grumble – that she had the misfortune to run a household after the servant era and before the invention of properly labour-saving machinery – had clearly become a reality.

But, housework apart, if they had married after the Second World War, Henry Slane would have had at least to *consider* his wife's wishes. He could not so easily have dismissed her painting as something he expected her to put aside, or assumed so automatically that her life would be spent ministering to his. Of course many, many men continued to coerce their wives – but it was not the norm in the same way as it had been. The climax of Dorothy Whipple's *Greenbanks* (1932) comes when Letty, who has been subdued and dominated by her husband all their married life, seizes her last chance of personal contentment. Ambrose announces that he proposes to use a legacy of his wife's to enable them to move.

'Well,' said Letty, drawing a long breath as if she were about to take a plunge. 'You must do as you like, of course, but I may as well tell you now as later, Ambrose, that I shall not go to Bournemouth.'

Ambrose stared fixedly at her.

'I've always made it clear that I should go to Bournemouth when I retired,' he said.

'I know. And there's nothing to stop you from going; but I shan't go.'

'You won't go!' He was astounded. 'You calmly suggest that I should go and that you should not go?'

Letty nodded her head.

'What on earth do you mean?' asked Ambrose.

'Simply that I shall not go Bournemouth.'

'You mean you want to stop here?'

'No.'

'What on earth do you mean then?' asked Ambrose again, his anger growing.

'Do you realize,' said Letty, 'that I am almost fifty? For thirty years I've done what you wanted; I've hardly done one thing I wanted to do, but I'm going to do it now. I've done my duty, I've had four children, I've looked after them and you and the house . . . you must look after yourself now for a bit . . .'

This was frightful. Ambrose perspired with horror. He could only stare at her and try to believe his ears. She was going to leave him — after thirty years of married life! But it was impossible! It couldn't happen. No one ever did that kind of thing .[2]

Letty's rebellion is remarkable because she has not been portrayed as a fighter: she is perfectly ordinary, rather meek and by nature a giver. She might not have had the courage to speak out if she had lived twenty years earlier — and even by the early 1930s it takes all her courage to strive for 'something for herself' and to refuse to hand her legacy over to her husband. But she does do it — she and many of her contemporaries have begun to refuse to submerge their identity in their husband's (although those with their own money have an easier time of it). In another novel by Dorothy Whipple, *The Priory* (1939), the heroine is only too well aware of the difficulties most married women face if they wish to be married no longer. Reading the newspapers in a vain hope of offers of employment she asks herself:

What did women in her position do? What did they *do*? If there was only marriage for girls brought up in the way she and Penelope had been brought up and marriage failed, what then?

It was a question parents, in her world, did not ask themselves . . .

'People say: "Oh, it's not like that for girls *now*." But it is, and it's going to be more like it than ever, it seems to me. According to these papers it is. Women are being pushed back into homes and told to have more babies. They're being told to make themselves helpless. Men are arming like mad, but women are expected to disarm, and make themselves more vulnerable than they already are by nature . . . In this newspaper, the headlines are about the necessity of preparations for war and the leader is about the necessity for an increase in the population. "The only hope," they say. They urge women to produce babies so they can wage war more successfully with them when their mothers have brought them up.'

What a world! For herself, for everybody, what a world!

'Well, this has taught me one thing,' she thought wearily, picking up another paper and turning to the advertisement columns. 'If I've to scrub floors or eat the bread of dependence all my life, Angela shall be educated to earn her own living. She shan't find herself in the hold I'm in now if I can help it.'[3]

The preceding chapters have shown that women enjoyed a new frame of mind in the inter-war period. They also enjoyed certain benefits undreamed of by their mothers, particularly birth control, the motor car, gas, electricity and the wireless. E. M. Delafield wrote about the latter, in 1937:

If I were asked to name a symbol of modern homelife I should choose the wireless . . . All over the country, in every house, sooner or later the well-known discussions arise. Jazz or no jazz. Symphony concert or variety. Henry Hall as a background to conversation: conversation as an interruption to Henry Hall. Absolute silence for The News, or The News ignored until next morning's paper.[4]

And it is instructive to reflect on the following figures: in 1923 there were 200,000 early valve receivers (wirelesses); in 1925, 1,200,000; in 1927, 2,269,644 (and very accurate records); and by 1939, 8,968,338. The number of cars shows a similar kind of rise, increasing within the decade from 200,000 to over a million.[5] Virginia Woolf wrote in her diary in 1927:

> We talk of nothing but cars . . . This is a great opening up in our lives. One may go to Bodiam, to Arundel, explore the Chichester downs, expand that curious thing, the map of the world in ones mind. It will I think demolish loneliness, & may of course imperil complete privacy . . . the motor is turning out the joy of our lives, an additional life, free & mobile & airy to live alongside our usual stationary industry . . . Soon we shall look back at our pre-motor days as we do now at our days in the caves.[6]

Any reader of her diaries will have been struck by the difficulty, in the pre-motor car days, that the two sisters, Virginia and Vanessa, had in seeing each other when they were in the country – a carefully planned expedition was inevitable if the short distance between Rodmell and Charleston was to be managed, and sheer logistics made life as complicated as the lack of a refrigerator or as the self-imposed rule which necessitated Virginia spending the first day of her monthly 'affaires' firmly in bed.

The reader of *A Very Great Profession*, aware of the effect of the 1914–18 war and its aftermath, will have been alert to the changes enjoyed by the women of the inter-war period. But for middle-class women who lived through it, the changes were not necessarily for the better – obviously they appreciated electric heating or the invention of antiseptics such as DDT (until the early 1920s most people would have endured the perpetually itchy scalp caused by nits) – but many advances were viewed as mere regressions. Most obviously this was so with the waning of the servant class, and middle-class women began to miss the way of life that had been made possible by their servants. Evelyn

Waugh captured their grievances when he described Mrs Scrope-Weld in *Unconditional Surrender* (1961) longing for a return to life as it had been before the Second World War.

> Almost all women in England at that time believed that peace would restore normality. Mrs Scrope-Weld in Staffordshire meant by 'normality' having her husband at home and the house to themselves; also certain, to her, rudimentary comforts to which she had always been used; nothing sumptuous; a full larder and cellar; a lady's maid (but one who did her bedroom and darned and sewed for the whole family), a butler, a footman (but one who chopped and carried fire-logs), a reliable, mediocre cook training a kitchen-maid to succeed her in simple skills, self-effacing house-maids to dust and tidy; one man in the stable, two in the garden; things she would never know again.[7]

While I love and admire the kind of women portrayed in *A Very Great Profession*, while I identify in so many ways with the *zeitgeist* of the inter-war period, I cannot but feel that the self-reliance of post-war women is far preferable to the helpless dependence on others which our mothers and grandmothers in the middle classes deemed to be their birthright. And indeed the majority of women adapted to the new demands made upon their energies and capabilities with complete calm and resilience, with the ironic good nature that Joyce Grenfell captured to such good effect, for example in 'The Countess of Coteley'. Her life was that of an aristocrat (in 1910 when 'she was at her zenith' she had three homes, twenty-seven servants and all the attendant trappings) but the changes in her life were not so different to those being felt, albeit on a smaller scale, by the entire middle class. After a verse describing the Countess's firmly upper-crust life, Joyce Grenfell takes us forward to 1947.

> When you see her in this flashback it is rather hard
>   to guess
> That she'll be a sort of typist in the W.V.S.
> She will learn to woo her grocer: she won't have a
>   cook to woo,

But a Czechoslovak cleaner may pop in from
    twelve to two.
Speaking worldlily she'll dwindle. She will change
    her books at Boots,
And lecture on Make-do-and-Mend to Women's
    Institutes. . . .
She will seldom dress for dinner, she will dote on
    Vera Lynn,
She will take in the *New Stateman*, but she won't
    be taken in.[8]

The implication is that the Countess, as a citizen of the Welfare State, has developed political antennae. This was probably not typical of most middle-class women, although many of them, unlike Mrs Scrope-Weld, had displayed a chameleon-like ability to adapt to new circumstances. Only very few were so attuned to the catastrophe of the Depression and the rise of fascism in the 1930s that they deliberately renounced all their former certainties – Storm Jameson was one exception who did resolve to give up her previous obsession with aesthetic, moral and philosophical comment in order to turn her undivided attention to the novel of social concern.[9] And few could have foreseen that the 'overwhelming influence of contemporary events' would have led, from about 1932 onwards, to 'a galloping consumption in the English novel'.[10]

Many women at this time were still trying to come to terms with the devastating after-effects of the First World War upon their lives. The pessimistic self-awareness that runs throughout the work of so many writers was an oblique expression of their sense of loss; and when another war loomed, many ceased to write (which is why there are fewer novels of note published at the end of the 1930s than might have been anticipated from the fertility of the previous years).

It was not until the Second World War was over that Mollie Panter-Downes wrote an elegy to the inter-war period which is so unique that the novel stands out as one of its greatest memorials. The line from *As You Like It*, 'True is it that we have seen better days' is written on the frontispiece of *One Fine Day* (1947) and runs as a *leitmotif* throughout the book – not in a mournful or complaining way, but rather in a resigned, tender, philosophical one. The world as it was has gone never to return; and for Laura, its heroine, it was a world of ease and comfort, cushioned by servants and domestic harmony. By showing how the world has changed for Laura, Mollie Panter-Downes shows how the world has changed for the middle classes: she wrote a social novel, one which went beyond the particular to change the reader's view of the world.

The plot is of a rare simplicity and, with a kind of classical unity as far as form is concerned, it is set during one day in the summer of 1946. The prologue describes a village nestling in the downs. Something had recently disturbed its placidity: 'there were signs of an occupation by something, an idea, an emotion'. War has come and gone and although the immediate danger has passed life has been disrupted: but not fatally.

Up here, on the empty hilltop, something said I am England. I will remain. The explosions in the valley, the muffled rumbles and distant flashes far our to sea, had sounded remote as the quarrelling voices of children some-where in the high, cool rooms of an ancient house from which they would soon be gone. But the house said I will stand when you are dust.[11]

Early on we are, immediately and obviously, with a middle-class couple for whom life has, irrevocably, changed. We are shown Stephen's dismay at the state of his garden, and his gloom prompts a brief but poignant vignette of life as it had been before 1939.

My man's good on roses, Stephen used to say to friends who motored down for lunch on Sundays before the war . . . and from the opposite deck-chair a guest would make a polite murmuring of approval. He liked that, he had to own it, but The soil suits 'em, he would say, as though they sprang up like buttercups. And they would sit there, look-

ing at the roses, talking idly, enjoying the hot sun – was it
imagination that all the summer Sunday afternoons before
the war had been hot? – until out from the house tripped
Ethel or Violet, smart in their pretty uniforms, to take
away the coffee-tray. He could see them now, making an
entrance as though the lovely afternoon were a ballet,
impossibly dancing across the smooth lawn, for ever lifting
the tray in that perpetual remembered sunlight and bear-
ing it away with a whisk of an apron streamer, a gleam of a
neat ankle.[12]

But the garden has run riot, and the house has assumed a different character. Laura reflects over her breakfast tea, in a
passage which is a faint echo of the one in which Mrs Dalloway
listens to the noises of her house, how she is more intimate with
her home than she ever was in the past.

Now, said the house to Laura, we are alone together. Now
I am yours again. The yellow roses in the bowl shed half a
rose in a sudden soft, fat slump on the polished wood, a
board creaked on the stairs, distant pipes chirped. She
knew all her house's little voices, as she had never done in
the old days when there had been more people under her
roof. Then there had been nothing but cheerful noises all
day long. In the kitchen, caps and aprons shrieked with
sudden merriment.[13]

But the noises have gone and the house is silent and 'here they
were awkwardly saddled with a house which, all those pleasant
years, had really been supported and nourished by squawks over
bread-and-cheese elevenses, by the sound of Chandler's boots on
the paths, by the smell of ironing and toast from the nursery'.
    Stephen and Laura find it hard to capitulate. 'Wretched
victims of their class, they still had dinner.' Certainly Mrs Prout
comes 'to circulate the dust a little' but even she cannot stop the
house looking down on its luck. For the house is a tyrant,
enslaving and enthralling Laura with its demands: 'my day is a
feeble, woman's day, following a domestic chalk line, bound to
the tyranny of my house with its voices saying, Clean me, polish

me, save me from the spider and the butterfly.' Food, too, is minimal and shoppers are grateful for anything, arriving early to strip the counters bare. 'After eleven, for those in the know, the little town had nothing much to offer. Sorry, the shaken heads would signal to those foolish virgins who came late with their baskets to seek the rare orange, the spotted plaice, the yellow and unyielding bun.'

But Laura has adapted to her changed circumstances in a way that her mother, for instance, has not. She realises that, for her mother,

> the war had flowed past her like a dark, strong river, never pulling her into its currents, simply washing to her feet the minor debris of evacuees who broke the statue's fingers and spoiled a mattress, of food shortages, or worry over Laura who was close to bombs, and worked too hard, and had tragically lost her fresh looks. Now, said Mrs Heriot, thank God it was over, and eveything could get back to normal again . . . Now, darling, said Mrs Heriot, the servants will be coming back, they will be glad to get out of those awful uniforms, out of those appalling huts into a decent house with hot baths and a nice bed. And when they did not, she simply could not understand it . . . So the mahogany continued to reflect the silver polo cups pleasantly, the Heriot world held together for a little longer in its deadness of glacial chintz strewn with violets and side tables strewn with the drooping moustached faces of yesteryear. The war had been horrible, really ghastly – had not the Carruthers lost three nephews, the Whyte-Jevons two airmen sons and a daughter drowned in a torpedoed ship, Colonel Heriot's niece Betty her husband in a Jap prison camp? But mercifully it was over, said Mrs Heriot, and Laura must really pay attention to her appearance a little more now that Stephen was home.[14]

During her day Laura tries and fails to get someone to help in the garden, then triumphs by finding oranges on her morning's shopping expedition. At tea time she goes to tea up at the Manor for the last time – it is being sold for development – and then wanders up on to the downs in search of her lost dog. There is no more action than this. But by the end of this marvellous novel, at the close of the day, Laura and Stephen have, almost unconsciously, perceived a new direction for themselves. They will cheerfully compromise: Stephen will stop mourning after the lost Ethels and Violets, for it has 'struck him as preposterous how dependent he and his class had been on the anonymous caps and aprons who lived out of sight and worked the strings'. And Laura, walking with the dog, stretches out on the hillside and, with a rush of happiness, gloats over her blessings and plans a carefree future: for the first time she can be truly and serenely grateful for the wonderful peace which had been bestowed upon England only a year before. Never had she felt 'quite this rush of overwhelming thankfulness, so that the land swam and misted and danced before her. She had had to lose a dog and climb a hill, a year later, to realize what it would have meant if England had lost. We are at peace, we still stand, we will stand when you are dust, sang the humming land in the summer evening.'

The tone of the novel is deeply optimistic. By the spring of 1945 much had been destroyed never to return, but a year later Stephen and Laura are able to lift their heads from their domestic round and realise that everything that mattered and lasted had survived unscarred. There are few other novels which are lyrical in quite this way, elegies to something lost, eulogies on something newly come to life. Laura is our final member of a very great profession – and she has all the qualities that have been continuously displayed throughout this book – staunchness, good humour and a deep appreciation of life.

> The long nightmare was over, the land sang its peaceful song. Thank God, thought Laura again as she had thought in the bus while the young man in the blue shirt read his map, but this time the feeling of thankfulness was so overwhelming that the view suddenly misted, gathered, and hung shining, and she rummaged in her bag for her handkerchief. Heavens knows, she thought sarcastically, the fact should have registered before, she had had occasions in plenty to get her weeping done with official sanction . . . Nothing better than this. A quiet evening, a house and a child in the valley, time to climb a hill by herself.

Notes

Introduction

1. Noel Coward, *Still Life* (1935), published in *To-night at 8.30* (Heinemann, 1936), p. 348 in *Plays: Three* (Eyre Methuen, 1979).
2. Virginia Woolf, *Night and Day* (Duckworth, 1919), p. 40 in Penguin edition, 1969.
3. Virginia Woolf, *A Room of One's Own* (The Hogarth Press, 1929), p. 44 in Penguin edition, 1963.
4. *Ibid.*, p. 45.
5. Elizabeth Bowen, 'Notes on Writing a Novel' (1945), *Collected Impressions* (Longmans, Green, 1950), p. 258.
6. Paul Bailey, *New Statesman* (London, 10 August 1973).
7. Anthony Burgess, *New York Times Book Review* (New York, 4 December 1966), quoted in Mary Ellmann, *Thinking about Women* (New York, 1968), p. 23 in Virago edition, 1979.
8. Rebecca West, *New Statesman* (London, 10 July 1920).
9. E. M. Forster, *A Room with a View* (Edward Arnold, 1908), p. 158 in Penguin edition, 1978.
10. Kay Dick, *Ivy and Stevie* (Duckworth, 1971), p. 7.
11. Rebecca West, *New Statesman* (London, 2 December 1922).
12. Vera Brittain, *Lady into Woman* (Andrew Dakers, 1953), p. 219.
13. Virginia Woolf, 'The Niece of an Earl' (1928), reprinted in *The Common Reader*, Second Series, (The Hogarth Press, 1932), p. 214.

14. E. M. Forster, 'Mrs Miniver', 1939, reprinted in *Two Cheers for Democracy* (Edward Arnold, 1951), p. 303 in Penguin edition, 1965.
15. E. M. Forster, *A Room with a View*, *op. cit.*, p. 129.
16. Virginia Woolf, *The Voyage Out* (Duckworth, 1915), p. 212 in Penguin edition, 1970.
17. Jan Struther, *Mrs Miniver* (Chatto & Windus, 1939), p. 221.
18. Noel Coward, *op. cit.*, p. 338.
19. John Betjeman, 'In Westminster Abbey', in *Old Lights for New Chancels* (1940), p. 85 in *Collected Poems* (John Murray, 1958).
20. Vera Brittain, *Thrice a Stranger* (Gollancz, 1938), p. 59.
21. Virginia Woolf, *The Diary of Virginia Woolf* Volume 1, ed. Anne Olivier Bell (The Hogarth Press, 1977), 13 January 1915, p. 17.
22. Elizabeth Bowen, *The Death of the Heart* (Gollancz, 1938); p. 157 in Penguin edition, 1962.
23. Denis Mackail, *Greenery Street* (Heinemann, 1925); p. 115 in Penguin edition, 1937.
24. Boots *First Literary Course*, pamphlet privately circulated in 1948.
25. Jan Struther, *op. cit.*, p. 6.

1 War

1. E. M. Forster, *Howards End* (Edward Arnold, 1910), p. 27 in Penguin edition, 1941.
2. R. Brimley Johnson, *Some Contemporary Novelists (Women)* (Leonard Parsons, 1920), p. x.
3. *The Question of Things Happening*, The Letters of Virginia Woolf, Volume II 1912–1922, ed. Nigel Nicolson (The Hogarth Press, 1976), p. xvii.
4. Rupert Brooke, 'Peace', 1914, *Collected Poems* (Sidgwick & Jackson, 1958), p. 146.
5. Nicholas Mosley, *Julian Grenfell* (Weidenfeld & Nicolson, 1976), p. 51.
6. *Ibid.*, p. 237.
7. H. G. Wells, *Mr Britling Sees It Through* (Cassell, 1916), p. 306.
8. Arthur Marwick, *Women at War 1914–1918* (Fontana, 1977), p. 166.

9. Vera Brittain, *Testament of Youth* (Gollancz, 1933), p. 104 in Virago edition, 1978.
10. *The Lady* (London, 13 August 1914.)
11. Lady Frances Balfour, *Dr Elsie Inglis* (Hodder & Stoughton, 1918), p. 144.
12. May Wedderburn Cannan, *Grey Ghosts and Voices* (Roundwood Press, 1976), p. 79.
13. Cicely Hamilton, *Life Errant* (J. M. Dent, 1935), p. 98.
14. Rose Macaulay, 'Many Sisters to Many Brothers', *Poems of Today* (English Association, 1915), p. 23.
15. Arthur Marwick, *op. cit.*, p. 73.
16. Cicely Hamilton, *The Englishwoman* (Longmans, 1940), p. 36.
17. Katharine Mansfield, in *The Atheneum* (London, 16 July 1920), reprinted in *Novels and Novelists* (Constable, 1930), p. 224.
18. Dorothy Canfield, *Home Fires in France* (Jonathan Cape, 1919), p. 275.
19. Vera Brittain, *Testament of Youth*, *op. cit.*, p. 429.
20. May Sinclair, *The Tree of Heaven* (Cassell, 1917), p. 71.
21. *Ibid.*, p. 330.
22. Enid Bagnold, *A Diary Without Dates* (Heinemann, 1918), p. 5 in Virago edition, 1978.
23. *Ibid.*, p. 114.
24. Lady Cynthia Asquith, *Diaries* 1915–18 (Hutchinson, 1968), p. 480.
25. *Ibid.*, p. 183.
26. *Ibid.*, p. 191.
27. *Ibid.*, p. 254.
28. *Ibid.*, p. 285.
29. H. G. Wells, *op. cit.*, p. 203.
30. *Ibid.*, p. 293.
31. F. Tennyson Jesse, *The Sword of Deborah* (Heinemann, 1919), p. 135.
32. Katharine Mansfield, in *The Atheneum*, (London, 21 November 1919), *op. cit.*, p. 111.
33. Katharine Mansfield, letter, 10 November 1919, *Letters and Journals of Katharine Mansfield: A Selection*, edited by C. K. Stead (Penguin, 1977), p. 147.
34. Cicely Hamilton, *William — An Englishman* (Skeffington & Son, 1919), p. 49.
35. *Ibid.*, p. 99.

36. Sheila Kaye-Smith, *Little England* (Nisbet, 1918), p. 293.
37. Sylvia Thompson, *The Hounds of Spring* (Heinemann, 1926), p. 124.
38. *Ibid.*, p. 326.
39. Mary Borden, *The Forbidden Zone* (Heinemann, 1929), Preface.
40. *Ibid.*, p. 142.
41. Mary Borden, *Sarah Gay* (Heinemann, 1931), p. 19.
42. Robert Wohl, *The Generation of 1914* (Weidenfeld & Nicolson, 1980), p. 121.
43. May Wedderburn Cannan, *The Lonely Generation* (Hutchinson, 1934), p. 287.
44. Marion Allen, 'The Wind on the Downs', in *The Wind on the Downs* (London, 1918), reprinted in *Scars Upon My Heart* (Virago, 1981), p. 1.

2 Surplus Women

1. R. C. K. Ensor, *England 1870–1914* (Oxford University Press, 1936), p. 272.
2. Eleanor Mordaunt, *The Family* (Methuen, 1915), p. 313.
3. Cecil Woodham-Smith, *Florence Nightingale* (Constable, 1950), pp. 60–61.
4. Ray Strachey, *The Cause* (G. Bell, 1928), p. 404 in Virago edition, 1979.
5. W. Thackeray, *Vanity Fair* (London, 1848), p. 501 in Penguin edition, 1982.
6. Virginia Woolf, *Night and Day*, *op. cit.*, p. 39.
7. *Ibid.*, p. 291.
8. Patricia Stubbs, *Women and Fiction* (Methuen, 1979), p. 6.
9. *The Edwardian Age*, ed. Alan O'Day (Macmillan, 1979), p. 135.
10. George Gissing, *The Odd Women* (Lawrence & Bullen, 1893), p. 152 in Virago edition, 1980.
11. Virginia Woolf, *Night and Day*, *op. cit.* p. 42.
12. H. G. Wells, *Ann Veronica* (Fisher Unwin, 1909), p. 5 in Virago edition, 1980.
13. E. Carpenter, *My Days and Dreams* (G. Allen & Unwin, 1916), p. 31.
14. F. Harrison, in *The Fortnightly Review* (London, October 1891), quoted Stubbs, *op. cit.*, p. 7.

15. F. M. Mayor, *The Rector's Daughter* (The Hogarth Press, 1924), p. 14 in Penguin edition, 1973.

16. *Ibid.*, p. 210.

17. E. M. Delafield, *Consequences* (Hodder & Stoughton, 1919), p. 74.

18. *Ibid.*, p. 142.

19. E. M. Delafield, *Thank Heaven Fasting* (Macmillan, 1932), p. 5.

20. *Ibid.*, p. 247.

21. *Ibid.*, p. 282.

22. E. M. Delafield, *The Heel of Achilles* (Hutchinson, 1921), p. 322.

23. Radclyffe Hall, *The Unlit Lamp* (Cassell, 1924), p. 128 in Virago edition, 1981.

24. *Ibid.*, p. 152.

25. *Ibid.*, p. 300.

26. *Ibid.*, p. 141.

27. Winifred Holtby, *The Crowded Street* (The Bodley Head, 1924), p. 16 in Virago edition, 1981.

28. *Ibid.*, p. 44.

29. Lettice Cooper, *The New House* (Gollancz, 1936), p. 75 in Penguin edition, 1946.

30. *Ibid.*, p. 116.

31. *Ibid.*, p. 129.

32. *Ibid.*, p. 163.

33. E. Arnot Robertson, *Ordinary Families* (Jonathan Cape, 1933), p. 217 in Virago edition, 1982.

34. Ruth Adam, *A Woman's Place* (Chatto & Windus, 1975), p. 100.

35. Muriel Spark, *The Prime of Miss Jean Brodie* (Macmillan, 1961), p. 42 in Penguin edition, 1965.

36. Virginia Woolf, *The Diary of Virginia Woolf* Volume 111, ed. Anne Olivier Bell (The Hogarth Press, 1980), 29 September 1930, p. 321.

37. Rosamond Lehmann, *Invitation to the Waltz* (Chatto & Windus, 1932), p. 52 in Virago edition, 1981.

38. Ruth Adam, *op. cit.*, p. 118.

39. Cicely Hamilton, *The Englishwoman*, *op. cit.*, p. 27.

3 Feminism

1. Cicely Hamilton, *Life Errant*, *op. cit.*, p. 65.

2. May Sinclair, *The Tree of Heaven, op. cit.*, p. 104.
3. *Ibid.*, p. 110.
4. E. M. Forster, *A Room with a View, op. cit.*, p. 214.
5. Mrs Havelock Ellis, *Attainment* (Alston Rivers, 1909),
    p. 106.
6. H. G. Wells, *Ann Veronica, op. cit.*, p. 24.
7. *Ibid.*, p. 20.
8. Vera Brittain, *Testament of Youth, op. cit.*, p. 51.
9. Vera Brittain, *Testament of Friendship* (Macmillan, 1942),
    p. 133 in Virago edition, 1980.
10. H. G. Wells, *Ann Veronica, op. cit.*, p. 205.
11. H. G. Wells, *An Experiment in Autobiography* Volume II
    (Gollancz/Cresset Press, 1934), p. 470.
12. Amy Cruse, *After the Victorians* (G. Allen & Unwin, 1938),
    p. 244.
13. Vera Brittain, *Testament of Friendship, op. cit.*, p. 134.
14. Mary Stocks, *Eleanor Rathbone*, (Gollancz, 1949), p. 116.
15. Jo van Ammers-Küller, *The Rebel Generation* (J. M. Dent,
    1928), p. 279 in Dent edition, 1932.
16. *Ibid.*, p. 345.
17. *Ibid.*, p. 365.
18. Rose Macaulay, *Told by an Idiot* (Collins, 1923), p. 39 in
    Penguin edition, 1940.
19. *Ibid.*, p. 21.
20. G. B. Stern, *Tents of Israel* (Chapman & Hall, 1924),
    p. 206.
21. Cicely Hamilton, *Modern England* (J. M. Dent, 1938), p. 185.
22. A. S. M. Hutchinson, *This Freedom* (Hodder & Stoughton,
    1922), p. 11.
23. *Ibid.*, p. 188.
24. *Ibid.*, p. 207.
25. *Ibid.*, p. 221.
26. Storm Jameson, *Three Kingdoms* (Constable, 1926), p. 336.
27. *Ibid.*, p. 396.
28. Olive Schreiner, *Woman and Labour* (Fisher Unwin, 1911),
    p. 49 in Virago edition, 1978.
29. *Ibid.*, p. 50.
30. *Ibid.*, p. 281.
31. Dorothy Canfield, *The Home-Maker* (Jonathan Cape, 1924),
    p. 257.
32. *Ibid.*, p. 276.
33. *Ibid.*, p. 280.

34. Winifred Holtby, *Letters to a Friend* (Collins, 1937), 27 September 1922, p. 128.

35. V. Friedlaender, *Mainspring* (Collins, 1922), p. 319.

36. Virginia Woolf, *A Room of One's Own, op. cit.*, p. 93.

37. Virginia Woolf, *The Voyage Out, op. cit.*, p. 210.

38. Virginia Woolf, *A Room of One's Own, op. cit.*, p. 89.

39. Virginia Woolf, *The Voyage Out, op. cit.*, p. 211.

40. Virginia Woolf, *The Years* (The Hogarth Press, 1937), p. 275 in Triad/Panther edition, 1977.

41. Virginia Woolf, 'Professions for Women', 1931, published in *The Death of the Moth* (The Hogarth Press, 1942), p. 152.

42. Virginia Woolf, *A Room of One's Own, op. cit.*, p. 93.

43. May Sinclair, *The Creators* (Constable, 1910), p. 334.

44. Cicely Hamilton, *Marriage as a Trade* (Chapman & Hall, 1909), p. 108 in The Women's Press edition, 1981.

45. Anne Morrow Lindbergh, *The Flower and the Nettle* (Harcourt Brace Jovanovich, 1976), p. 123.

46. *Ibid.*, p. 126.

47. E. M. Delafield, *Diary of a Provincial Lady* (Macmillan, 1930), p. 179.

48. *A Reflection of the Other Person*, The Letters of Virginia Woolf, Volume IV 1929–1931, ed. Nigel Nicolson (The Hogarth Press, 1978), 8 June 1930, p. 176.

49. Elizabeth Cambridge, *Hostages to Fortune* (Jonathan Cape, 1933), p. 41.

50. Virginia Woolf, 'Professions for women', 1931, in *The Death of the Moth, op. cit.*, p. 150.

51. Rebecca West, in the *Bookman* (London, May 1922).

52. Katharine Mansfield, *Letters and Journals, op. cit.*, p. 43, letter, summer 1913.

53. R. Ellis Roberts, *Portrait of Stella Benson* (Macmillan, 1939), p. 215.

54. John Gawsworth, ed. *Ten Contemporaries* (Ernest Benn, 1932), p. 59.

55. Vita Sackville-West, *All Passion Spent* (The Hogarth Press, 1931), p. 164.

56. *Ibid.*, p. 175.

4 Domesticity

1. George Eliot, *Amos Barton* in *Scenes of Clerical Life* (Edinburgh: Blackwoods, 1857), p. 80 in Penguin edition, 1980.

2. Cicely Hamilton, *Marriage as a Trade*, *op. cit.*, p. 113.

3. Rosamond Lehmann, *A Note in Music* (Chatto & Windus, 1930), p. 52 in Virago edition, 1982.

4. E. M. Delafield, *The Way Things Are* (Hutchinson, 1927), p. 16.

5. *Ibid.*, p. 12.

6. *Ibid.*, p. 31.

7. Virginia Woolf, 'Life and the Novelist', 1926, published in *Granite and Rainbow* (The Hogarth Press, 1958), p. 46.

8. E. M. Delafield, *The Way Things Are*, *op. cit.*, p. 287.

9. Virginia Woolf, *A Room of One's Own*, *op. cit.*, p. 89.

10. Virginia Woolf, *Mrs Dalloway* (The Hogarth Press, 1925), p. 33 in Penguin edition, 1964.

11. Leonora Eyles, *The Woman in the Little House* (Grant· Richards, 1922), p. 110.

12. *Ibid.*, p. 38.

13. Edith Sitwell, *English Women* (Collins, 1942), p. 8.

14. Enid Bagnold, quoted in the Introduction to *The Girl's Journey*, reissue of *The Happy Foreigner* and *The Squire* (Heinemann, 1954), p. xi.

15. Naomi Mitchison, *You May Well Ask* (Gollancz, 1979), p. 28.

16. Quentin Bell, *Virginia Woolf* Volume Two (The Hogarth Press, 1972), p. 55.

17. Maureen Duffy, *The Emancipation of Women* (Oxford: Basil Blackwell, 1967), p. 32.

18. Quentin Bell, *op. cit.*, p. 57.

19. Martin Armstrong, *St Christopher's Day* (Gollancz, 1928), p. 34.

20. *Ibid.*, p. 179.

21. Cynthia Asquith, *Diaries*, *op. cit.*, p. 150.

22. Stella Gibbons, *Miss Linsey and Pa* (Longmans, 1936), p. 217.

23. *New Statesman*, (London, 17 October 1925).

24. Lettice Cooper, *The New House*, *op. cit.*, p. 82

25. Virginia Woolf, *The Diary of Virginia Woolf* Volume 111, *op. cit.*, 13 April 1929, p. 220.

26. *Ibid.*, 6 August 1930, p. 311.

27. Cynthia White, *Women's Magazines 1693–1968* (Michael Joseph, 1970), p. 99, quoting *Woman's Life*, (London, 1920).

28. *Ibid.*, p. 104, quoting *The Lady*, (London, 1938).

29. *Our Homes and Gardens*, London, February 1920, reprinted in *Homes and Gardens*, London, June 1979.
30. *Ibid.*
31. Kay Smallshaw, *How to Run Your Home without Help* (John Lehmann, 1949), p. 153.
32. Rose Macaulay, *Crewe Train* (Collins, 1926), p. 305.
33. E. M. Delafield, *Diary of a Provincial Lady*, *op. cit.*, p. 6.
34. Interview with Janet Graham Rance, Jan Struther's daughter, 17 September 1980, Radio Four, 'Woman's Hour'.
35. Jan Struther, *Mrs Miniver*, *op. cit.*, p. 47.
36. *Ibid.*, p. 220.
37. Elizabeth Cambridge, *Hostages to Fortune*, *op. cit.*, p. 88.
38. *Ibid.*, p. 253.
39. *Ibid.*, p. 256.
40. Enid Bagnold, *The Squire* (Heinemann, 1938), p. 145.
41. *Ibid.*, p. 154.
42. Enid Bagnold, *Autobiography* (Heinemann, 1969), p. 179.
43. Dorothy Canfield, *The Brimming Cup* (Jonathan Cape, 1921), p. 250.
44. Frances Cornford, 'Ode on the Whole Duty of Parents' in *Mountains and Molehills* (1934), *Collected Poems* (Cresset Press, 1954), p. 59.

5 Sex

1. Virginia Woolf, 'Professions for Women', *The Death of the Moth*, *op. cit.*, p. 152.
2. Acton, *The Functions and Disorders of the Reproductive Organs* (London, 1857), quoted Steven Marcus, *The Other Victorians* (Weidenfeld & Nicolson, 1966), p. 31 in Corgi edition, 1969.
3. Patricia Stubbs, *Women and Fiction*, *op. cit.*, p. xiv.
4. Barbara Low, *Psycho-Analysis* (G. Allen & Unwin, 1920), p. 96.
5. Winifred Holtby, *Virginia Woolf* (Wishart, 1932), p. 29.
6. Katharine Mansfield, *Letters*, Vol. II, edited by J. Middleton Murry (Constable, 1928), 17 October 1920, p. 57.
7. *Ibid.*, December 1921, p. 159.
8. John Montgomery, *The Twenties* (G. Allen & Unwin, 1957), p. 216.
9. Virginia Woolf, *A Room of One's Own*, *op. cit.*, p. 88.
10. Virginia Woolf, *Mrs Dalloway*, *op. cit.*, p. 36.
11. *Ibid.*, p. 36.

12. Sylvia Thompson, *Third Act in Venice* (Heinemann, 1936), p. 103.

13. Rosamond Lehmann, *The Weather in the Streets* (Collins, 1936), p. 158 in Virago edition, 1981.

14. Margaret Lawrence, *We Write as Women* (Michael Joseph, 1937), p. 220.

15. Rebecca West, *The Thinking Reed* (Hutchinson, 1936), p. 28 in Macmillan edition, 1966.

16. Stella Gibbons, *Cold Comfort Farm* (Longmans, 1932), p. 112 in Penguin edition, 1956.

17. Rebecca West, *The Thinking Reed*, *op. cit.*, p. 12.

18. Michael Arlen, *The Green Hat* (Collins, 1924), p. 47.

19. Enid Bagnold, *Autobiography*, *op. cit.*, p. 92.

20. May Sinclair, *The Romantic* (Collins, 1920), p. 12.

21. Beatrice Kean Seymour, *The Romantic Tradition* (Chapman & Hall, 1925), p. 21.

22. Ellen Glasgow, in the *New York Herald-Tribune Books* (New York, 27 May 1928).

23. May Sinclair, *The Allinghams* (Hutchinson, 1927), p. 279.

24. Marie Stopes, *Literary Guide* (London, 1939), quoted in Vincent Brome, *Havelock Ellis* (Routledge & Kegan Paul, 1979), p. 147.

25. Ruth Hall, *Marie Stopes* (André Deutsch, 1977), p. 93 in Virago edition.

26. Aylmer Maude, *The Authorized Life of Marie Stopes* (London, 1924), quoted Ruth Hall, *Marie Stopes*, *op. cit.*, p. 101.

27. *Ibid.*, p. 109.

28. Marie Stopes, *Married Love* (Putnam, 1918), p. 108 in 1924 edition.

29. Ruth Hall (ed.), *Dear Dr Stopes* (André Deutsch, 1978), p. 170 in Penguin edition, 1981.

30. Enid Starkie, letter to Rosamond Lehmann, 1945, quoted Joanna Richardson, *Enid Starkie* (John Murray, 1973), p. 78.

31. Bernhard Bauer, *Woman* (Jonathan Cape, 1927), p. 7.

32. *Ibid.*, p. 227.

33. Helena Wright, *The Sex Factor in Marriage* (Noel Douglas, 1930), p. 65.

34. *Ibid.*, p. 59.

35. *Ibid.*, p. 50.

36. R. Lewis and A. Maude, *The English Middle Classes* (Phoenix House, 1949), p. 222.

37. A. J. P. Taylor, *English History 1914–45* (Oxford University Press, 1965), p. 218, in Pelican edition, 1970.
38. Letter to author from LRC.
39. Mrs C. Peel, *Life's Enchanted Cup* (John Lane, 1933), p. 262.
40. Leonora Eyles, *Margaret Protests* (Erskine Macdonald, 1919), p. 46.
41. Rosalind Wade, *Treasure in Heaven* (Collins, 1937), p. 249.
42. Leonora Eyles, *The Woman in the Little House, op. cit.*, p. 130.
43. *Ibid.*, p. 144.
44. Sheila Rowbotham, *Hidden from History* (Pluto Press, 1973), p. 142.
45. Irene Clephane, *Towards Sex Freedom* (The Bodley Head, 1935), p. 212.
46. *Ibid.*, p. 221.
47. Naomi Mitchison, *You May Well Ask, op. cit.*, p. 69.
48. Naomi Mitchison, *All Change Here* (The Bodley Head, 1975), p. 157.
49. Robert Graves and Alan Hodge, *The Long Weekend* (Faber & Faber, 1940), p. 103 in Penguin edition, 1971.
50. Naomi Mitchison, *You May Well Ask, op. cit.*, p. 179.
51. Naomi Mitchison, *The Delicate Fire* (Jonathan Cape, 1933), p. 161.
52. Pamela Hansford Johnson, *Important To Me* (Macmillan, 1974), p. 118.
53. Pamela Hansford Johnson, *This Bed Thy Centre* (Chapman & Hall, 1935), p. 249.
54. E. Arnot Robertson, *Four Frightened People* (Jonathan Cape, 1931), p. 147 in Virago edition, 1982.
55. *Ibid.*, p. 226.
56. *Ibid.*, p. 238.
57. Rose Macaulay, *Potterism* (Collins, 1920), p. 7.
58. Noel Coward, *Still Life, op. cit.*, p. 376.
59. Cynthia White, *Women's Magazines, op. cit.*, p. 108.
60. Nancy Mitford, *The Pursuit of Love* (Hamish Hamilton, 1945), p. 138 in Penguin edition, 1976.

6 Psychoanalysis

1. Samuel Butler, *The Way of all Flesh* (Grant Richards, 1903), p. 54 in Penguin edition, 1980.

2. W. H. Auden, 'In Memory of Sigmund Freud', p. 66, in *W. H. Auden*, A Selection by the Author (Penguin, 1958).

3. Barbara Low, *op. cit.*, p. 61.

4. Dora Russell, *The Tamarisk Tree 2* (Virago, 1980), p. 21.

5. Frank Swinnerton, *The Georgian Literary Scene* (Heinemann, 1935), p. 402.

6. Katharine Mansfield, in *The Atheneum* (London, 22 October 1920), *Novels and Novelists, op. cit.*, p. 274.

7. Virginia Woolf, 'Freudian Fiction', 1920, reprinted in *Contemporary Writers* (The Hogarth Press, 1965), p. 152.

8. May Sinclair, *Far End* (Hutchinson, 1926), pp. 106–110.

9. William James, *Principles of Psychology* (London, 1890), quoted in Walter Allen, *The English Novel* (Phoenix House, 1954), p. 345 in Penguin edition, 1958.

10. May Sinclair, 'The Novels of Dorothy Richardson', *The Little Review* (London, April 1918).

11. Virginia Woolf, review of *The Tunnel*, February 1919, reprinted in *Contemporary Writers, op. cit.*, p. 120.

12. Frank Swinnerton, *The Georgian Literary Scene, op. cit.*, p. 403.

13. Virginia Woolf, 'Modern Fiction', *The Common Reader* (London, 1925), p. 188.

14. Dorothy Richardson, Foreword to *Pilgrimage* 1938, quoted in R. A. Scott-James, *Fifty Years of English Literature* (Longmans, 1951), p. 137.

15. Virginia Woolf, 'Mr Bennett and Mrs Brown', May 1924, reprinted in *Collected Essays* Volume One (The Hogarth Press, 1966), p. 330.

16. Dorothy Richardson, *Revolving Lights* (Duckworth, 1923), the seventh novel in the *Pilgrimage* sequence, p. 304 of Volume Three of the Virago edition, 1979.

17. Patrick Braybrooke, *Some Goddesses of the Pen* (C. W. Daniel, 1927), p. 45.

18. Rosamond Lehmann, *The Weather in the Streets, op. cit.*, p. 263.

19. *Ibid.*, p. 303.

20. Rosamond Lehmann, 'The Future of the Novel', in *Britain Today* (London, June 1946).

21. Rosamond Lehmann, 'Rosamond Lehmann Reading', in *New World Writing* Number Two (London, 1952).

22. Katharine Mansfield, *Letters, op. cit.*, 13 October 1920, p. 53.

23. Ethel Colburn Mayne, 'Light', *Nine of Hearts* (London, 1923), p. 180.

24. Letter from G. B. Stern to May Sinclair, 15 June 1919, quoted in T. E. M. Boll, *Miss May Sinclair: Novelist* (Rutherford, New Jersey, Fairleigh Dickinson University Press, 1973), p. 122.

25. Virginia Woolf, review of *Revolving Lights*, May 1923, reprinted in *Contemporary Writers, op. cit.,* p. 124.

26. Katharine Mansfield, in *The Atheneum* (London, 20 June 1919), *Novels and Novelists, op. cit.,* p. 42.

27. May Sinclair, *Mary Olivier* (Cassell, 1919), p. 249 in Virago edition, 1980.

28. *E. M. Forster, A Life* by P. N. Furbank (Secker & Warburg, 1977), Volume One, p. 193.

29. Virginia Woolf, 'Mr Bennett and Mrs Brown', May 1924, *Collected Essays* Volume One, *op. cit.,* p. 320.

30. May Sinclair, *The Romantic, op. cit.,* p. 245.

31. Rebecca West, *The Return of the Soldier* (Nisbet, 1918); p. 187 in Virago edition, 1980.

32. *Ibid.,* p. 163.

33. E. M. Delafield, *The Way Things Are, op. cit.,* p. 100.

34. Rosalind Wade, *Treasure in Heaven, op. cit.,* p. 377.

35. Rebecca West, 'The Long Chain of Criticism', 1926, reprinted in *The Strange Necessity* (Jonathan Cape, 1928), p. 262.

36. *The Sickle Sidē of the Moon*, The Letters of Virginia Woolf Volume V 1932–1935, ed. Nigel Nicolson (The Hogarth Press, 1979), 19 March 1932, p. 36.

37. Winifred Holtby, *Virginia Woolf, op. cit.,* p. 29.

38. Rose Macaulay, *Dangerous Ages* (Collins, 1921), p. 112.

39. *Ibid.,* p. 265.

40. George Egerton, in John Gawsworth, ed., *Ten Contemporaries, op. cit.,* p. 58.

7 Romance

1. Rebecca West, review of Ethel M. Dell's *Charles Rex, New Statesman* (London, 16 September 1922), reprinted in *The Strange Necessity, op. cit.,* p. 320 as 'The Tosh Horse'.

2. Storm Jameson, 'The Craft of the Novelist', 1932, reprinted in *Civil Journey* (Cassell, 1939), pp. 58–61.

3. Q. D. Leavis, *Fiction and the Reading Public* (Chatto & Windus, 1932), p. 74.

4. Mary McCarthy, 'On Madame Bovary', 1964, in *The Writing on the Wall* (Weidenfeld & Nicolson, 1970), p. 72.

5. Michael Joseph, *The Commercial Side of Literature* (Hutchinson, 1925), p. 9.

6. Georgette Heyer, *Regency Buck* (Heinemann, 1935), p. 316 in Pan edition, 1972.

7. George Orwell, 'In Defence of the Novel', 1936, reprinted in *The Collected Essays, Journalism and Letters of George Orwell* Volume One (Secker & Warburg, 1968), p. 284 in Penguin edition, 1970.

8. George Orwell, 'Inside the Whale' 1940, reprinted, *op. cit.*, p. 570.

9. Ethel M. Dell, *The Way of an Eagle* (Fisher Unwin, 1912), p. 27.

10. *Ibid.*, p. 56.

11. *Ibid.*, p. 298.

12. *Ibid.*, p. 313.

13. *Ibid.*, p. 354.

14. *Ibid.*, p. 355.

15. A. C. Ward, *The Nineteen-Twenties* (Methuen, 1930), p. 193.

16. A. P. Herbert, *Riverside Nights* (London, 1926) quoted in A. C. Ward, *ibid.*, p. 191.

17. Rebecca West, *The Strange Necessity, op. cit* ., p. 325.

18. Q. D. Leavis, *Fiction and the Reading Public, op. cit.*, p. 64.

19. Anthony Glyn, *Elinor Glyn* (Hutchinson, 1955), p. 129 in 1968 edition.

20. Radio interview, 15 January 1975.

21. Elinor Glyn, *Three Weeks* (Duckworth, 1907), p. 127.

22. *Ibid.*, p. 173.

23. *Ibid.*, p. 199.

24. Alec Craig, *The Banned Books of England* (G. Allen & Unwin, 1962), p. 73.

25. Victoria Cross, *Anna Lombard* (John Long, 1901), p. 167 in Queensway Library edition n.d.

26. The *Bookman* (London, July 1922).

27. E. M. Hull, *The Sheik* (Eveleigh Nash, 1919), p. 59.

28. Rebecca West, *The Strange Necessity, op. cit* ., p. 323.

29. Norah James, *Sleeveless Errand* (New York: Morrow, 1929), p. 227.

30. E. M. Hull, *The Desert Healer* (Grayson & Grayson, 1923), p. 277.
31. The *Bookman* (London, June 1923).
32. Bernhard Bauer, *Women, op. cit.*, p. 260.
33. D. H. Lawrence, *Lady Chatterley's Lover* (privately printed abroad, 1928), p. 7 in Penguin edition, 1961.
34. *Ibid.*, p. 131.
35. George Eliot, 'Silly Novels by Lady Novelists', 1856, reprinted in *Collected Essays*, ed. T. Pinney (Routledge & Kegan Paul, 1963), p. 300.
36. Berta Ruck, *A Story-Teller Tells the Truth* (Hutchinson, 1935), p. 406.
37. Angela Thirkell, *High Rising* (Hamish Hamilton, 1933), p. 14 in Penguin edition, 1941.
38. *My Weekly*, January 1920, quoted in Cynthia White, *Women's Magazines, op. cit.*, p. 98.
39. Boots *First Literary Course, op. cit.*

8 Love

1. Nancy Mitford, *The Pursuit of Love, op. cit.*, p. 125.
2. *Ibid.*, p. 129.
3. *Ibid.*, p. 192.
4. *Ibid.*, p. 159.
5. Vera Brittain, *Honourable Estate* (Gollancz, 1936), p. 13.
6. *Ibid.*, p. 328.
7. *Ibid.*, p. 425.
8. *Ibid.*, p. 440.
9. Molly Haskell, *From Reverence to Rape* (New English Library, 1975), p. 158.
10. Noel Coward, *Still Life, op. cit.*, p. 363.
11. E. M. Delafield, *The Way Things Are, op. cit.*, p. 240.
12. E. M. Delafield, *Three Marriages* (Macmillan, 1939), p. 339.
13. Ann Bridge, *Four-Part Setting* (Chatto & Windus, 1939), p. 393.
14. Rosamond Lehmann, *The Weather in the Streets, op. cit.*, p. 165.
15. Rosamond Lehmann, *Dusty Answer* (Chatto & Windus, 1927), p. 302 in Penguin edition, 1981.
16. Simon Raven, in the *London Magazine* (London, April 1963), p. 62.

17. Elizabeth von Arnim, *Vera* (Macmillan, 1921), p. 58.
18. *Ibid.*, p. 63.
19. *Ibid.*, p. 147.
20. Rosamond Lehmann, *A Note in Music*, *op. cit.*, p. 251.
21. Margaret Kennedy, *Together and Apart* (Cassell, 1936), p. 25 in Virago edition, 1981.
22. *Ibid.*, p. 59.
23. Helena Wright, *The Sex Factor in Marriage*, *op. cit.*, p. 77.
24. H. G. Wells, *Mr Britling Sees It Through*, *op. cit.*, p. 105.
25. Katharine Mansfield, in *The Atheneum*, 19 November 1920, reprinted in *Novels and Novelists*, *op. cit.*, p. 296.
26. E. B. C. Jones, *Quiet Interior* (Richard Cobden-Sanderson, 1920), p. 264.
27. Ethel Mannin, *Hunger of the Sea* (Jarrolds, 1924), p. 216.
28. E. Arnot Robertson, *Ordinary Families*, *op. cit.*, p. 330.
29. Stella Gibbons, *Miss Linsey and Pa*, *op. cit.*, p. 116.
30. *Ibid.*, p. 141.
31. Vita Sackville-West, *The Edwardians* (The Hogarth Press, 1930), p. 15 in Penguin edition, 1935.
32. *Ibid.*, p. 171.
33. Rebecca West, *The Thinking Reed*, *op. cit.*, p. 308.
34. Kate O'Brien, *Pray for the Wanderer* (Heinemann, 1938), p. 88.
35. Bill Webb in the *Guardian* (London, 14 December 1967).
36. F. M. Mayor, *The Rector's Daughter*, *op. cit.*, p. 76.

Epilogue

1. Vita Sackville-West, *All Passion Spent*, *op. cit.*, p. 178.
2. Dorothy Whipple, *Greenbanks* (John Murray, 1932), p. 330.
3. Dorothy Whipple, *The Priory* (John Murray, 1939), p. 424.
4. E. M. Delafield, *Ladies and Gentlemen in Victorian Fiction* (The Hogarth Press, 1937), p. 12.
5. Jonathan Hill, *The Cat's Whiskers — Fifty Years of Wireless Design* (Oresko Books, 1978), p. 53 and Ruth Adam, *A Woman's Place*, *op. cit.*, p. 98.
6. Virginia Woolf, *The Diary of Virginia Woolf* Volume 111, *op. cit.*, 11 July and 10 August 1927, p. 146 and p. 151.
7. Evelyn Waugh, *Unconditional Surrender* (Chapman & Hall, 1961), p. 146 in Penguin edition, 1964.

8. Joyce Grenfell, 'The Countess of Coteley', reprinted in *Stately as a Galleon* (Macmillan, 1978), p. 32 in Futura edition, 1979.
9. Storm Jameson, *Journey from the North* I (Collins, 1969), p. 301.
10. Philip Toynbee, 'The Decline and Future of the English Novel', in *The Penguin New Writing* Number 23 (Penguin, 1945), p. 128.
11. Mollie Panter-Downes, *One Fine Day* (Hamish Hamilton, 1947), p. 9.
12. *Ibid.*, p. 11.
13. *Ibid.*, p. 17.
14. *Ibid.*, p. 74.
15. *Ibid.*, p. 148.

Glossary

This glossary is not comprehensive, but gives some salient facts about most of the English women novelists mentioned in *A Very Great Profession*. It omits those novelists who, because of the author's personal taste, or because they failed to 'fit in', have not been included in this book – such as Antonia White, Julia Strachey, Ivy Compton-Burnett, Jean Rhys or Edith Olivier; all of them excellent writers who, through no fault of their prose, did not seem relevant to any of the eight chapters.

There is no bibliography in the conventional sense because nearly all the books used are referred to in the notes. There are a few that have been indirectly useful and that would be essential reading for anyone interested in pursuing the subject further, such as Colin Watson's *Snobbery with Violence* (Eyre & Spottiswoode, 1971) or Rachel Anderson's *The Purple Heart Throbs* (Hodder & Stoughton, 1974). It will become rapidly evident from the notes that I have tried to use primary sources throughout – partly because there are very few secondary sources (the two examples just given are rare exceptions) and partly to convey a sense of period.

Elizabeth von Arnim, also known as Elizabeth, Countess von Arnim and Countess Russell, 1866–1941: a cousin of Katharine Mansfield, she had a great success with her first novel *Elizabeth and her German Garden* (1898) about her life with her first husband on their estate in Pomerania. Later she was briefly married to Earl Russell – Wemyss in

Vera (1921) is thought to have something of his character. *Love* (1925) is a memorable novel about an older woman and a younger man. Her daughter Leslie de Charms has written a good biography, *Elizabeth of the German Garden* (1958).

Cynthia Asquith 1887–1960: daughter of the 11th Earl of Wemyss, she married Herbert Asquith, the son of H. H. Asquith (Prime Minister 1908–16). During the First World War she kept a detailed and fascinating diary which was published in 1968. She was for a while a close friend of D. H. Lawrence and was secretary to J. M. Barrie for nearly twenty years; she herself wrote and edited many books, mostly for children and on subjects connected with royalty. Her novel *The Spring House* (1936) draws on the material in her diary.

Enid Bagnold 1889–1981: wrote *A Diary without Dates* (1918) about her nursing experiences and *The Happy Foreigner* (1920) about serving with a French transport unit. She lived with her family in London and in the beautiful house in Rottingdean in Sussex which is the setting for *The Squire* (1938). She wrote a few other novels and some successful plays; *Serena Blandish* (1925) is by 'A Lady of Quality'.

Mary Borden 1886–1968: an American who settled in England upon her marriage. She worked with a mobile hospital in France and was awarded the Croix de Guerre and made a member of the Legion of Honour. *The Forbidden Zone* (1929), about the war, is her best work, but her novels are very readable, especially *Passport for a Girl* (1939) about English attitudes to the rise of Nazism. A favourite subject was the impact of the Old World on an arrival from the New.

Elizabeth Bowen 1889–1973: born in Ireland, she lived in England with her husband and began writing in the early 1920s. She is a novelist of outstanding technique and verbal power. *The Death of the Heart* (1938) and *The Heat of the Day* (1949) are her best novels, although *Friends and Relations* (1931) is her most readable; it makes an interesting comparison with her friend Rosamond Lehmann's *The Echoing Grove* (1953).

Ann Bridge 1891–1974: pseudonym of Mary, later Lady O'Malley. Lived with relations in Italy as a child and, upon her marriage to a diplomat, lived in China, Dalmatia, Turkey etc; these countries provided the settings for her excellent novels. Like so many of her contemporaries she 'fitted in' her writing when she could, usually writing for a mere couple of hours a day before breakfast; she, too, was very shy of personal publicity. It is interesting to compare her novels of

Foreign Office life with that other excellent example of the genre, Mary McMinnies's *The Visitors* (1958), which is about the wife of a diplomat in Poland.

Vera Brittain 1896–1970: her experiences during the First World War are described in *Testament of Youth* (1933), her most famous work. After a provincial upbringing in Buxton and a career at Somerville interrupted by the war, she devoted her energies to political causes, especially pacifism, and to freelance journalism and writing novels. Her friendship with Winifred Holtby is well documented; her daughter is the politician Shirley Williams. Many of her novels are reworkings of the cataclysm of the First World War in one form or another.

Elizabeth Cambridge 1893–1949: pseudonym of Barbara Hodges. She was both the daughter and the wife of country doctors, and almost all of her novels have a medical background. *The Two Doctors* (1936) is about the petty jealousies of village life; *Hostages to Fortune* (1933) decribes the harshness of this life during the 1920s and is perceptive on the subject of child-rearing.

Dorothy Canfield, also known as Dorothy Canfield Fisher, 1879–1958: an American author with a deep interest in family life, education and the New England farming community in which she lived. *Home Fires in France* (1918) consists of stories based on her own experience of life in France during the First World War. *The Brimming Cup* (1921), *The Home-Maker* (1924) and *Her Son's Wife* (1926) are all excellent novels on domestic themes.

E. M. Delafield 1890–1943: pseudonym of Edmée Elizabeth Monica de la Pasture, daughter of Mrs Henry de la Pasture who also wrote novels. *The War-Workers* (1918) drew on her experiences as a VAD. In 1921 she settled with her husband in Devon and wrote many very witty novels, *The Way Things Are* (1927), *The Diary of a Provincial Lady* (1930) and *Thank Heaven Fasting* (1932) being her best. She often satirised the kind of life she herself lived – the JP, mother, pillar of the community role. She also wrote some plays, some non-fiction and a great deal of journalism.

Ethel M. Dell 1881–1939: an extremely popular novelist who achieved her first success with *The Way of an Eagle* (1912). Thirty-four other novels followed, all with the same salient characteristics. She led an extraordinarily retiring life, locking herself into the bathroom to write and knitting her own clothes rather than having to face the publicity of a changing room. Her life has been well described by her adopted daughter Penelope Dell in *Nettie and Sissie* (1977).

Leonora Eyles 1889–1960: the daughter of the owner of a Staffordshire pottery works, she had a deep understanding of working men and women. *Margaret Protests* (1919) is a powerful novel about the difficulties of women's lives, and *The Woman in the Little House* (1922) pursues the same theme in a documentary form. She also wrote more novels, books on women's careers and home economics, e.g. *Eat Well in Wartime* (1940) and, finally, *Commonsense About Sex* (1956).

Stella Gibbons 1902 – : worked as a journalist before publishing her highly successful *Cold Comfort Farm* (1932), a very funny novel which parodies 'rural' novelists such as Mary Webb and the Powys brothers. Although she has written thirty-four other books, none of them ever had quite the success of her first. *Here Be Dragons* (1956) should not be overlooked.

Elinor Glyn 1864–1943: her career as a novelist began in 1900 but it was *Three Weeks* (1907) that brought her fame and success, for it was an overnight sensation, eventually selling over two million copies. She continued to produce extravagantly romantic novels, writing over forty in all, and was renowned for her personal charisma and rather caustic wit. Her grandson, Anthony Glyn, wrote her biography in 1955.

Radclyffe Hall 1883–1943: began by writing poetry and then turned to novels, of which her best is *The Unlit Lamp* (1924) and her most notorious *The Well of Loneliness* (1928). This was a study of lesbianism, and although it was far less explicit than Rosamond Lehmann's *Dusty Answer*, published the year before, it attracted far more attention because of its plea for tolerance, and was banned in Britain as an obscene libel. *Miss Ogilvie Finds Herself* (1934) is a volume of short stories on the theme in which she had a lifelong interest – psychical research.

Cicely Hamilton 1872–1952: worked as a teacher, actress and journalist, was active in the suffrage movement and fought for other causes such as birth control and pacifism. *Marriage as a Trade* (1909) is as anti-romantic as its title suggests. *William – An Englishman* (1919) is an excellent novel about the First World War, while *Theodore Savage* (1922) is a grim vision of anarchy. She also wrote plays, travel books, a very good authobiography, *Life Errant* (1935), and, during the Second World War, *Lament for Democracy*.

Georgette Heyer 1902–74: like Ethel M. Dell and E. M. Hull, she had a horror of personal publicity and was virtually a recluse, although, like many very private people, was intensely loyal to her small circle of friends. Her success as a novelist began with *These Old Shades* (1926) and all her subsequent novels were either popular historical romances set largely in the Regency period, or detective novels.

Winifred Holtby 1898–1935: born in Yorkshire, she was at Somerville with, among others, Vera Brittain. She joined the staff of Lady Rhondda's *Time and Tide* and was a director from 1926. Her novel *The Crowded Street* (1924) is very fine, although her reputation rests on *South Riding* (1936).

E. M. Hull (no dates available): the shy, retiring wife of a gentleman-farmer in Derbyshire, she wrote her bestsellers to make money for her family; she started writing her most famous novel *The Sheik* (1919) to alleviate boredom while her husband was away during the First World War. All her subsequent novels had desert settings although she is alleged never to have been there (just as Ethel M. Dell never went to India).

Norah James 1901–79: was organising secretary to the Civil Service Clerical Association and worked in publishing. She wrote many novels, often one a year, and specialised in hospital romances; her most notorious was *Sleeveless Errand* (1929) because it was banned in England. Every bookshop known to have copies in stock was raided – although no one was ever quite sure why.

Storm Jameson 1891– : born in Yorkshire, she married Professor Guy Chapman and wrote many books, short stories, plays, criticism and forty-five novels. A lifelong and passionate liberal, her *In the Second Year* (1936) is a horrifying indictment of fascism.

F. Tennyson Jesse 1889–1958: was a freelance correspondent in the First World War and wrote many novels of which *The Lacquer Lady* (1929) is perhaps the best. She often wrote about murders and murder trials and, like E. M. Delafield, wrote a book about the Thompson-Bywaters murder trial, *A Pin to see the Peepshow* (1934).

E. B. C. Jones 1893–1966: was for a while married to the Cambridge don F. L. Lucas and was known as 'Topsy'. She is sometimes mentioned in rather cutting tones in Virginia Woolf's letters and diaries; Lytton Strachey was, however, fond of her. Her first novel *Quiet Interior* (1920) has great power and charm and her other novels deserve attention as well.

Sheila Kaye-Smith 1887–1956: married an Anglican clergyman, but both became Roman Catholics in 1929. Her novels are regional ones set in the Sussex she knew and loved. *Joanna Godden* (1921) is one of her best, revealing her deep affection for the countryside and its people. She is one of that group of novelists (Mary Webb and Constance Holme are others) whose work was satirised by, among others, Stella Gibbons in *Cold Comfort Farm* (1932). Her novels were once much more popular than those of most of her contemporaries.

Margaret Kennedy 1896–1967: after reading history at Oxford during the First World War she wrote the superb *The Ladies of Lyndon* (1923), but achieved overnight success with *The Constant Nymph* (1924). She wrote many other novels and had a wide following but never wrote another novel which caught the public imagination in quite the same way.

Rosamond Lehmann 1901– : a renowned beauty and Girton scholar, her first novel *Dusty Answer* (1927) was an immediate success, partly because of the delicate yet sensuous manner in which it handled the theme of lesbianism. All her novels reveal great insight into the feminine mind and are indeed wonderfully readable works of fiction; until recently she was probably one of the most underrated novelists of the interwar period.

Rose Macaulay 1881–1958: spent her childhood in Italy and after Oxford started to write the satirical novels with which she had such a great success. *Told by an Idiot* (1923) and the historical *They Were Defeated* (1932) are among her best novels; she is another novelist whose fame has been greatly eclipsed in recent years and whose novels, almost more than anyone else's, have become period pieces. Her possessions having been destroyed in the Blitz, she wrote a brilliant short story 'Miss Anstruther's Letters' based on this disaster.

Ethel Mannin 1900– : a very popular and prolific novelist whose books have stayed in demand. She joined the Independent Labour Party in 1932 and has been a lifelong campaigner for sexual freedom. Born in London of working-class origins, she worked in advertising and journalism before turning to writing her very readable novels.

Katharine Mansfield 1888–1923: a short story writer whose life, curtailed by tuberculosis, has been exhaustively documented. *Prelude* (1918) was her first story published in book form and is considered by many to be her finest achievement. Her letters, journals and reviews are outstanding literary works, the latter proving fascinating comparison with the reviews of Rebecca West and Virginia Woolf.

Ethel Colburn Mayne 1870–1941: best known as a short story writer, she also wrote biographies. During the second decade of the century her work was very well known. *Nine of Hearts* (1923) has one or two very touching stories; her Irish background is often apparent in her writing.

F. M. Mayor 1872–1932: she came from an academic background and went up to Newnham to read history. Forced by ill-health to give up the idea of acting, she published her first novel in 1901. Her second, *The Third Miss Symons* (1913), was praised by reviewers, more so than *The Rector's Daughter* (1924), her masterpiece. Because of illness, she led a very retiring life.

Naomi Mitchison 1897– : married at the age of nineteen, she led an elaborate domestic and social life, but managed to become a well-known historical novelist, often using ancient Greece and Rome as settings. *The Corn King and the Spring Queen* (1931) is one of her best-known novels. Much of her energies were devoted to political and social causes. Her autobiographies give a fascinating picture of her own life and of the society in which she lived.

Nancy Mitford 1904–73: the daughter of Lord Redesdale, she was educated at home and grew up in the inimitable atmosphere which is familiar to readers of her most famous novel *The Pursuit of Love* (1945). She moved to Paris after the war, partly in order to be near her lover (who evidently had many similarities to Fabrice in *The Pursuit of Love*.) In later years she wrote biographies and studies in French history, and helped to edit *Noblesse Oblige* (1956) about the definition of 'U' and 'non-U'.

Elinor Mordaunt 1877–1942: her life with her first husband, a planter in Mauritius, provided the settings for some of her novels, giving them overtones not dissimilar from those found in the novels of her contemporary Jean Rhys. *The Family* (1915) and *The Park Wall* (1916) are excellent, very underrated novels on domestic themes. Her life was very varied, full of death and disaster, and all her novels are worth reading. Her work influenced that of Rosamond Lehmann.

Kate O'Brien 1897–1974: most of her novels were set either in Ireland (where she was born) or Spain, since she knew both countries intimately. She saw deeply into the psychology of the Irish middle-class, and also often wrote about religious conflict. *Without my Cloak* (1931) and *That Lady* (1946) are among her best novels. Laura Jesson appears to have one of her novels in her shopping basket in the film *Brief Encounter*.

Mollie Panter-Downes 1906– : another novelist with an Irish background, her first novel was published when she was eighteen. She seems to have written a few popular novels when young, but ignores these in her list of publications in *Who's Who*. From 1939 onwards she was the *New Yorker*'s London Correspondent. In my opinion *One Fine Day* (1947) is one of the few great novels of the 1940s.

Dorothy Richardson 1873–1957: author of one novel *Pilgrimage* which was published in thirteen parts from 1915–1938. Her detailed exploration of the life and mind of her *alter ego* Miriam Henderson can appear daunting but her technique anticipated that of James Joyce. Her life has been well documented by biographers. She was a close friend of Mrs H. G. Wells.

E. Arnot Robertson 1903–61: a novelist whose light, ironic, sometimes bitter, touch disguised a woman of fiercely independent feeling. She wrote her best novels in the five years 1928–1933; *Ordinary Families* (1933) has had a lasting success. Her descriptive powers were outstanding, particularly in *Four Frightened People* (1931) in which she brilliantly evoked the Malay jungle without ever having been there. In her later years she wrote trenchant film criticism. By some she is remembered with affection for her remark that Hampstead is not just a place but a way of life.

Berta Ruck 1878–1978: after a childhood in Wales, she married another writer, Oliver Onions, and turned to writing romantic novels. She was at the height of her popularity in the 1930s and earned enormous advances, often larger than those of her rivals Ruby M. Ayres, May Christie and Margaret Pedlar. (She is mentioned in Virginia Woolf's letters and diaries: there was an incident when the latter used her name unconsciously in one of her novels, presumably because she had, again unconsciously, noticed the name Berta Ruck on the side of an omnibus, where it often appeared advertising her latest book.)

Vita Sackville-West 1892–1962: born at Knole, she married Harold Nicolson but this is no way diminished the varied nature of her private life. Her love affair with Violet Trefusis has been described by her son Nigel Nicolson in *Portrait of a Marriage* (1973), while her relationship with Virginia Woolf is recorded in great detail in the latter's diaries and letters. Virginia Woolf's *Orlando* (1928) is a fictional portrait of her; *The Edwardians* (1930) and *All Passion Spent* (1931) are her best novels. The last twenty-five years of her life were devoted to gardening and to writing about it.

Beatrice Kean Seymour 1890–1955: married to a fellow writer William Kean Seymour, she wrote many novels which were popular at the time but are now hard to find; usually she wrote a new novel every two years. *The Romantic Tradition* (1925) and *Youth Rides Out* (1928) have charm and power but never pretend to be profound. She was one of the many women novelists (G. B. Stern, Sheila Kaye-Smith, Margaret Kennedy and Elizabeth Jenkins are among the others) who wrote a study of Jane Austen.

May Sinclair 1870–1946: one of the most important novelists of the early twentieth century, she has been largely forgotten until the last few years, although she exercised a profound influence on, for example, Rosamond Lehmann and Rebecca West. *Mary Olivier* (1919) is her outstanding achievement, but all her novels have memorable qualities, being about the life of the mind rather than a world of action and excitement. No life of her has so far been written except that by the American T. E. M. Boll (1973).

G. B. Stern 1890–1973: a novelist who gained a wide following for her 'Matriarch' novels about the Jewish Rakonitz family, of which the first was *Tents of Israel* (1924). She was a friend of May Sinclair's, and was once highly regarded as a writer, for example Somerset Maugham considered her one of the great novelists of the century.

Jan Struther 1901–53: pseudonym of Joyce Anstruther. She contributed to *Punch* for many years from 1927, and also wrote for other publications. Her outstanding success was *Mrs Miniver* (1939), originally a series for *The Times*, based on her own family life. The film on which it was based is alleged to have helped precipitate American entry into World War Two.

Angela Thirkell 1890–1961: only after two failed marriages did she begin to write her popular middlebrow novels, often set in Trollope's imaginary Barsetshire. Burne-Jones was her grandfather, Rudyard Kipling a cousin, and she used to spend childhood holidays at Rottingdean (cf. Enid Bagnold) and wrote *Three Houses* (1930) about it. Denis Mackail, author of *Greenery Street* (1925) and a close friend of J. M. Barrie, was her brother.

Sylvia Thompson 1902–68: soon after she came down from Oxford she published the very successful *The Hounds of Spring* (1926). She wrote many subsequent novels but never recaptured the bestselling magic. In 1926 she married an American artist and lived in Venice until the

Second World War. Almost all her novels are about young people between the wars.

Rosalind Wade 1909– : was the second wife of William Kean Seymour (cf. Beatrice Kean Seymour). She has written many novels and has led an active public life connected with writing. *Treasure in Heaven* (1937) deserves to be remembered, and all her novels are readable.

Rebecca West 1892– : pseudonym of Cicily Fairfield. Began her long and distinguished career as a journalist when she was nineteen and soon gained a reputation for clarity and wit. Her book reviews, especially those in the *New Statesman* in the 1920s, have for far too long remained uncollected. The short novels contained in *The Harsh Voice* (1935) are perhaps her most memorable works of fiction, although all her novels are, in their way, excellent; the post-war *The Fountain Overflows* (1957) is considered by some to be her best work of fiction.

Dorothy Whipple 1890–1966: a once popular writer who is now largely forgotten, although she has been called 'a North-Country Jane Austen.' *Greenbanks* (1932) has a great deal of period charm. She wrote her autobiography in 1936.

Virginia Woolf 1882–1941: her reputation eclipsed for many years after her death, but she has become in recent years the best-known woman writer of the twentieth century. Her novels are sometimes thought difficult, although most enjoy *The Voyage Out* (1915) and *Night and Day* (1919). Her literary criticism was of the highest quality and her letters and diaries, now nearing complete publication, are among the great documents of the century; few other women, except perhaps Anaïs Nin and Anne Morrow Lindbergh, have kept such a detailed and absorbing record of their day-to-day existence. *A Room of One's Own* (1929) has rightly had a far-reaching influence on women's perceptions of themselves.

Index

abortion, 136

acceptance of limitations by middle class, 44–51

Acton, 121

adultery, 125–7, 139–40, 204–10

age difference in love affairs, 220

Age of Innocence, The (Wharton) 203–4

Alas, Poor Lady (Ferguson), 60–1

Allen, Grant
The Woman Who Did (1895), 41

Allinghams, The (Sinclair), 55, 130–1

All Passion Spent (Sackville-West), 54, 92–3, 225

Anna Karenina (Tolstoy), 204

Anna Lombard (Cross), 187–8, 191, 194

Ann Veronica (Wells), 43, 66–9, 191

Arlen, Michael
The Green Hat (1924), 129

Armstrong, Martin, 6
St Christopher's Day (1928), 105–6

Arnim, *see* von Arnim

Asquith, Lady Cynthia
Diaries (1915–18), 24–5, 106
The Spring House (1936), 25–6

Attainment (Ellis), 66

Auden, W.H., 147

Austen, Jane, 14, 175

autonomy of women, 226–8

Ayres, Ruby M., 124, 174, 195

babies, *see* children

Bagnold, Enid, 104, 118, 129
A Diary Without Dates (1918) 22–4
The Happy Foreigner (1920), 19
The Squire (1938), 91, 117–19

Bauer, Bernhard
Woman (1927), 133–4, 192–3

Bell, Quentin, 103–4

Below Stairs (Powell), 109

Benson, Stella, 92

bestseller, definition of, 73–4, 177

Betjeman, John, 10

birth control, 122, 123, 134–41

Bland, Rosalind, 67

Boots, 9, 10, 13, 173–4, 197

Borden, Mary
  The Forbidden Zone (1929), 32–4
  Sarah Gay (1931), 34–5

Bowen, Elizabeth 3–4
  Death of the Heart (1938), 11

Boyle, Kay
  Plagued by the Nightingale (1931), 155

Braddon, Miss, 124

Bradlaugh-Besant, 122

Braybrooke, Patrick, 155

Brideshead Revisited (Waugh), 157, 211

Bridge, Ann
  Four-Part Setting (1939), 208

Brief Encounter, 1, 144, 204–5

Brimming Cup, The (Canfield), 91, 119–20

Brittain, Vera, 16, 20, 107
  Testament of Youth (1933), 35, 202
  Honourable Estate (1936), 202–3
  Testament of Friendship (1942), 67

Broughton, Rhoda, 124

Butler, Samuel, 147

Cambridge, Elizabeth
  Hostages to Fortune (1933), 90–1, 116–17

Canfield, Dorothy
  Home Fires in France (1919), 20
  The Brimming Cup (1921), 91, 119–20
  The Home-Maker (1924), 80–2

Cannan, May Wedderburn, 16, 35–6
  The Lonely Generation (1934), 36

careers, women with, 59–60, 74–82; *see also* creative women

Carpenter, Edward
  Love's Coming of Age (1906), 131

cars as benefit to women, 229

Cassandra (Nightingale), 38

Cause, The (Strachey), 38

Challenge (Sackville-West), 190

Charles Rex (Dell), 190

children, 80–2
  and careers, 75–82, 226
  and creativity, 87–91, 120
  and pleasure, 115–20
  and servants, 106–7
  their sexual fantasies, 148

class distinction in taste in literature, 173–9

Clephane, Irene, 144
  Towards Sex Freedom (1935), 139–40

Cold Comfort Farm (Gibbons), 55, 127–8

Commercial Side of Literature, The (Joseph), 176–8

Company Parade (Jameson), 79

Compton-Burnett, Ivy, 6

conclusions drawn from this book, 225–6

conformity, sexual, 128–9

Connolly, Cyril, 82

Consequences (Delafield), 46–9

contraception, *see* birth control

convention, influence of, 46–8

Cooper, Lettice
  The New House (1936), 56–8, 107–8

Corelli, Marie, 124

Cornford, Frances, 120

Coward, Noel
  Still Life, 1, 9, 144–5, 163
  Brief Encounter, 1, 144, 204–5

creative women, 86–93

Creators, The (Sinclair), 86–7

Crewe Train (Macaulay), 112–13, 155

Cross, Victoria
  Anna Lombard (1901), 187–8, 191, 194

Crowded Street, The (Holtby), 54–6, 74
Cullum (Robertson), 218

Dane, Clemence
  Regiment of Women (1917), 19
Dangerous Ages (Macaulay), 170–1
Death of the Heart (Bowen), 11
Delafield, E.M., 46, 90, 96, 103, 104, 112, 228
  The War-Workers (1918), 18
  Consequences (1919), 46–9
  The Heel of Achilles (1921), 50–1
  The Way Things Are (1927), 96–7, 99–100, 166, 205–6
  Diary of a Provincial Lady (1930), 9, 89–90, 113–14
  Thank Heaven Fasting (1932), 49–50
  Faster, Faster (1936), 79–80
  We Meant to Be Happy (1939), 206–7
The Delicate Fire (Mitchison), 141–2
Dell, Ethel M., 174, 179, 190
  The Way of an Eagle (1912), 178–83, 194
  Charles Rex (1922), 190
Desert Healer, The (Hull), 191–2
Diana of the Crossways (Meredith) 41
Diaries (Asquith), 24–5, 106
Diary of a Provincial Lady (Delafield), 9, 89–90, 113–14
Diary Without Dates, A (Bagnold), 22–4
Diver, Maud, 194
domesticity, 94–120
double standards, 204
du Maurier, Daphne,
  Rebecca (1938), 178, 200, 211
Dusty Answer (Lehmann), 210–11
duty, restrictions of, 57–8, 61

Edwardians, The (Sackville-West), 220–1
Egerton, George, 69, 92, 171–2
  Keynotes (1893), 41
Ellis, Havelock, 123, 131, 143
  Studies in the Psychology of Sex (1910), 131
Ellis, Mrs Havelock
  Attainment (1909), 66
Eliot, George, 94–5, 195
Emma (Austen), 123
equality, fight for, 69–70
erotic novels, 124, 185–90
Esther Waters (Moore), 122
Eyles, Leonora
  Margaret Protests (1919), 136–7
  The Woman in the Little House (1922), 101–2, 137, 138–9

Family, The (Mordaunt), 37
Family History (Sackville-West), 220
Far End (Sinclair), 89, 150–1
Farewell to Arms, A (Hemingway), 33
Faster, Faster (Delafield), 79–80
feminism, 63–93
  'old' and 'new', 69–70
Ferber, Edna
  So Big (1924), 90
Ferguson, Rachel
  Alas, Poor Lady (1937), 60–1
Fiction and the Reading Public (Leavis), 175
Firth, Violet
  The Psychology of the Servant Problem (1925), 107
Flaubert, Gustave, 175–6
Forbidden Zone, The (Borden), 32–4
formula for romances, 196–7
Forster, E.M. 6, 7, 161–2
  A Room With a View (1908), 6, 7–8, 65–6
  A Passage to India (1924), 194–5

Four Frightened People (Robertson), 143
Four-Part Setting (Bridge), 208
Freud, Sigmund, 123, 125–6, 143, 147–9, 169
Friedlaender, V.H.
  Mainspring (1922), 82–3
Fruits of Knowledge, The (pamphlet), 122

Gibbons, Stella
  Cold Comfort Farm (1932), 55, 127–8
  Miss Linsey and Pa (1936), 106–7, 219–20
Gissing, George
  The Old Women (1893), 41–2
Give and Take (Reeves), 18–19
Glasgow, Ellen, 130
Glyn, Elinor, 124, 185–6, 191
  Three Weeks (1907), 186–7
  His Hour (1910), 185
  Six Days (1924), 187
Gone With the Wind (Mitchell), 178
Good Housekeeping (magazine), 145
good novel, definition of, 5
Goodbye to All That (Graves), 31
Grand, Sarah, 68–9
  The Heavenly Twins (1893), 41
Graves, Robert
  Goodbye to All That (1929), 31
Green Hat, The (Arlen), 129
Greenbanks (Whipple), 226–7
Greenery Street (Mackail), 11–13
Grenfell, Joyce, 230–1
Grier, Sydney C., 194

Haire, Norman, 133–4
Hall, Radclyffe
  The Unlit Lamp (1924), 51–3, 54
  The Well of Loneliness (1928), 190, 191, 192, 219
Hall, Ruth, 132

Hamilton, Cicely, 17, 18, 62, 73, 95
  on suffragism, 63–4
  Marriage as a Trade (1909), 88
  William – An Englishman (1919), 28–31
Happy Foreigner, The (Bagnold), 19
Hardy, Thomas
  Tess of the D'Urbervilles (1890) 122
  Jude the Obscure (1895), 122
Harrison, Frederick, 44–5
Heavenly Twins, The (Grand), 41
Heel of Achilles, The (Delafield), 50–1
Hemingway, Ernest
  A Farewell to Arms (1929), 33
Henrey, Madeleine, 6–7
Herbert, A.P.
  The Water Gypsies (1930), 184
Heritage (Sackville-West), 190
Heyer, Georgette, 177
  Regency Buck (1935), 177
High Rising (Thirkell), 196
history, traditional teaching of, 1–2
Hogarth Press, 169
Holtby, Winifred, 69–70, 82–3, 123, 169–70
  The Crowded Street (1924), 54–6, 74
  South Riding (1935), 59
Home Fires in France (Canfield), 20
Home-Maker, The (Canfield), 80–2
Homes and Gardens (magazine), 109
Honourable Estate (Brittain), 202–3
Hostages to Fortune (Cambridge), 90–1, 116–17
Hounds of Spring, The (Thompson), 31–2
How to Run Your Home Without

Help, 111
Hughes, Molly
  A London Child of the 1870s, 3
Hull, E.M., 124, 189
  The Sheik (1919), 188–90
  The Desert Healer (1923), 191–2
Hunger of the Sea (Mannin) 217–18
Hunt, Violet, 66–7
husbands, 126–7; *see also* marriage
Hutchinson, A.S.M., 6
  This Freedom (1922), 73–6
Hypatia (Russell), 142

independence, failure to achieve, 65–8, 70–82
India as setting for novels, 194–5
Inglis, Elsie, 16
Invitation to the Waltz (Lehmann), 61, 209–10

Jacob's Room (Woolf), 85
James, Norah
  Sleeveless Errand (1929), 190–1
Jameson, Storm, 175, 231
  Three Kingdoms (1926), 76–7, 79
  Company Parade (1934), 79
Jane Eyre (Brontë), 178
jealousy, 216–9
Jesse F. Tennyson
  The Sword of Deborah (1919), 27–8
Joanna Godden (Kaye-Smith), 90
Johnson, Pamela Hansford
  This Bed Thy Centre (1935), 142
Johnson, R. Brimley, 14
Jones, E.B.C.
  Quiet Interior (1920), 216–17
Joseph, Michael
  The Commercial Side of Literature, 176–8

Joyce, James, 143
Jude the Obscure (Hardy), 122
Judge, The (West), 64, 169
Julian Grenfell (Mosley), 15

Kaye-Smith, Sheila, 31
  Joanna Godden (1921), 90
Kennedy, Margaret, 92
  Long Time Ago, A (1932), 213
  Together and Apart (1936), 61, 213–15
Keynotes (Egerton), 41
Krafft-Ebing, 123

Lady and Her Husband, A (Reeves), 90
Lady, The (magazine), 16, 109, 110
Lady, Chatterley's Lover (Lawrence) 190, 193–4
language, sexual, 185, 194
Laslett, Peter
  The World We Have Lost, 3
Lawrence, D.H., 143
  Lady Chatterley's Lover (1928) 190, 193–4
Leavis, Queenie, 4, 185
  Fiction and the Reading Public (1932), 175
lesbianism, 191, 219–20
Lehmann, Rosamond, 4, 153, 157–8, 210–11
  Dusty Answer (1927), 210–11
  A Note in Music (1930), 95, 184, 213
  Invitation to the Waltz (1932), 61, 209–10
  The Weather in the Streets (1936), 54, 126–7, 155–7, 209
libraries, circulating, 10–13
Life and Death of Harriett Frean (Sinclair), 149, 162–3
'Light' (Mayne), 159
Lindbergh, Anne Morrow, 88–9
London Child of the 1870s, A (Hughes), 3

Lonely Generation, The (Cannan), 36
Long Time Ago, A (Kennedy), 213
love, 198–224
Love (von Arnim), 220
Love's Coming of Age (Carpenter), 131
Low, Barbara
  Psycho-Analysis (1920), 148–9

Macaulay, Rose, 17, 143, 170–1
  Dangerous Ages (1921), 170–1
  Told by an Idiot (1923), 72
  Crewe Train (1926), 112–13, 155
  Towers of Trebizond (1956), 171
Mackail, Denis, 6
  Greenery Street (1925), 11–13
Madame Bovary (Flaubert), 175–6
magazines, women's 109–11, 145
Mainspring (Friedlaender), 82–3
Mannin, Ethel
  Hunger of the Sea (1924), 217–18
Mansfield, Katherine, 19, 28, 91–2, 123, 149, 158–9, 160, 216
Marcella (Ward), 65
Margaret Protests (Eyles), 136–7
marriage, 201–2
  and infidelity, 125–7, 204–10
  prospects of middle-class women, 40–1
Marriage as a Trade (Hamilton), 88
Married Love (Stopes), 131–2, 140
martyrdom, female, 79–80; *see also* self-sacrifice
Mary Lavalle (O'Brien), 208–9
Mary Olivier (Sinclair), 51, 159, 160–2
masochism, 186

Matriarch, The (Stern), 72
Mayne, Ethel Colburn
  'Light', 159
Mayor, F.M.
  The Rector's Daughter (1924), 45–6, 223–4
McCarthy, Mary, 176
Memoirs of a Fox-Hunting Man (Sassoon), 31
men
  as lovers, 126–8
  in romantic novels, 184–5
Merchant of Prato (Origo), 3
Meredith, George
  Diana of the Crossways (1895), 41
middlebrow taste in literature, 173–4
middle-class women
  acceptance of limitations by, 44–51
  after Second World War, 232–5
  and careers, 59–60
  expectations of, 43
  in First World War, 17–18, 20
  growing freedom of, 40–1
  marriage prospects of, 40–1
  as subject of this book, 3
Middlemarch (Eliot), 94–5
Miss Linsey and Pa (Gibbons), 106–7, 219–20
Mitchison, Naomi, 102–3, 140–2, 143
  Delicate Fire, The (1933) 141–2
  We Have Been Warned (1935), 98–9, 141
Mitford, Nancy, 210
  The Pursuit of Love (1945), 145–6, 198–201
Moore, George
  Esther Waters (1894), 122
Mordaunt, Eleanor
  The Family (1915), 37
Mosley, Nicholas

Julian Grenfell (1976), 15

Mother (magazine), 109

mothers in fiction, 49–57, 61, 160–1

Mr Britling Sees it Through (Wells) 15–16, 26–7, 215–16

Mrs Dalloway (Woolf), 100, 124–6, 154–5

Mrs Miniver (book – Struther), 9, 13, 114–17

(film), 114

Murry, John Middleton, 91

My Weekly (magazine), 196–7

New House, The (Cooper), 56–8, 107–8

new feminism, 70

'New Woman' novels, 41–4, 65, 122

Night and Day (Woolf), 1, 7, 28, 39–40, 42, 124

Nightingale, Florence, 38, 39

Cassandra (1852), 38

Northanger Abbey (Austen), 175

Note in Music, A (Lehmann), 95, 184, 213

novel, *see under* good novel, propaganda novel, women's novel.

nursing as subject of novels, 22–4, 33–5

O'Brien, Kate

Mary Lavalle (1936), 208–9

Pray for the Wanderer (1938), 222–3

Odd Women, The (Gissing), 41–2

old feminism, 69–70

One Fine Day (Panter-Downes), 231–5

Ordinary Families (Robertson), 58–9, 142–3, 218

Origo, Iris,

The Merchant of Prato, 3

Orlando (Woolf), 124

Orwell, George, 178–9

Ouida, 124

Our Homes and Gardens (magazine), 110–11

Pall Mall Gazette, 150

Pankhurst, Christabel, 122

Panter-Downes, Molly

One Fine Day (1947), 231–5

Passage to India, A (Forster), 194–5

passion and marriage, 201–2

Pedlar, Margaret, 174

Peel, Mrs C., 136

Perrin, Alice, 194

personal revolt, failures in, 65–8, 70–82

Pilgrimage (Richardson), 151–5, 160

Plagued by the Nightingale (Boyle), 155

pleasure, sexual, 125, 128–35

Powell, Margaret, 109

Pray for the Wanderer (O'Brien) 222–3

pregnancy sickness, 155–6

Priory, The (Whipple), 227–8

propaganda novels, 22

Proust, Marcel, 161, 216

psychoanalysis, 147–72

Psycho-Analysis (Low), 148–9

psychological novels, 149–53, 167–71

jargon in, 164

Psychology of the Servant Problem, The (Firth), 107

'pulp' fiction, 174, 178, 202

Pursuit of Love, The (Mitford), 145–6, 198–201

Queen, The (magazine), 109

Quiet Interior (Jones), 216–17

Rachel Moon (Rea), 52–3

Rathbone, Eleanor, 70

Rea, Lorna

Rachel Moon (1931), 52–3

realism, dislike for, 191–2
reality in psychological novels, 165–8
Rebecca (du Maurier), 178, 200, 211
Rebel Generation, The (van Ammers-Küller), 70–2, 79
Rector's Daughter, The (Mayor), 45–6, 223–4
Reeves, Amber, 67
  A Lady and Her Husband (1914), 90
  Give and Take (1923), 18–19
Reeves, Maud Pember
  Round About a Pound a Week (1913), 3, 100
Regency Buck (Heyer), 177
Regiment of Women (Dane), 19
restrictions, slackening of, 122–3
Return of the Soldier, The, (West) 164–6
reverence for war dead, 36
Rice, Margery Spring
  Working-Class Wives, Their Health and Conditions (1939), 100
Richardson, Dorothy, 66–7, 152–5
  Pilgrimage (1915–38), 151–5, 160
Riddell, Lord, 124
Robertson, E. Arnot
  Cullum (1928), 218
  Four Frightened People (1931), 143
  Ordinary Families (1933), 58–9, 142–3, 218
Robins, Denise, 174, 195, 211
Robins, Elizabeth,
  The Convert (1905), 63–4
Romantic, The (Sinclair), 19, 22, 129, 150, 158, 163
romantic novels, 173–97
  increase of psychology in, 195–6
Romantic Tradition, The (Seymour), 129–30
Room of One's Own, A (Woolf), 2, 41, 83
Room With A View, A (Forster), 6, 7–8, 65–6
Round About a Pound a Week (Reeves), 3, 100
Ruck, Berta, 195
Russell, Dora, 70, 144, 149
  Hypatia (1925), 142

Sackville-West, Vita, 92
  Heritage (1919), 190
  Challenge (1923), 190
  The Edwardians (1930), 220–1
  All Passion Spent (1931), 54, 92–3, 225
  Family History (1932), 220
sadism, 188–90
St Christopher's Day (Armstrong) 105–6
'Salt of the Earth, The' (West), 79, 168–9
Sarah Gay (Borden), 34–5
Sassoon, Siegfried
  Memoirs of a Fox-Hunting Man (1928), 31
Schreiner, Olive, 69
  Story of an African Farm (1883), 41
  Woman and Labour (1911), 77–9
self-sacrifice in women, 22–4, 161, 162, 208; *see also* martyrdom
servants, 97, 102–9
Seton, Anya, 177
sex, 121–46
  in romantic novels, 185–90
Sex Factor in Marriage, The (Wright), 134–5, 215
Seymour, Beatrice Kean
  The Romantic Tradition (1925), 129–30
Sheik, The (Hull), 188–90
Sinclair, May, 92, 149–55,

158–60, 163, 213
The Creators (1910), 86–7
The Three Sisters (1914), 160
Tasker Jeavons (1916), 22
The Tree of Heaven (1917), 21, 27, 64–5
Mary Olivier (1919), 160–2
The Romantic (1920), 19, 129, 150, 163–4
The Life and Death of Harriett Frean (1922), 149, 162–3
Far End (1926), 89, 150–1
The Allinghams (1927), 55, 130–1
Sitwell, Edith, 102
Six Days (Glyn), 187
Sleeveless Errand (James), 190–1
So Big (Ferber), 90
South Riding (Holtby), 59
Spark, Muriel, 59–60
Spring House, The (Asquith), 25–6
Squire, The (Bagnold), 91, 117–19, 222
Starkie, Enid, 133
Steel, Flora Annie, 194
Stern, G.B., 160
Tents of Israel (1924), 72–3
Still Life (Coward), 1, 9, 144–5, 163
Stopes, Marie, 131–3, 135
Married Love, (1918), 131–2, 140
Wise Parenthood (1918), 132
Story of an African Farm, The (Schreiner) 41
Strachey, Ray
The Cause (1928), 38
stream of consciousness novels, 150–1, 152
Struther, Jan
Mrs Miniver (1939), 9, 13, 114–17
Studies in the Psychology of Sex (Ellis), 131

suffragettes, during First World War, 17–18
suffragism and feminism, 63–4, 67–8
surplus women, 37–62
Swinnerton, Frank, 149, 151–2
Sword of Deborah, The (Jesse), 27–8

Tasker Jeavons (Sinclair), 22
taste in literature, class distinction in, 173–9
Taylor, A.J.P., 135
Taylor, Elizabeth, 4
Tents of Israel (Stern), 72–3
Tess of the D'Urbervilles (Hardy) 122
Testament of Friendship (Brittain) 67
Testament of Youth (Brittain), 35, 202
Thank Heaven Fasting (Delafield), 49–50
Thinking Reed, The (West), 127, 128–9, 221–2
Third Act in Venice (Thompson), 126
Thirkell, Angela
High Rising (1933), 196
This Bed Thy Centre (Johnson), 142
This Freedom (Hutchinson), 73–6, 109
Thompson, Sylvia
The Hounds of Spring (1926) 31–2
Third Act in Venice (1936), 126
Three Kingdoms (Jameson), 76–7, 79
Three Sisters, The (Sinclair), 160
Three Weeks (Glyn), 186–7
Times, The, 53
Together and Apart (Kennedy), 61, 213–15

Told By An Idiot (Macaulay), 72
'Tommy' casualties in First World War, 35
To The Lighthouse (Woolf), 54, 124
Towards Sex Freedom (Clephane), 139–40
Towers of Trebizond, The (Macaulay), 171
Treasure in Heaven (Wade), 137, 167–8
Tree of Heaven, The (Sinclair), 21, 27, 64–5

unhappy endings, 202
Unlit Lamp, The (Hall), 51–3, 54
unmarried women *see* surplus women

van Ammers-Küller, Jo
The Rebel Generation (1925), 70–2
Vanity Fair (Thackeray), 39
Vera (von Arnim), 211–12
von Arnim, Elizabeth, 66–7
Vera (1921), 211–12
Love (1925), 220
Voyage Out, The (Woolf), 8–9, 83–4, 124

Wade, Rosalind
Treasure in Heaven (1937), 137, 167–8
war novels, 14–36
Ward, Mrs Humphry, 65, 122
Marcella (1894), 65
War-Workers, The (Delafield), 18
Water Gipsies, The (Herbert), 184
Waugh, Evelyn
Brideshead Revisited (1945), 157, 211
Unconditional Surrender (1961), 230

Way of an Eagle, The (Dell), 178–83
Way Things Are, The (Delafield), 96–7, 99–100, 166, 205–6
Weather in the Streets, The (Lehmann), 54, 126–7, 155–7, 209
We Have Been Warned (Mitchison), 98–9, 141
Well of Loneliness, The (Hall), 190, 191, 192, 219
We Meant to be Happy (Delafield), 206–7
Wells, H.G., 6
Ann Veronica (1909), 43, 66–9, 191
Mr Britling Sees It Through (1916), 15–16, 26–7, 215–16
West, Rebecca, 5, 6, 66–7, 91, 119, 160, 168–9, 174–5, 190
The Return of the Soldier, (1918) 164–6
The Judge (1922), 64, 169
'The Salt of the Earth' (1935), 79, 168–9
The Thinking Reed (1936), 127, 128–9, 221–2
Wharton, Edith
The Age of Innocence (1920), 203–4
Whipple, Dorothy
Greenbanks (1932), 226–7
The Priory (1939), 227–8
Wife and Home (magazine), 109
William – An Englishman (Hamilton), 28–31
wireless as benefit to women, 228–9
Wise Parenthood (Stopes), 132
wish-fulfilment, 195
Woman (Bauer), 133–4, 192–3
Woman and Labour (Schreiner), 77–9
Woman in the Little House, The

(Eyles), 101–2, 137, 138–9
Woman Who Did, The (Allen), 41
Woman's Own (magazine), 145
women,
  autonomy of, 226–8
  and careers, 59–60, 74–82
  creative, 86–93
  during First World War, 16–18
  failures in personal revolt, 65–8, 70–82
  working class, 100–2, 136–9
  see also middle-class women
women's magazines, 109–11
women's novel, definition of, 5
women's sexual pleasures, 125, 128–35
Woolf, Virginia, 4, 14, 61, 85, 90, 92, 98, 103–4, 121, 150, 151, 152, 162, 169
  The Voyage Out (1915), 8–9, 83–4, 124
  Night and Day (1919), 1, 7, 28, 39–40, 42, 124

Jacob's Room (1922), 85
Mrs Dalloway (1925), 100, 124–6, 154–5
To the Lighthouse (1927), 54, 124
Orlando (1928), 124
A Room of One's Own (1929), 2, 41, 83
The Years (1937), 85–6, 124
Diaries, 99, 108, 229
and sex in fiction, 124–6
Working-Class Wives, Their Health and Conditions (Rice), 100
working-class women, 100–2, 136–9
World We Have Lost, The (Laslett), 3
Wright, Helena
  The Sex Factor in Marriage (1930), 134–5, 215

Years, The (Woolf), 85–6, 124

If you would like to know more about Virago books, write to us at Ely House, 37 Dover Street, London W1X 4HS for a full catalogue.

Please send a stamped addressed envelope

VIRAGO
Advisory Group

Andrea Adam	Zoë Fairbairns
Carol Adams	Carolyn Faulder
Sally Alexander	Germaine Greer
Rosalyn Baxandall (USA)	Jane Gregory
Anita Bennett	Suzanne Lowry
Liz Calder	Jean McCrindle
Beatrix Campbell	Cathy Porter
Angela Carter	Alison Rimmer
Mary Chamberlain	Elaine Showalter (USA)
Anna Coote	Spare Rib Collective
Jane Cousins	Mary Stott
Jill Craigie	Rosalie Swedlin
Anna Davin	Margaret Walters
Rosalind Delmar	Elizabeth Wilson
Christine Downer (Australia)	Barbara Wynn

Book Tokens

Give them the pleasure of choosing

Book Tokens can be bought and exchanged at most bookshops